Facts, Fallacies and Frauds in Psychology

Psychology Editor Brian Foss
Professor of Psychology, Royal Holloway and Bedford New
College

Facts, Fallacies and Frauds in Psychology

Andrew M. Colman

London and New York

First published in 1987 by Hutchinson Education
Reprinted 1988

Reprinted 1993
by Routledge
11 New Fetter Lane, London EC4P 4EE

Simultaneously published in the USA and Canada
by Routledge
29 West 35th Street, New York, NY 10001

Printed and bound in Great Britain by
Richard Clay Ltd, Bungay, Suffolk

British Library Cataloguing in Publication Data

A catalogue record for this book is available from the British Library.

ISBN 0–415–09871–8

Contents

Preface   7

1 **Introduction**   9
   Notes

2 **Intelligence and IQ: nature or nurture?**   15
   History of IQ testing – Is intelligence inherited? –
   Separated identical twins – Kinship correlations –
   Adoption studies – Zero heritability? – Notes

3 **Intelligence and race: are black people genetically
   inferior?**   53
   A priori arguments – Racial admixture and crossing studies
   – The heritability argument – Test bias – Comparing
   minority groups – Environmental influences on IQ –
   Psychology and ideology – Notes

4 **Obedience and cruelty: are most people potential
   killers?**   81
   Milgram's study of obedience – Ethical justification of
   obedience research – Validity of obedience experiments –
   Further research – Notes

5 **Hypnosis: are hypnotic effects genuine?**   109
   Historical background – Hypnotic analgesia: credulous
   versus sceptical views – Is there a hypnotic state? – Trance
   logic – Notes

6 **Eating disorders: are anorexia nervosa and bulimia
   nervosa forms of depression?**   141
   Anorexia nervosa: 'the slimmer's disease' – How is
   anorexia nervosa diagnosed? – What is 'normal' body
   weight? A digression – How common is anorexia nervosa?
   – Body image disturbance – Bulimia nervosa – Eating
   disorders and depression – Notes

7 **Extra-sensory perception: is there any solid
   evidence?**   166
   Classification and historical background – The
   Soal–Goldney experiments – The Pearce–Pratt
   experiments – Precognition in rodents – Psi Ganzfeld
   experiments – Remote viewing experiments – ESP: errors
   surely present? – Notes

References   201

Index   219

Preface

This book is suited to short courses in psychology for non-specialists; it can also be used as background reading by psychology students. It contains detailed discussions of debates and arguments about a small number of controversial issues that intrigue most people, and it will therefore, I hope, stimulate lively classroom discussions. Its non-technical treatment of popular topics should make it accessible to the general reading public. For those who wish to pursue the topics in greater depth, detailed notes and references to primary sources and useful texts are supplied.

In the interests of accuracy and clarity I have quoted extensively from the primary sources whenever there seemed to be a danger of distorting or clouding the original authors' ideas by paraphrasing them. Important new ideas are almost invariably expressed more lucidly and vigorously by their originators than by later commentators. As an additional precaution, preliminary drafts of the chapters were critically examined and commented upon by friends, colleagues, and acknowledged experts in the various fields of research, as a result of which I was able to make numerous improvements in the final versions.

The following people, in particular, deserve special thanks for helping me in various ways: Kate Aucott, Sue Blackmore, John Brookfield, Peter Cooper, Alison Dunbar-Dempsey, Susan Dye, Brian Foss, Chris French, Ernest Hilgard, Clive Hollin, Bambos Kyriacou, Eric Liknaitzky, Nicholas Mackintosh, and Ian Pountney. In addition, Claire L'Enfant and Sarah Conibear of Hutchinson Education helped to make the writing a much pleasanter task than it might otherwise have been, and were very patient in waiting two years for the manuscript.

A.M.C.
October 1986

1 Introduction

The best way to approach any new subject is to start with topics that interest you already. This advice is based on sound psychological principles: a person whose curiosity is already aroused is likely to be especially receptive to pertinent facts and ideas, and especially appreciative of the contributions that experts have made to the relevant topics. Active reading, stimulated by questions to which the reader wants to know the answers, is more fun than passive assimilation of unwanted information, and what is read with curiosity is normally understood and remembered with clarity. A reader whose appetite has first been whetted in this way will probably develop interests in other branches of the subject and will certainly be better equipped to cope with them.

With these principles in mind, I have chosen for this volume psychological topics that interest most students and members of the general reading public. A second criterion of choice has been the amount of debate, argument, and controversy that the topics have generated within the psychological community itself. My reason for choosing controversial topics is twofold. First, most of us enjoy lively controversies, at least when we are not personally involved in them. Oscar Wilde's tongue was firmly in his cheek when he said: 'Arguments are to be avoided; they are always vulgar, and often convincing.' A little vulgarity can do no harm, and it is a positive boon when it helps us to see things more clearly. Second, to develop an intuitive 'feel' for any subject, it is not enough to know the key facts and one author's interpretation of them, which is what one finds in standard texts and popular psychology books; it is essential also to understand how these facts came to be discovered and how the leading authorities argued over their interpretation. My aim is to provide a clearer, deeper, and more balanced understanding of a small number of intriguing psychological questions that can be gained from other popular books. Instead of ignoring or sidestepping differences of opinion among experts, this book traces the evolution of each controversy in fine detail, in the hope of giving the reader the sensation of actually participating in the process of scientific discovery and a realistic insight into how psychologists think. Theories and experiments that have been cleverly refuted or fatally damaged by criticism, and research that has been exposed as fraudulent – there are several embarrassing examples of this in the following chapters – are all grist to my mill. In some cases the evidence that has come to light has swung the argument decisively in favour of one or other interpretation, so that I feel justified in drawing definite conclusions. Where the issues have remained unresolved, on the other hand, I offer tentative interpretations of the existing evidence or – in a few cases – leave the final verdicts open. By focusing on debates and arguments, I hope at least to encourage a healthy scepticism about expert opinion and a realization that psychological research, like any other branch of scientific inquiry, is a problem-solving activity.

Psychology is an unusually varied discipline, and the diversity of its subject matter is reflected in the contents of this book. The research areas that are touched upon include individual differences, cognition, social psychology, motivation, abnormal psychology, physiological psychology, states of consciousness, and perception. The specific topics discussed in this book are all taught to undergraduates in universities and colleges, and some are in the core curriculum of all reputable degree courses. But this is not a textbook: its coverage of psychology is riddled with holes, like a Gruyère cheese. (It is a book, none the less, just as Gruyère is a cheese.)

The chapters that follow are sufficiently self-contained to be readable in any order, or for one or more of them to be skipped. The basic ideas and research findings surrounding each controversy are presented in mainly non-technical language, without assuming familiarity with earlier chapters or any specialized knowledge beyond a handful of concepts that are explained in this introductory chapter. Jargon terms cannot be avoided entirely, partly because they sometimes serve as a useful form of shorthand without which the text would become intolerably verbose, repetitive, and imprecise, and partly because they are often used by the authorities whose original words I wish to quote; but I define all the necessary jargon terms when they first appear.

What is psychology? The word itself was coined three centuries ago by merging the Greek words *psyche* and *logos*. *Psyche* originally meant 'breath', and later also 'spirit' or 'soul' (because breathing was believed to indicate that the soul had not left the body), and later still 'mind'. *Logos* originally meant 'word', and later, by extension, 'discourse' or 'study'. A natural definition of psychology would therefore seem to be 'the study of mind'. But this definition is considered unsatisfactory nowadays because some of the things that psychologists study have more to do with behaviour than with mind. A rough working definition which corresponds more closely to what psychologists actually do is 'the study of cognition (thinking, remembering, and perceiving), emotion, and behaviour'.[1]*

Academic psychologists engaged in basic research devote themselves to trying to explain mental processes and behaviour, and they regard understanding as an end in itself. Applied psychologists, on the other hand, are concerned with applications of research to practical problems of everyday life – to mental disorders and their treatment, to learning and adjustment of children in school, and to well-being and efficiency of people in work. Psychological research generally focuses on problems that, in principle at least, can be solved by *empirical* methods – by observations of actual behaviour – rather than by reasoning alone. The main research methods in psychology are controlled experiments and quasi-experiments, survey methods, and case studies. These methods are all represented in this book, and a few words of explanation will help to clarify their fundamental aims and to introduce a few technical terms.

Controlled experiments are designed to investigate cause–effect relationships. Their defining properties are *manipulation* and *control*. After formulating a hypothesis about some causal process, such as the effect of a specified hypnotic procedure on the sensation of pain, the investigator manipulates the *independent variable* (the conjectured cause, in this case the hypnotic procedure) by, for example, exposing subjects in an *experimental group* to it and comparing their pain responses with those of a *control group* of subjects not exposed to it. Some objective measure of the effect, called the *dependent variable*, is obviously needed if accurate comparisons between the groups are to be made. Extraneous factors which might also influence the dependent variable must be controlled, otherwise the observed effect will not be clearly attributable to the independent variable. In psychology, control is usually achieved by *randomization*, that is, by assigning subjects to experimental and control groups by tossing a coin or using some other randomizing device. This ensures that sex differences, for example, are controlled: roughly the same proportions of male and female subjects will end up in the experimental and control groups, and consequently differences between the groups on the dependent variable will not be due to any difference that might exist between the sexes in pain responses. Randomization ensures that sex, age, socio-economic status, variations in skin thickness, and *all* other extraneous factors, including ones that the investigator has not even dreamt of, will be distributed in roughly the same proportions in the experimental and

* Superior figures refer to Notes at the ends of chapters.

control groups, so that any difference on the dependent variable will necessarily be due to the independent variable or to chance.

That is where statistics comes in. It is possible, though unlikely, that by chance all the female subjects will end up in one group, even if the assignment of subjects to groups is strictly random. Analogously, if you toss a coin many times, it is possible that you will get an unbroken string of heads. This implies that any observed difference between the average scores of the groups might have nothing at all to do with the independent variable; it might be a purely chance occurrence arising from unknown extraneous factors. Statistical methods enable a researcher to calculate the numerical probability or odds that the observed difference is due to chance, given the size of the difference and the number of subjects in each group. By convention, an experimental effect with a probability of less than one in twenty of being due to chance is called *statistically significant* (or simply *significant*) and is assumed to be due to the independent variable. If an experimental result is non-significant, one cannot conclude with confidence that the hypothesized effect has been corroborated by the evidence.

It often happens that causal questions arise which are not amenable to strict experimental investigation, either because the independent variable cannot be manipulated (cannot be varied independently) or because complete control of extraneous factors is impossible. In psychological comparisons between racial groups, for example, genetic differences, which have been hypothesized as causes of certain psychological differences, cannot be varied independently of differences in social circumstances between the groups. To be specific, black and white people are exposed to different environmental influences, and an investigator cannot assign subjects to racial groups at random in order to exercise control over these environmental differences. Some, but not all, of the extraneous factors can be controlled: differences between the socio-economic status of black and white people can, for example, be controlled by matching every black subject with a white subject of similar socio-economic standing. Investigations of this kind are called *quasi-experiments*, and for obvious reasons their findings carry less weight than those obtained by strictly experimental methods.

Survey methods are designed to determine how factors of psychological interest are distributed in specific sections of a population or in different populations. These methods are usually applied to questions about the distribution or prevalence of mental disorders (such as eating disorders), opinions, attitudes, beliefs, or behavioural patterns. Special techniques have to be used to ensure that the samples that are investigated are truly representative of the populations in question.

A psychological case study is a detailed investigation of a single person, or occasionally a single organized group. Case studies are especially useful in the field of abnormal psychology, where detailed descriptions of the background, symptoms, and responses to treatment of individuals with unusual mental disorders can be illuminating. They are occasionally used in other fields of research. A great deal of the early research into extra-sensory perception was based on case studies of hauntings, apparitions, and other supposedly paranormal happenings. In general, this research method is more useful for suggesting hypotheses than for testing them, because experimental control is entirely lacking.

Psychological research, and in particular quasi-experimentation and survey research, makes frequent use of techniques of *correlation*, which are worth discussing briefly. Two variables are said to be positively correlated if high scores on one of them tend to go together with high scores on the other, and vice versa, like the sizes of houses and their prices. If high scores on one variable tend to go with low scores on the other, then the correlation is negative. The usual statistical measure of correlation ranges from 1.00, which represents perfect positive correlation, through zero for no correlation, to −1.00 for perfect negative correlation. As an illustration, consider the heights and weights of adult human beings. Tall people tend to be heavy and short people tend to be light, which suggests that the two variables are positively correlated. The correlation between height and weight among adults in Britain is, in fact, 0.47 for men and 0.35 for women.[2] These correlations are positive and statistically significant (they are evidently not due to chance), but they are not perfect, and the correlation is stronger among men than among women. A second illustration is the correlation between the fulness of the moon and admissions to mental hospitals. This correlation is not significantly different from zero, contrary to popular superstition.[3] A third illustration is the correlation between the number of lynchings of black men per annum and the farm value of cotton in the American deep south from 1882 to 1930. This correlation turns out to be −0.72, which is strongly negative, showing that lynchings tended to increase when the value of cotton was low and to decrease when the value of cotton was high.[4]

Techniques of correlation are invaluable tools in psychological research, but they can never establish that a *causal* relationship exists between variables – only experimental methods can achieve that. A useful lesson can be learnt by considering the age of the Statue of Liberty in years and the average price of residential properties in London in pounds sterling. The correlation between these two variables over the past century would certainly turn out to be strongly positive, probably quite close to 1.00, if anyone bothered to calculate it; but no intelligent person would suggest any causal connection between them.

If you are looking bewildered and scratching your head, then relax. Correlation and the other technical concepts that I have been discussing are mere tools of the psychological trade; you will understand them better, and appreciate their usefulness, when you see them in action in the chapters that follow.

Notes

1 See Colman (1988) for an introduction to psychology aimed at interested general readers and intending students.
2 Knight (1984), p. 29. The data are derived from a fully representative survey of heights and weights in a sample of 10,000 men and women in Great Britain. The correlations are very similar in the United States, according to data summarized by Knight.
3 Rotton and Kelly (1985).
4 Hovland and Sears (1940).

2 Intelligence and IQ: nature or nurture?

Here is a problem of a type that will be familiar to most people: 'Which of the following is the odd one out: cricket, football, billiards, hockey?' This problem first cropped up in an IQ test that formed part of a school entrance examination in England. It provoked a puzzled parent to write a letter to *The Times*:

I said billiards because it is the only one played indoors. A colleague said football because it is the only one in which a ball is not struck by an implement. A neighbour says cricket because in all the other games the object is to put the ball in a net; and my son, with the confidence of nine summers, plumps for hockey 'because it is the only one that is a girl's game'. Could any of your readers put me out of my misery by stating what is the correct answer, and further enlighten me by explaining how questions of this sort prove anything, especially when the scholar has merely to underline the odd one out without giving any reason?[1]

The four sports problem stirred up a lively controversy in the correspondence columns of *The Times*.[2] One correspondent thought that ' "billiards" is the obvious answer ... because it is the only one of the games listed which is not a team game .... I should have thought it a very suitable question for an intelligence test'. Another suggested that 'football is the odd one out because ... it is played with an inflated ball compared with the solid ball used in each of the other [games]'. An eminent philosopher then joined the fray. He began by commenting that 'billiards is the only one in which the colour of the balls matters, the only one played with more than one ball at once, the only one played on a green cloth and not on a field, and the only one whose name has more than eight letters in it'; but he went on to argue that equally logical reasons could be adduced on behalf of any of the other games. Summing up the controversy in his book, *The Tyranny of Testing*, the mathematician Banesh Hoffmann noted that the correspondents to *The Times* had offered excellent reasons for choosing cricket, football, or billiards, but that their arguments for choosing hockey were dubious at best. At first he thought that hockey was therefore the worst of the four choices, and that it could be ruled out. But then it occurred to him that 'the very fact that hockey was the only one that could thus be ruled out gave it so striking a quality of separateness as to make it an excellent answer after all – perhaps the best'.[3]

The controversy over the four sports problem illustrates something that applies to all IQ test questions of the odd-one-out type: logically valid arguments can generally be found for *any* of the listed options. The problem is to guess which of the answers the test constructors had in mind. A similar difficulty arises with mathematical questions of the following familiar type: 'What is the next number in the sequence 2, 4, 8 … ?' A good case can, of course, be made for 16 (which is probably the 'right' answer) because each number is twice its predecessor in the sequence. But 14 is an equally valid answer, even if it is likely to be marked wrong, because in that case the differences between neighbouring pairs of numbers are 2, 4, 6 – the even numbers. It is a fact that for any short sequence of numbers there are infinitely many mathematical rules that generate it. The problem is to find the rule – probably the 'simplest', although simplicity is ill-defined in mathematics – that the test constructors had in mind. Actually, there is a childishly simple procedure that enables anyone who knows it to score at genius level on number-sequence IQ problems.[4] (Ambitious readers who wish to raise their IQs at a stroke should consult my endnote.)

IQ tests are designed to measure intelligence, of course, and there is great controversy over whether they achieve this objective in any meaningful sense. I am not going to discuss that controversy in depth, but a few words are in order about the definition of intelligence. Roughly speaking, intelligence is the ability to think abstractly, and since it is itself an abstraction, it cannot be observed directly. *Intelligent behaviour*, on the other hand, can be observed directly: solving *The Times* crossword in less than half an hour, getting good marks in school examinations, and answering difficult questions in IQ tests are observable instances of it. It is an important (and perhaps surprising) fact of life that people who are good at some types of abstract thinking are generally good at others, and that people who are bad at some are generally bad at others. It is hard to devise *any* set of intellectual problems that are not more easily solved by people with high IQs than by those with low IQs. Some psychologists have inferred from this that intelligence is a global, unitary factor rather than a set of specific (though overlapping) abilities, but that inference remains controversial.

There is no precise definition of intelligence that would satisfy all psychologists, and dictionary definitions are not very definitive either. The *Oxford English Dictionary* lists twelve definitions of 'intelligence'; but it also lists eight definitions of 'definition' and no fewer than 114 definitions of 'of'. What a muddle! But quibbles about the precise meaning of words are nearly always a waste of time, and there are controversies surrounding intelligence, notably those bearing on the nature–nurture question, which are more interesting and worthy of detailed examination. Since these controversies did not spring fully formed from the head of Zeus, it will be helpful to begin by placing them in their historical context, although the history of IQ testing is a shameful and unedifying saga.[5]

History of IQ testing

The concepts of nature and nurture are at least as old as western civilization. In Plato's *Republic*, for example, discussions of courage and justice are based on the assumption that human character is determined by nature (*physis*) and nurture (*trophe*). The modern phase of the nature–nurture debate, especially in relation to intelligence, can be traced to the writings of Francis Galton, grandson of the poet and physician Erasmus Darwin and half-cousin of the biologist Charles Darwin. Galton was responsible for the first statistical study, based on kinship correlations, of the inheritance of intelligence, and for the first adoption and twin studies designed to disentangle hereditary and environmental influences on intelligence. He also constructed the world's first intelligence test, he founded and named the *eugenics* movement whose purpose was to improve the hereditary quality of the human race by selective breeding, and he was the first to propose that human races differ in innate intelligence.

In his book *Hereditary Genius*,[6] published in 1869, Galton examined the family trees of 415 highly distinguished judges, statesmen, military commanders, literary figures, scientists (modestly omitting himself), poets, artists, and divines. He found that a much larger proportion of these eminent people than would be expected by chance had blood relatives who were also eminent, and that their close relatives were more often eminent than their distant relatives. For example, 48 per cent of their sons, 7 per cent of their grandsons, and only 1 per cent of their great-grandsons were eminent. Eminence seemed to run in families in much the same way as unusual physical attributes such as exceptional height which were already known to be largely hereditary. Galton concluded that genius is also largely hereditary. To put it bluntly, he regarded the British upper class as a highly productive intellectual stud farm.

Galton discounted the alternative possibility that members of these brilliant families were successful because of superior nurture, in the form of better education, opportunities, and personal connections. But he was well aware of this alternative environmental explanation for his findings, and he realized that his kinship data might not convince all his readers that intelligence is largely determined by heredity. To strengthen his argument he therefore reported the results of an adoption study designed to disentangle hereditary and environmental effects. His adoption study focused on the effects of nepotism, the common practice among Popes and other Roman Catholic dignitaries of adopting distantly related young boys and raising them in their own homes as 'nephews'. These boys, Galton argued, shared the environmental but not the genetic advantages of natural sons raised by eminent parents: 'If social help is really of the highest importance, the nephews of the Popes will attain eminence as frequently, or nearly so, as the sons of other eminent men; otherwise, they will not.' Galton's evidence showed that they did not. The natural sons of other eminent men went on to attain eminence far more often than the Popes' adopted 'nephews': 'The social helps are the same, but hereditary gifts are wanting in the latter case.'[7]

Six years later Galton published his pioneering twin study. He guessed (correctly) that identical twins are identical in heredity and that non-identical twins differ in heredity to the same degree as ordinary siblings. The evidence he collected showed identical twins to be much more alike in mental ability than non-identical twins. This lent further weight to his theory that intelligence is largely hereditary.

At the International Health Exhibition at the South Kensington Museum in 1884, Galton set up a stall where visitors could have their natural mental abilities tested for the modest fee of 3 pence. No fewer than 9000 men and women volunteered as subjects in this pioneering intelligence testing project. The tests measured reaction times to sounds, lights, and touches of the skin; keenness of visual judgement; the number of taps a person could make in half a minute; and other aspects of sensory and motor functions that could easily be measured accurately. Galton believed intelligence to be an all-round global capacity, and he expected superior people to perform better on all his tests. But the tests consistently failed to correlate with one another and with independent signs of intelligence or accomplishment, so later researchers had to invent more direct tests of thinking ability. Whether there is any connection between sensory-motor functioning and intelligence is still a matter of controversy.[8]

The first useful intelligence test was developed in France by Alfred

Binet and Theodore Simon in 1905. Binet had been commissioned by the Minister of Public Instruction to devise a means by which mentally subnormal children could be detected and classified as *débiles*, later called morons (mildly subnormal), imbeciles (severely subnormal), or idiots (profoundly subnormal), with a view to screening them out and putting them in special classes or schools where teaching could be geared to their abilities. The Binet–Simon scale consisted of a series of thirty items carefully arranged in order of difficulty and complexity, from following the movement of a lighted match with the eyes to working out what time a clock face would show if the hour and minute hands were interchanged – for example, five minutes to two would become ten minutes past eleven. By administering the scale to representative groups of normal children of all ages, Binet and Simon established test norms – that is to say, they *standardized* their scale – and introduced the idea of mental age. Then, for example, if the scale was administered to a 12-year-old child, and the child passed only those items that most normal 5-year-olds had been found to pass, it was possible to infer that the child was functioning at a mental age of 5 years and was therefore mentally retarded by about 7 years. Binet defined morons (*débiles*) as people whose mental age did not increase beyond 11 years, imbeciles as those who did not develop past 5 years, and idiots as those who got stuck at a mental age of 2 years.

Binet did not believe that a person's intelligence is necessarily static and unalterable. He fiercely criticized the 'deplorable verdicts' of those who regarded intelligence as a fixed quantity: 'We must protest and react against this brutal pessimism .... With practice, enthusiasm, and especially method, one can succeed in increasing one's attention, memory, and judgement, and in becoming literally more intelligent than one was before.'[9] He even designed a programme of 'mental orthopaedics' to improve the intelligence of mentally retarded children.

The concept of the intelligence quotient, or IQ, was introduced by the German psychologist William Stern in 1912. Stern pointed out that a person's mental age gives an indication of intelligence only when it is related appropriately to that person's actual (chronological) age. Consider three hypothetical children, Matthew, Mark, and Lucy, who each have a mental age of 10 years. Suppose Matthew's chronological age is 20 years, Mark's is 10 years, and Lucy's is 5 years. Then Matthew is severely retarded, Mark is average, and Lucy is a genius. Stern therefore proposed that the ratio of mental age to chronological age – in symbols MA/CA – should be the index of intelligence, and he named this index the intelligence quotient. The American psychologist Lewis Terman later introduced the abbreviation IQ and suggested multiplying the ratio MA/CA by 100, that is, expressing it as a percentage, to eliminate inconvenient decimal places. According to this formula, which was soon adopted universally, Matthew's IQ is $(10/20) \times 100 = 50$; Mark's IQ is $(10/10) \times 100 = 100$; and Lucy's IQ is $(10/5) \times 100 = 200$, which is way above Einstein's. Note that a person with an IQ of 100 is average by definition; IQs less than 100 are below average, and IQs higher than 100 are above average.

Binet's method of intelligence testing and Stern's concept of IQ were enthusiastically adopted by the pioneer mental testers in the United States. Lewis Terman of Stanford University, whose adaptation of the Binet–Simon scale, known as the Stanford–Binet, was the prototype of virtually all subsequent IQ tests, Henry Goddard of the Vineland Training School for the Feebleminded in New Jersey, and Robert Yerkes of Harvard University, President of the American Psychological Association, all believed that IQ tests provided a measure of fixed and innate intelligence, and they were active members of various eugenic societies. In other words, they continued to propagate the 'brutal pessimism' that Binet had protested and reacted against. They believed that genetically inferior people posed a menace to the social, economic, and moral welfare of the state, and that IQ tests could and should be used to weed them out. Terman, for example, prophesied in 1916 that 'in the near future intelligence tests will bring tens of thousands of high-grade defectives under the surveillance and protection of society. This will ultimately result in curtailing the reproduction of feeble-mindedness and in the elimination of an enormous amount of crime, pauperism, and industrial inefficiency'.[10] He thought that mental defectives were especially common among black people and other racial minorities, and commented: 'There is no possibility at present of convincing society that they should not be allowed to reproduce, although from a eugenic point of view they constitute a grave problem because of their unusually prolific breeding.'[11]

The rise of the mental testing movement in the United States contributed to the enactment in more than thirty states of sterilization laws designed to prevent people of low intelligence from reproducing. The first sterilization act to be passed by a state legislature was the Act for the Prevention of Idiocy in Pennsylvania in 1905, but it was vetoed by the governor and never became law. The first fully enacted law took effect in Indiana in 1907; its preamble began with the dogmatic premise: 'Whereas, heredity plays a most important part in the transmission of crime, idiocy, and imbecility ....' New Jersey followed in 1911, and in the same year the Iowa state legislature provided for the 'unsexing of criminals, idiots, etc.'. A sterilization law passed by the Washington state legislature was challenged in the Supreme Court in 1912, but the court upheld the law on the grounds that 'modern scientific investigation shows that idiocy, insanity, imbecility, and criminality are congenital and hereditary .... There appears to be a wonderful unanimity of [experts] favoring the prevention of their future propagation'. A California law of 1918 allowed compulsory sterilization provided it was approved by a board including a psychologist holding a PhD degree – at a time when Terman was one of the few people in California with that qualification. A similar law passed in Virginia led to more than 7500 compulsory sterilizations between 1924 and 1972. Doris Buck Figgins, a young woman compulsorily sterilized for mental deficiency under this law in 1928, and told at the time that she was having an appendix operation, discovered only in 1980 that she had been sterilized: 'I broke down and cried. My husband and me wanted children desperately. We were crazy about them. I never knew what they'd done to me.'[12] Involuntary sterilization of mental defectives is seldom if ever practised today, but some American states still retain sterilization laws on their statute books.

The pioneering mental testers were also concerned about immigration into the United States. The earliest European immigrants had been mainly of British, German, and Scandinavian stock, but after 1890 Italian, Polish, Russian, and Jewish immigrants began to predominate. In 1912 Henry Goddard administered IQ tests to large numbers of immigrants at the receiving station in New York harbour, ironically at the base of the Statue of Liberty, and reported the astonishing conclusion that 79 per cent of the Italians, 87 per cent of the Russians, and 83 per cent of the Jews were feeble-minded. These findings fuelled existing prejudices, and immigration rules were systematically tightened up. The Immigration Act of 1917 provided specifically for the exclusion of 'persons of constitutional psychopathic inferiority'. Goddard reported with obvious pride in 1917 that large numbers of aliens had been deported because of feeble-mindedness, and that 'this was due to the untiring efforts of the physicians who were inspired by the belief that mental tests could be used for the detection of feeble-minded aliens'. Finally, as a direct result of lobbying by various groups and individuals opposed to immigration from southern, central, and eastern Europe, the Immigration Restriction Act of 1924 was passed. It stipulated that the quota of immigrants per annum from any country could not exceed 2 per cent of the number of people from that country already resident in the United States in 1890, that is, before the wave of immigration from southern, central, and eastern Europe began. During the 1930s hundreds of thousands of Jewish refugees from the Nazi Holocaust tried to enter the United States, but many were deported back to Germany to meet their ghastly fate because the central and eastern European quotas were filled, although quotas from other countries were vastly undersubscribed. A significant number of those who perished in Nazi concentration camps might have survived but for the 1924 Act, to which the 'scientific' racism of Terman, Goddard, and other influential American psychologists lent intellectual respectability.[13]

The pioneers of the mental testing movement in Britain were also followers of Galton rather than Binet inasmuch as they considered intelligence to be a fixed and hereditary factor. Cyril Burt, later to be knighted for his services as Britain's first educational psychologist, gave expert evidence to the Consultative Committee on Secondary Education which reported in 1938: 'Our psychological witnesses assured us that [intelligence] can be measured approximately by means of intelligence tests .... We are informed that, with few exceptions, it is possible at a very early age to predict with some degree of accuracy the ultimate level of a child's intellectual powers .... Different children from the age of 11, if justice is to be done to their varying capacities, require types of education varying in certain important respects.'[14] The recommendations of this committee were implemented in the Education Act of 1944 which introduced the divisive 'eleven-plus' examination based largely on intelligence tests. All children were required to sit this examination at the age of 11; only the top-scoring minority were allowed to proceed to elite grammar schools, while the majority were sent to academically inferior secondary modern schools, and it was virtually impossible for a late developer to transfer from a secondary modern to a grammar school. This notorious abuse of psychology was rigorously implemented throughout England and Wales for more than a generation.

Is intelligence inherited?

It is misleading to ask what proportion of *an individual's* intelligence is inherited. In order to be able to think abstractly, or at all, a person must first possess a brain, and must therefore have inherited the necessary genes for the growth of that indispensable organ. The correct form of the question is: To what extent are *differences* in intelligence *between people* genetically determined? Psychologists and population geneticists generally phrase the question more precisely as follows: what proportion of the *variance* in IQ scores in a specified population is explained by genetic factors? A more concise version of the same question is: what is the *heritability* of IQ in a specified population? There are some technical terms that need to be explained.

Variance is a statistical concept, closely related to the common-sense notion of variation or differences. Suppose that an IQ test has been administered to five individuals and their scores are 85, 95, 100, 106, and 114. The *mean* (average), which is obtained by adding up the scores and then dividing by five, is 100, but there is considerable variation around this mean. How would you express the variation as a number? You might think that a measure of the variation among the scores could be obtained by simply adding up their deviations from the mean: $(85 - 100) + (95 - 100) + (100 - 100) + (106 - 100) + (114 - 100)$. But positive and negative deviations cancel one another out and the answer comes out as zero; that will not do because there is obviously some variation among the scores. Statisticians therefore square the deviations to eliminate negative terms – the square of any number, even a negative number, is positive – and define the *variance* as the mean of the squared deviations from the mean. Adding up the squared deviations from the mean of the five scores in my example we get $(-15)^2 + (-5)^2 + (0)^2 + (6)^2 + (14)^2 = 482$, and dividing this by 5 we get the 'mean square' or variance: $482/5 = 96.4$. The reason for taking the mean of the squared deviations rather than their sum is to obtain an index of variation that is independent of the number of scores. Variance is an index of the average amount of dispersion or scatter or spread in a set of scores, irrespective of the number of scores.

The heritability of IQ in a given population is the proportion of the total variance in IQ scores that is due to genetic variance. The following *Gedankenexperiment* (imaginary experiment) will clarify this idea. Imagine that we were able to raise a random sample of individuals in identical environments from conception, and then to measure their IQs with a perfectly reliable IQ test. The variance in their IQ scores would obviously be due entirely to genetic differences because environmental factors would be held constant – there would be no environmental variance. If the variance in IQ scores turned out to be 96.4, for example, and the variance in IQ scores in another random sample raised in the normal range of environments was 192.8, then we could estimate the proportion of IQ variance due to genetic differences – the heritability of IQ – to be 96.4/192.8, which works out as 0.50. This means that 50 per cent of the variance in IQ is due to genetic variance. Alternatively, suppose that we raised a sample of clones (individuals with identical genes) from conception in a random selection of environments and found the variance in their IQs to be 38.56; this variance would, of course, be due entirely to environmental factors. If the IQ variance in a random sample from the normal population was once again 192.8, then the proportion of variance due to environmental factors could be estimated as 38.56/192.8, which is 0.20 or 20 per cent. We could therefore estimate the heritability of IQ to be 0.80 or 80 per cent.

In the real world, of course, neither of these experiments is feasible, so researchers have to use indirect methods to estimate heritability. Evidence is available from three main methods of investigation: the study of separated identical twins, kinship correlations, and adoption studies. In 1969 Arthur Jensen of the University of California, Berkeley, reviewed the evidence from all three sources in a long article entitled 'How Much Can We Boost IQ and Scholastic Achievement?', and reached the conclusion that the heritability of IQ is about 80 per cent.[15] He also reviewed evidence showing that black Americans score, on average, 15 points below white Americans on IQ tests, and he commented: 'We are left with ... various lines of evidence, none of which is definitive alone, but which, viewed all together, make it a not unreasonable hypothesis that genetic factors are strongly implicated in the Negro–white intelligence difference.' (The debate over race and intelligence is discussed in Chapter 3.) Jensen's article aroused angry emotions in both academic and non-academic circles. Literally hundreds of criticisms appeared in print, there were calls for Jensen's dismissal from membership of the American Psychological Association, students began disrupting his lectures and seminars, and his university hired a personal bodyguard to protect him.

In 1971 Hans Eysenck of the University of London, a former teacher of Arthur Jensen, published a book entitled *Race, Intelligence and Education* in the United Kingdom and *The IQ Argument* in the United States[16] which reached essentially identical conclusions about the heritability of IQ and race differences and created a similar storm of protest in Britain. Eysenck quoted Jensen's 80 per cent estimate of the heritability of IQ and added: 'I can only report that among experts the conclusion I mentioned above is pretty universally accepted.' But Eysenck's own claim to expertise was somewhat dented by his misunderstanding of heritability. He repeatedly misinterpreted heritability, which as I have explained is a statistical concept, as if it applied to individuals, so that 80 per cent heritability was taken to mean 80 per cent of an average person's IQ is genetically determined. According to Eysenck, 'the figure of 80 per cent heritability is an average; it does not apply equally to every person in the country. For some people environment may play a much bigger part than is suggested by the figure; for others it may be even less .... An average is an average is an average'. But a number is a number is a number, and it is easy to see that the variance of a single number is always zero; therefore the heritability of one person's IQ is quite meaningless. Eysenck was being rather modest in claiming that 80 per cent of the variance in an average person's IQ is determined genetically; he could have said 200 per cent is, because after all 200 per cent of zero is zero. But then the nonsense would have been obvious.

In 1974 the Princeton psychologist Leon Kamin published a stinging critique of the 80 per cent heritability estimate, and the research on which it was based, in a book entitled *The Science and Politics of IQ*.[17] His conclusion was startling: 'There exist no data which should lead a prudent man to accept the hypothesis that I.Q. test scores are in any degree heritable.' In a debate with Eysenck published in 1981 he re-emphasized this radical conclusion and amplified his critique of the evidence, and Eysenck defended his original claims.[18] It is astonishing that a large and diverse body of evidence should lead to such sharply differing interpretations. Let us therefore examine the three lines of evidence and the controversies they have generated.

Separated identical twins

Identical or monozygotic (MZ) twins are formed when a single sperm fertilizes a single ovum, which then divides in two and grows into two separate individuals. The individuals have identical genes; they are therefore necessarily of the same sex, and they resemble each other in all other characteristics that depend on heredity. Non-identical or dizygotic (DZ) twins are formed when two separate sperms fertilize two separate ova at about the same time. Although DZ twins are born together like MZ twins, they are in fact no more genetically alike than ordinary siblings: they may be of the same or opposite sex and they normally share, on average, a little over half their genes in common. (In the rare cases of DZ twins with different natural fathers, the twins share, on average, a little over one-quarter of their genes in common.)

A crucial experiment of nature occurs when MZ twins are separated soon after birth and raised in different homes. This may happen if their mother dies in childbirth, or if the authorities consider her incompetent to raise children, or if she decides that she cannot cope with both of them. Even in these circumstances separation is unusual, so it is hardly surprising that the psychological literature contains IQ data on only 121 pairs of separated MZ twins. Their significance lies in the fact that separated MZ twins share only their heredity – and not their environments – in common, so that if they resemble each other more than would be expected by chance, this must be due to their common genes. The usual index of resemblance is called the *intraclass correlation coefficient*,[19] which is 0.00 when there is no resemblance and rises to a maximum of 1.00 when there is complete resemblance. It can be proved that this correlation coefficient measures the heritability of the trait in question provided that certain mathematical assumptions are met; a correlation of 0.50 between separated MZ twins, for example, indicates that 50 per cent of the variance is due to genetic differences. But this inference is strictly valid only if the MZ twins were separated at conception, which is never the case because all twin pairs spend their first nine months together in the shared environment of their mother's womb, and if they were raised in environments that were completely uncorrelated, which is seldom, if ever, the case as we shall see.

The most influential study of separated MZ twins was undoubtedly the life's work of Sir Cyril Burt of University College London.[20] Jensen described Burt's work as 'the most satisfactory attempt to estimate the separate variance components',[21] and Eysenck 'drew rather heavily' on Burt's work 'because of the outstanding quality of the design and the statistical treatment in his studies'.[22] There are two main reasons for the enormous influence of Burt's twin study. The first is its sheer size: Burt reported data on fifty-three pairs of separated MZ twins – far more than any other investigator. The second is that Burt's was the only study that investigated the correlation between the environments of the twins: Burt rated the socio-economic status on a six-point scale from 'higher professional' to 'unskilled' of the families in which the twins were raised, and found the correlation to be very close to zero. The correlation between the twins' IQ scores, however, was reported to be 0.86 – by far the highest correlation in any of the published studies of separated MZ twins – which suggests that 86 per cent of the variance in IQ is genetically determined.

The first person to raise serious doubts about Burt's data was Leon Kamin, whose book was published in 1974, three years after Burt's death.[23] Kamin pointed out that Burt's published papers contain no specific details about the twins he claimed to have investigated or the IQ tests he supposedly administered. Burt always referred his readers to earlier publications or unpublished documents for details, but the earlier publications did not contain the promised details and the unpublished documents were impossible to locate. Kamin was also the first to notice certain numerical impossibilities in Burt's data. For example, in 1955, after collecting his first twenty-one pairs of separated MZ twins, Burt reported a correlation of 0.843 between their IQs as measured on unnamed 'individual tests'. In 1958, by which time he claimed to have collected 'over 30 such cases', the correlation for the enlarged sample was still 0.843, which is an incredible coincidence. Finally, in 1966, by which time his sample had grown to fifty-three pairs, the correlation was 0.863, which looks like a typing error. Burt also tested his twins on a (presumably less reliable) 'group test', and the correlations reported over the years were 0.771 (twenty-one pairs), 0.771 ('over 30 such cases') and – what is the next number in the sequence? – 0.771 (fifty-three pairs). Kamin found numerous other examples in Burt's papers of invariant correlations which strain the laws of probability. Kamin's conclusion was that 'the numbers left behind by Professor Burt are simply not worthy of our current scientific attention'.[24]

Soon after discovering Burt's invariant correlations, Kamin wrote to Jensen about the matter. Jensen immediately wrote an article admitting that the peculiarities in Burt's data, which he attributed to carelessness rather than fraud, rendered them 'useless for hypothesis testing'. In a footnote he credited Kamin with discovering the invariant correlations. Eysenck immediately wrote a bizarre letter to the *Bulletin of the British Psychological Society* claiming that his protégé Jensen should be given priority for exposing Burt, because Jensen's article appeared in print before Kamin's book. Kamin replied in the *Bulletin* that 'to squabble about "priority" is unseemly, especially when no intellectual accomplishment is involved'.[25]

Kamin had not openly accused Burt of deliberate fraud, and Burt's devotees continued to insist that Kamin's findings showed nothing more than carelessness on Burt's part. But on 24 October 1976 the *Sunday Times* ran a front-page story under the headline 'Crucial Data Was [sic] Faked by Eminent Scientist'. The reporter was Oliver Gillie, the newspaper's medical correspondent and, incidentally, a qualified geneticist. Gillie reported, among other things, that Burt's two collaborators, Margaret Howard and J. Conway, who according to Burt had actually tested the twins and processed the data, either did not exist or at least had not been in contact with Burt when he co-authored papers with them in the journal that he edited. Jensen immediately wrote an angry letter to *The Times*: 'The desperate scorched-earth style of criticism that we have come to know in this debate has finally gone to the limit, with charges of "fraud" and "fakery" now that Burt is no longer here to answer for himself or take warranted legal action against such unfounded defamation.'[26] Eysenck, a faithful disciple of Burt's, at least in print, described Gillie's allegations as 'unspeakably mean' and redolent of 'McCarthyism, smear campaigns, and witch-hunting'. He wrote to Burt's sister: 'I think the whole affair is just a determined effort on the part of some very left-wing environmentalists determined to play a political game with scientific facts. I am sure that the future will uphold the honour and integrity of Sir Cyril without any question.'[27]

Eysenck's optimistic prediction was decisively refuted by subsequent events. All lingering doubts about Burt's fraud were quelled when Leslie Hearnshaw's official biography of Burt appeared in 1979.[28] Hearnshaw had been commissioned by Burt's sister to write the biography before the allegations of fraud had been levelled, and he was given access to Burt's private diaries, letters, and files. Starting as an unqualified admirer of Burt's, Hearnshaw gradually discovered that all the allegations were true. He could find no trace of the shadowy Miss Conway or Miss Howard, or any concrete evidence that Burt ever tested the IQs of any twins. He discovered several instances of evasion and outright dishonesty in Burt's letters to colleagues who asked questions about his data. He even uncovered frauds that had not previously been suspected.

What is perhaps most scandalous about the Burt scandal is that Jensen, Eysenck, and other specialists in IQ testing accepted Burt's data at face value for so long. As the Cambridge psychologist Nicholas Mackintosh pointed out in his review of Hearnshaw's biography, the fact that Burt's data are scientifically unacceptable is patently evident in the data themselves. 'It was, indeed, clear to anyone with eyes to see in 1958. But it was not seen until ... Kamin first pointed to Burt's totally inadequate reporting of his data and to the impossible consistencies in his correlation coefficients.'[29]

Burt's was not only the largest of the four published studies of separated MZ twins, and the one reporting the highest correlation, but it was also the only one that provided quantitative information purporting to show that there was no correlation between the environments in which the twins were raised. Now that Burt's data have been rejected, we are therefore left with three smaller studies, none of which can claim to provide such an accurate and valid estimate of the heritability of IQ.

The largest of the three remaining studies, also performed in England, was reported by James Shields in 1962.[30] Shields found a correlation of 0.77 between the intelligence test scores of thirty-seven pairs of separated MZ twins. This correlation is lower than Burt's 0.86, but it is very high nevertheless. Unlike Burt, Shields included mountains of detailed biographical information about his twins, and this provided a springboard for a devastating critique by Kamin. Kamin's main allegations were that Shields unconsciously biased his results and that the twins were not really separated – that their environments were highly correlated.

On the question of unconscious bias, Kamin focused on the fact that Shields did not test all the twins himself. In five cases the two individuals belonging to a twin pair were tested by two independent examiners. Kamin noticed that the average difference in scores in these five pairs was a massive 22.4 points, compared with an average difference of only 8.5 points in the remaining pairs tested by Shields alone. Kamin calculated the intraclass correlation between the pairs tested by different examiners. It turned out to be 0.11, compared with 0.84 between the pairs tested by Shields alone. Kamin concluded that 'there is clearly a strong suggestion that unconscious experimenter expectation may have influenced these results'.[31]

This conclusion was swiftly challenged by Kamin's critics.[32] They argued that in two of the five pairs tested by independent examiners the difference in scores was no larger than the average of all the pairs, and that the evidence for bias must therefore rest on only three pairs. This argument is unconvincing, because clearly the two pairs whose scores were no more discrepant than average might have shown an *even smaller* discrepancy had they both been tested by Shields. The critics also drew attention to the fact that among the remaining three pairs was one which Shields excluded from his own analysis because one member of the pair seemed to have misunderstood the test instructions. But the exclusion of this pair could be interpreted as further evidence of bias on Shields's part, because the discrepancy was quite large in this case and remained so even when the pair was later given a completely different intelligence test. Perhaps Shields excluded this pair because he could not believe that one member of an MZ pair could score so much worse than the other without having misunderstood the instructions. Lastly, Kamin's critics argued that the large discrepancy in one of the other pairs tested by independent examiners could be satisfactorily explained by the fact that one member had congenital syphilis, amnesia, and recurrent blindness. But Kamin replied to this by pointing out that it was the blind, amnesic, syphilitic individual who had by far the higher IQ![33] In summary, Kamin's claim that 'there is clearly a strong suggestion' of unconscious bias in the Shields study seems a little overstated in view of the scanty evidence on which it is based, but the evidence is not negligible and it has not been convincingly explained away by Kamin's critics.

Kamin's second major criticism of the Shields study – that the twins were not really separated – is even more damaging. More than half the 'separated' twins were in fact raised in different branches of the same family; often one member of the pair stayed with its mother while the other was raised by its maternal grandmother or aunt. Only thirteen of the thirty-seven pairs were raised in unrelated families, and Kamin calculated the correlation between their test scores to be 0.51. Even some of these thirteen pairs had highly correlated environments. One of the pairs raised in unrelated families, for example, were Jessie and Winifred, who were 8 years old when they were tested. Shields's biographical information reveals that they were brought up a few hundred metres from each other, played together often, and went to the same school where they sat at the same desk. According to Shields 'they were never apart', and their intelligence test scores were very similar. Kamin selected seven 'not wholly atypical cases' such as Jessie and Winifred in which the environments were highly correlated, and calculated the correlation between their test scores to be 0.99. He commented: 'That seems incredible. Tests are never that reliable, nor are *non-separated* twins so highly correlated.'[34] It does indeed seem incredible, and even suspicious, until one begins to wonder how Kamin selected the seven cases. Mackintosh was the first to notice that Kamin appears to have selected the pairs, not only on the basis of their strikingly similar environments, but also because they had very similar test scores.[35] Mackintosh examined Shields's data and found two more pairs who had had at least as much contact with each other as the seven selected by Kamin, but whose test scores differed markedly. When they were added to

Kamin's seven pairs, the correlation dropped to 0.92, well within the bounds of test reliability and no higher than correlations reported for some non-separated twins. As Mackintosh commented, 'so much for Kamin's accusations of unconscious bias'. But in spite of Kamin's unconsciously biased calculation, the inescapable fact remains that most of Shields's 'separated' twins were not really separated at all. Their environments were highly correlated, and the correlation of 0.77 between their intelligence test scores therefore overestimates the heritability of IQ to an unknown degree, even if we ignore the real possibility of unconscious experimenter bias.

The next largest study of separated MZ twins is the earliest of the four and the only one carried out in the United States. The Newman, Freeman, and Holzinger study, often called NFH for short, was published in 1937.[36] The correlation between the IQ scores of the nineteen pairs in this study was 0.67. Apart from the problem of correlated environments, which was clearly evident in the NFH data, Kamin had two other major objections to the study: the method of recruiting the twins, and the confounding of IQ with age.

The NFH researchers recruited their twins through radio and newspaper appeals for identical twins who had been raised separately. Potential volunteers were accepted only if they agreed, in reply to a letter from the researchers, that they were 'so strikingly similar' that 'even friends and relatives' confused them. (One wonders how separated a pair of twins could be if they associated with the same friends and relatives.) In their zeal to avoid accidentally including DZ twins in their sample, the researchers rigorously excluded all pairs who seemed at all dissimilar in appearance or behaviour. One pair, for example, was excluded because, even though they looked identical, they said they were 'as different as can be in disposition'. Kamin pointed out that this method of recruitment is likely to have spuriously inflated the IQ correlation, because it biased the sample from the outset in favour of twins who were similar. This is a serious methodological error in a study in which it is precisely the degree of similarity between the twins that is at issue. A second source of bias in the recruiting method was the inducement offered to volunteers of an all-expenses-paid trip to the Century of Progress Exposition in Chicago. Such an attractive offer, in the midst of the Great Depression, may have tempted some twins to lie about (or to exaggerate) their separate upbringing in order to be included in the sample, and this may also have inflated the IQ correlation spuriously. A third problem, not mentioned by Kamin, was that twins who were separated by great distances (as, for example, one pair who lived in Alaska and California) were excluded for reasons of cost. This probably biased the sample in favour of pairs with relatively similar environments, and may also have inflated the IQ correlation spuriously. Everything considered, the NFH method of recruiting twins was seriously flawed.

Kamin's main objection to the NFH study concerned the confounding of IQ with age. The test used in the study was the original 1916 Stanford–Binet IQ test, which is notorious for its faulty standardization. A properly standardized IQ test should, of course, yield an average score of 100 in a random sample of the population at any age level, but the 1916 Stanford–Binet yields higher average scores at younger than at older age levels; in other words it is easier for younger than for older subjects to obtain high scores on the test. Since twins are, by definition, identical in age, the correlation between their IQ scores in the NFH study may be partly or wholly due to their identical ages rather than to their identical genes. Kamin showed that the unwanted correlation between IQ and age was clearly present in the NFH data, and he went on to perform a statistical calculation, which he admitted was rough and ready, to estimate the effect of age on the IQ correlation. His conclusion was that 'the 0.67 correlation reported for separated MZs by NFH was to some considerable extent inflated by an age bias'.[37] Kamin's critics have argued about the likely extent of this inflation, but not with its probable existence.

The last and smallest study of separated MZ twins can be dealt with rather briefly. It was carried out in Denmark on twelve pairs of twins and published by Juel-Nielsen in 1965,[38] and it reported a correlation of 0.62. The IQ test used was a Danish translation of the Wechsler Adult Intelligence Scale which had never been standardized on a Danish population. Kamin found a very large correlation between IQ and age in the Juel-Nielsen data, and he concluded that 'the correlation between I.Q. score and age contributes mightily to the reported I.Q. resemblance of twins'.[39] He also showed that the environments of the twins were much more similar than one might expect in a study of 'separated' twins. To mention two examples. Ingegerd and Monika were cared for by different relatives until the age of 7, but they then lived with their mother until they were 14; Martha and Marie grew up in the same neighbourhood and attended the same school for a number of years.

The problem of correlated environments due to incomplete separation (and other causes) is common to all published studies of separated MZ twins, apart from Burt's study which has to be disregarded for other reasons. When students read about separated MZ twins in textbooks they probably imagine (as I did) individuals who are separated during the first year of life and live independent lives, unaware of each other's existence, until they are discovered by psychologists and given IQ tests. Susan Farber, in her book *Identical Twins Reared Apart: A Reanalysis*,[40] examined all 121 published cases and discovered that such truly separated MZ twins can be counted on one hand.

Howard Taylor of Princeton University attempted to estimate the inflation in heritability estimates due to environmental correlation in twin studies.[41] He re-analysed all existing studies, excluding Burt's, in the light of four potentially important environmental factors. The first factor was age of separation. Only thirty-five of the twin pairs in the Shields, NFH, and Juel-Nielsen studies had been separated at or before six months of age. Rather surprisingly, the correlation between their IQ scores, averaged across studies, was only slightly lower than the correlation for the thirty-three pairs separated later (often much later) in life – the correlations were 0.61 and 0.71 respectively. The second factor, reunion prior to testing, had a much larger effect. The average correlation for the twenty-four pairs who had not been reunited – who had not lived together or associated regularly after separation – was 0.55, compared with 0.85 for the forty-four reunited pairs. Living together or associating regularly clearly has a large influence on IQ similarity, and if this aspect of environmental correlation alone is eliminated, the estimate of heritability falls to 55 per cent. Taylor's third factor was the relatedness of the twins' adoptive families. For the twenty pairs raised in families that were not obviously close relatives the correlation was 0.61; for the forty-eight raised in definitely related families it was 0.77. The fourth and last factor was the similarity of the twins' educational and socio-economic environments, which Taylor coded according to whether the twins attended the same school, were raised in homes with similar social class characteristics, and so forth. The IQ correlation for the twenty-two pairs in relatively dissimilar environments was 0.43, and for the forty-six pairs in relatively similar environments it was 0.87.

The correlation of 0.43 between the IQ scores of MZ twins raised in dissimilar educational and socio-economic environments looks, at first sight, like a suitable direct estimate of the heritability of IQ. But Taylor pointed out that eleven of these twenty-two pairs were reunited after separation or raised in related families (or both), and there are other factors that are also likely to have inflated the IQ correlation, such as the confounding of IQ with age, unconscious experimenter bias, and faulty methods of recruiting subjects. Taylor managed to find five pairs (in the Shields study) who at least had dissimilar educational and socio-economic environments, were not reunited after separation, and were raised in unrelated families. The IQ correlation for these five pairs of reasonably well separated MZ twins turned out to be 0.24. Although it is based on very meagre data, and is possibly unreliable for other reasons, this figure is the best available estimate of heritability from twin studies, and it is a long way down from Jensen and Eysenck's 0.80. Taylor rounded off his interesting analysis like this: 'It seems reasonable to suggest that the IQ correlation characterizing pairs of individuals with absolutely identical genes and absolutely uncorrelated environments would be extremely low. If this is in fact true, then the identical genes of monozygotic twins would have little to do with their comparative IQs.'[42] It is difficult to disagree; the heritability of IQ estimated from a perfect twin study might be even less than 24 per cent, which is the best estimate we have from existing twin data. But the safest conclusion is that twin studies have cast very little light on the heritability of IQ.

Kinship correlations

The method of estimating heritability via kinship correlations is based on the obvious fact that hereditary traits run in families. In the case of polygenic traits – traits like intelligence that are governed by many genes – relatives tend to resemble one another in proportion to how closely they are related. The degree of genetic relatedness between two people can be rigorously defined in terms of the proportion of genes that they share in common, but the estimation of this quantity is not as straightforward as it is sometimes thought to be. A child acquires half its genes from each of its parents, and it therefore shares approximately half its genes in common with each of them. For the same reason, DZ twins and ordinary siblings share, on average, approximately half their genes in common with each other. But in reality these figures underestimate the degree of genetic relatedness between children and their parents and between DZ twins or siblings because they ignore *assortative mating*. People do not choose sexual and marriage partners at random; they generally choose people who resemble themselves in various ways, with the result that parents tend to share a small proportion of their genes in common. Consequently, a child shares slightly more than half the genes of each of its parents, and DZ twins or siblings share, on average, slightly more than half their genes in common.[43]

From these basic facts it is possible to work out the theoretical degrees of genetic relatedness between pairs of relatives arranged in decreasing order of closeness, from MZ twins to unrelated individuals. These figures can then be compared with the IQ correlations between the pairs. If the IQ correlations are found to decrease in an orderly fashion corresponding to the decrease in genetic relatedness, this may be interpreted as strong evidence that IQ is highly heritable. In spite of what is stated in many textbooks, this inference is not entirely safe, because genetic relatedness is inevitably correlated with environmental relatedness. For one thing, the more closely people are related, the more they tend to look alike and to be treated similarly by family members, friends, and strangers. If, for example, physical attractiveness affects how a person is treated by others, then close relatives will be treated more similarly than distant relatives because physical attractiveness is highly heritable (and polygenic). Another reason for the correlation between genetic relatedness and environmental relatedness is that close relatives are more likely than distant relatives to associate with one another. The upshot of all this is that high IQ correlations among close relatives may be due to shared experiences (environmental similarity) rather than shared genes (genetic similarity).

Jensen based his argument for 80 per cent heritability of IQ largely on an impressive table of kinship correlations which displayed a very orderly pattern indeed, and Eysenck reproduced Jensen's table in his book and drew the same conclusion from it.[44] The table shows the expected decrease in IQ correlations: 0.87 between MZ twins raised together, 0.75 between MZ twins raised apart, 0.55 between siblings raised together, 0.50 between parents and children, 0.49 between DZ twins (different sexes), 0.47 between siblings raised apart, and so on down to 0.16 between second cousins, and −0.01 between unrelated children raised apart. These correlations are astonishingly close to the values predicted by an extremely crude genetic model which assumes that each correlation should be a direct estimate of the proportion of genes shared by the kinship pair if IQ is highly heritable. Jensen claimed that the table summarized 'over 30,000 correlational pairings from 8 countries in 4 continents'.[45] It was based almost entirely on a chart published by Erlenmeyer–Kimling and Jarvik in 1963,[46] with more recent data, all reported by Burt, added to it.

Erlenmeyer–Kimling and Jarvik (EKJ) culled their kinship correlations from fifty-two separate published studies, but they did not list their sources. Kamin managed to get a list of the studies from the authors, and after a great deal of detective work he concluded that the EKJ chart, and therefore the Jensen–Eysenck table, was bristling with errors, omissions, and unmistakable signs of bias. In the category of siblings reared apart, for example, Jensen's (and Eysenck's) table shows a correlation of 0.47 based on thirty-three separate studies. But the EKJ list includes only three studies containing the relevant data, so presumably 'thirty-three' should read 'three', which is rather less impressive. In fact, although the EKJ list contains three studies, data from only two (one of them from a paper by Burt and Howard) are shown on their chart. The two correlations shown on the chart are 0.46 and 0.34; the median or average of these two figures is 0.40, not 0.47 as it appears in the Jensen–Eysenck table. The third study, which was omitted from the EKJ chart, reported a correlation of 0.23. Had it been included, it would have reduced the median correlation to 0.34, or (weighting for sample sizes) to 0.25 – way below the theoretical figure of about 0.50 or 0.55 predicted by the crude genetic model when heritability is very high. The omission of this study from the EKJ chart is indeed suspicious, especially when it is viewed in the context of numerous other errors and omissions which invariably bias the figures towards the theoretical predictions of the crude genetic model. The Jensen–Eysenck correlation of 0.47 for siblings raised apart, which 'improved' the EKJ figure still further, was only one of several errors noted by Kamin and other critics. Another serious problem with the EKJ chart (and therefore also the Jensen–Eysenck table) is that much of the information in it consists of data fabricated by Burt. This includes all correlations between second cousins, uncles/aunts and nephews/nieces, and grandparents and grand-children, together with some of the crucial correlations between various categories of twins and siblings.

After Kamin's demolition of the EKJ chart, all researchers into the genetics of intelligence, including those who rejected many of Kamin's other conclusions, conceded that the chart was thoroughly discredited. Diane Paul of the University of Massachusetts was therefore astonished to discover that introductory textbooks of genetics published between 1978 (four years after Kamin's book) and 1984 continued to cite the EKJ chart uncritically.[47] Of the nineteen genetics textbooks published in the United States that devoted more than a paragraph to the heritability of intelligence, eleven cited the EKJ chart as evidence. A twelfth provided a table, which may have come via Jensen or Eysenck and was certainly based on EKJ, but did not mention its source. Ten of the textbooks prominently displayed the EKJ chart or a slightly simplified version of it. In several textbooks the EKJ chart was the *only* evidence presented on the heritability of intelligence, although the authors apparently knew that Burt's data, which were incorporated in the chart, were spurious. One textbook, published in 1982, included a dramatic insert on 'Scientific Fraud: The Case Against Sir Cyril Burt', but also asserted, on the basis of the EKJ chart, that 'the measured heritability of IQ is relatively high'. Another textbook, published in 1983, reproduced the EKJ chart and commented on it as follows: 'It points out clearly the strength of the genetic component of IQ. As the genetic relatedness diminishes between pairs of individuals, the IQ correlation also goes down .... With such information available, it is hard to deny the importance of the genotype to the IQ trait.' But this same textbook remarked that Burt's data were 'manipulated', and that this necessitated their 'exclusion from current reviews'! Paul summed up her review in these words: 'A majority of genetics students are being taught that intelligence is highly heritable (often linked to an incorrect and ideologically loaded concept of heritability) on the basis of evidence from studies that more properly belong in histories of science, or pseudo-science, than in contemporary textbooks.'

Some researchers have tried to give a precise figure for the heritability of IQ on the basis of kinship correlations. In order to do this it is necessary to develop a mathematical model of the manner in which genetic, environmental, and random error factors combine to produce the observed pattern of correlations. The mathematical details need not detain us;[48] what is important to bear in mind is that all of the models are based on a large number of assumptions, and that several of these assumptions are considered ludicrously implausible by Taylor and other critics. The assumptions have to be made because without them the models would have more unknown than measurable variables. Among the more dubious assumptions built into the models are these:

1   That MZ twins, DZ twins, ordinary sibling pairs, and unrelated adopted pairs raised together in the same family experience the same degree of environmental similarity. For example, it is assumed that MZ twins are treated no more similarly (in ways that influence IQ) than DZ twins, ordinary sibling pairs, or unrelated adopted pairs.
2   That the correlation between the environments of separated MZ twins is zero or nearly zero.
3   That for any degree of kinship the IQ of one pair member has no direct causal effect on the IQ of the other. For example, having a

bright or a dull brother or sister is assumed to have no effect on a child's IQ.

4   That the IQ tests used in different studies of kinship correlations all measure the same unitary trait.

The most influential early model was developed by Burt and Howard. When it was applied to the EKJ kinship correlations it yielded an estimate of heritability slightly over 80 per cent, and the close fit of the model's predictions with the EKJ correlations was repeatedly stressed by Jensen, Eysenck, and others. This fact is less impressive in the light of evidence that many of the EKJ correlations were from Burt's own studies, and were presumably fabricated so as to fit his model closely. When the model was applied to more reliable data from recent studies it failed completely by generating impossible predictions.[49]

More sophisticated models have been developed by Rao, Morton, and Yee in Honolulu (United States) and by Jinks, Eaves, and Fulker in Birmingham (United Kingdom). These models have been severely criticized, not only by outsiders like Kamin and Taylor, but also by the protagonists of the competing models; perhaps there is an element of transatlantic rivalry in this field of research. The Honolulu models always assume random mating and zero genetic dominance – no tendency for 'high-IQ' genes to suppress the effect of 'low-IQ' genes in a person who inherits both. The Birmingham models always assume assortative mating and positive dominance. The Birmingham researchers have claimed that the Honolulu assumption of random mating is demonstrably false, and the Honolulu researchers have commented scathingly on the Birmingham assumption of dominance: 'Today the geneticist who ... ascribes any excess of sib correlation over parent–offspring correlation to dominance must defend his integrity and intelligence.'[50] The truth is that all models depend on arbitrary and often dubious assumptions.

One very popular method of estimating heritability via kinship correlations is based on just two correlations – between MZ twins raised together and DZ twins raised together. Several different mathematical models have been proposed even for this relatively simple case. Jensen used the following formula: MZ correlation minus DZ correlation divided by $(1.00 - 0.50)$, or by $(1.00 - 0.55)$ to correct for assortative mating. The denominator represents the proportion of genes shared by MZ twins minus the proportion of genes shared by DZ twins. This formula has been used by many other researchers, but it is obvious that it depends crucially on the first of the assumptions listed above: it yields an inflated estimate of heritability to the degree that environmental similarity is greater for MZ than for DZ twins.

Jensen applied his formula to the results of several studies and obtained estimates of heritability ranging from 47 to 91 per cent. Kamin noticed that Jensen had omitted one published study that would have yielded a nonsensical heritability of *minus* 7 per cent, and another that would have yielded an equally nonsensical estimate higher than 100 per cent. More importantly, Kamin cited evidence, seriously damaging to this method of estimation, showing that environmental similarity is significantly greater for MZ than for DZ twins. The evidence is clear that MZ twins more often spend time together, study together, and share the same friends than DZ twins. This is the familiar problem of genetic relatedness being correlated with environmental relatedness; it is a problem that bedevils all heritability estimates based on kinship correlations.

Kamin's summation of this line of research was dismissive: 'The orderliness attributed to median kinship correlations, and the cross-validating consistency said to characterize different methods of estimating heritability, are in part the product of systematic bias and in part wholly imaginary.'[51] Norman Henderson of Oberlin College has provided a more sophisticated and balanced evaluation. While admitting that the assumptions built into the genetic models are arbitrary and the data contradictory, he concluded that the heritability of IQ probably lies somewhere between 30 and 60 per cent, and that there is no reason to believe that a middle value is any more likely than either of these extremes.[52] Taylor's summary comment was more dismissive: 'Given the number of required assumptions and the implausibility of the important ones, I see no reason to argue that the genetic heritability of IQ is a reliably estimable quantity .... The alternative is not to waste one's time in attempting to estimate the heritability of IQ.'

Adoption studies

The practice of adoption seems, on the face of it, to provide a golden opportunity to tease out hereditary and environmental influences, because adopted children are raised almost exactly like natural children, but the parents who raise them do not share any of their genes. If IQ is highly heritable, then the IQs of adopted children should certainly correlate moderately highly with those of their *natural* mothers, with whom they share a little over half their genes, even if they were sent for adoption very early in life.

Conversely, if the variance in IQ is determined mainly by environmental differences, then the IQs of adopted children should probably correlate highly with those of their *adoptive* parents and with other relevant features of their adoptive environments. On the basis of evidence from adoption studies, Eysenck estimated the heritability of IQ to be between 75 and 80 per cent.[53]

The classic adoption studies carried out by Barbara Burks in 1928 and Alice Leahy in 1935 focused on the second prediction.[54] Both studies investigated the correlation between the IQs of adopted children and the IQs of their adoptive parents, on the assumption that adoptive parents with high IQs provide environments favourable to the development of their adopted children's IQs and vice versa. This correlation, which they assumed to be entirely due to environmental factors, was then compared with the correlation, in a matched group of ordinary families, between the IQs of children and the IQs of their natural parents. This second correlation was assumed to be due to both genetic and environmental factors, and should be much higher than the first if the heritability of IQ is high. In both studies it was: the average parent–child correlations in adoptive families were 0.13 (Burks) and 0.18 (Leahy), whereas in natural families the average parent–child correlations were 0.46 (Burks) and 0.51 (Leahy). The conclusion drawn from these findings was that IQ must be highly heritable because ordinary children resemble their natural parents in IQ much more closely than adopted children resemble their adoptive parents. Burks applied a mathematical model of kinship correlations to her findings and estimated the heritability of IQ to be between 75 and 80 per cent.

Conclusions about heritability are valid only if the adoptive and natural families were satisfactorily matched on all other factors that might influence the parent–child IQ correlation. Kamin argued vigorously that they were not.[55] In the Burks study, each adoptive family was matched with a natural family according to the age and sex of the child, the ocupational category of the father, and the type of neighbourhood in which the home was situated. But the adoptive parents were much older, and there were fewer children in their homes, as might be expected of people who have usually spent some years trying unsuccessfully to have natural children of their own before deciding to adopt. Despite the matching for occupational category, the average income of the adoptive families was more than one and a half times as high as that of the natural families; in other words the adoptive families were much more affluent. The adoptive parents more often owned their own homes, and their homes were much larger and more expensive than those of the matched group of natural parents. Similar differences existed in the Leahy study.

Most importantly, Kamin calculated that in both studies, in terms of environmental advantages, *'the variance in adoptive homes was significantly lower than in [natural] homes*. The adoptive homes were closely bunched near the top .... This fact alone could account for the failure to find strong correlations between IQ of adopted children and measures of home environment'.[56] This bunching near the top is, of course, to be expected, because adoption agencies try to place children in 'good' homes. To show why it reduces the parent–child IQ correlation in adoptive homes, Kamin used an analogy from boxing. There would be a very high correlation between success in boxing and body weight if competitors were not divided into weight classes, because heavier boxers would generally beat lighter opponents. Weight classes were established precisely to remove this correlation; fights are allowed only between competitors of roughly similar weight, and the correlation between boxing success and body weight is therefore low. Kamin argued that, in terms of the environments they provide for their children, almost all adoptive homes are bunched in the heavyweight class, whereas natural homes are spread across all classes.

The logic of Kamin's argument, which he does not make very clear, is as follows. The IQ correlation between parents and children in natural families is due to both genetic and environmental factors, but in adoptive families it is due to environmental factors alone. It might seem, therefore, that the parent–child correlation in natural families minus the correlation in adoptive families could provide an estimate of heritability. But Kamin's boxing analogy shows that a correlation is artificially reduced if one of the variables is restricted in variance, and this is the case for the environmental variable in adoptive homes. This means that the parent–child correlation would be higher in natural than adoptive families *even if there were no genetic influences operating*. The calculations of Burks and Leahy, and others who have used this method, therefore overestimate heritability to an unknown degree.

The British geneticist David Fulker defended the Burks and Leahy studies against Kamin's onslaught.[57] He argued that if the restricted environmental variance in adoptive homes was as important as Kamin made it out to be, then we should expect it to be reflected in a restricted variance in the adopted children's IQs. This is a very good point; what are the facts? The variance in IQs was indeed less among adopted than natural children in the Leahy study – Kamin called the difference 'significant' and Fulker called it 'small' – but in the Burks study the variances were almost identical. The restricted environmental variance in the adoptive homes, which Kamin took such pains to prove, seems to have had virtually no effect on the variance of the children's IQs. Kamin's explanation was that the variance in the IQs of the adopted children was inflated by the presence of a few children with *very* low IQs, entirely outside the range of the natural children, and probably due to organic brain damage. If these children are excluded, then the variance in the adopted group is indeed much smaller than that of the natural group. Fulker rejected this argument as arbitrary, and I for one find it difficult to reach a clear conclusion on it. But even if Kamin's explanation is debatable, it is fair to conclude that the Burks and Leahy studies do not provide any very persuasive evidence concerning the heritability of IQ.

An adoption study reported by Harry Munsinger of the University of California, San Diego, in 1975 yielded an apparently much more persuasive result.[58] His forty-one Californian children had all been adopted in earliest infancy. Munsinger correlated their IQs with estimates of natural and adoptive parents' intelligence based on socio-economic status (SES) – the adults' IQ scores were not available. The correlation with the adoptive parents' SES turned out to be very small and non-significant, but the correlation with the natural parents' SES was a thumping 0.70 – higher even than the correlation normally found for children living with their natural parents when a direct measure of IQ is available. Munsinger's results seemed to show that upper-class parents have genes for high intelligence which are passed on and expressed in their children's IQs even if their children are separated from them in earliest infancy, and also that environment plays a negligible role in the development of intelligence.

When this study was published Kamin wrote to Munsinger inquiring whether the ratings of parental SES were reliable and whether they were done 'blindly', that is, by someone ignorant of the children's IQs. Munsinger replied: 'If you mean the translation from occupation to numbers, then the reliability is over 0.98 based on two different blind judges – All the ratings of SES were done by two people independently, and with no knowledge of the child's IQ.'[59] But when Kamin trained his eagle eye on Munsinger's data he discovered something very odd indeed. In many cases the husband and wife had been given the same SES rating on a six-point scale; but in all thirty-four cases where the SES was not identical the husband and wife differed by exactly *two* social classes – never by one, or by three, four, or five, but always by exactly two. Kamin commented sarcastically that 'such a strange reluctance to mate with members of adjacent social classes – while succumbing to the charms of individuals precisely two social classes removed – is clearly nonsensical.'

Kamin drew attention to this suspicious anomaly in Munsinger's data in a paper in 1977.[60] A reply from Munsinger was published alongside Kamin's critique, together with a further comment from Kamin. Munsinger's reply contained the following astonishing admission: 'I cannot report precisely how the original parental intellectual level ratings [the SES ratings] were generated.' His explanation for this was that the adoption records were confidential and he had not had personal access to them. It was the staff of the adoption agency, Munsinger revealed, who had rated the parents' SES. This turned out to be a 'difficult, subjective, and sometimes ambiguous procedure'. Remember that Munsinger had previously assured Kamin in private correspondence that the ratings had been done blindly by two judges with almost perfect reliability!

Regarding the 'unusual distributions of parental intellectual level' – the fact that every couple received either the same SES rating or ratings separated by exactly two social classes – Munsinger offered the following explanation: 'I believe that the ... ratings were produced by first obtaining a family rating and then generating individual ratings consistent with the midparent rating.' In other words, the raters decided first which social class the couple belonged to, and then, if one parent was judged to be of higher social class than the other, the rating of the higher-class parent was raised by one class and that of the lower-class parent was reduced by one class. This would explain why the pairs of ratings were all either identical or separated by exactly two classes, although it is not clear why the raters should have adopted this silly procedure. Kamin was unimpressed with Munsinger's explanation: 'I can only reiterate that Munsinger's study is rife with error, and is invalid. When a scientist indicates that he "cannot report precisely" how his data were obtained, he has nothing to report – and less than nothing if those data fall into "unusual distributions".'

An impartial reader should, in my view, be hesitant about accepting Munsinger's data and his attempted justification of them. At the very least Munsinger was guilty of prevarication in his correspondence with Kamin about the way the SES ratings were done. Although Munsinger's adoption study continues to be cited in textbooks as persuasive evidence for the high heritability of IQ, many scholars believe that the results, like Burt's, are literally too good to be true. It is worth noting that Munsinger is an even more rabid hereditarian than Burt: he is the only psychologist ever to have gone on record with the preposterous claim that the true heritability of IQ is 100 per cent.[61]

Neither Burks nor Leahy (nor Munsinger) investigated the correlation between the IQs of adopted children and the IQs of their natural parents. If such a correlation does indeed exist, it would seem to provide very powerful support to the hereditarian position; and if it does not, the hereditarian position would seem to be severely weakened since, after all, children inherit more than half their genes from each parent. The classic study providing the relevant information was reported by Skodak and Skeels in 1949.[62] They found that the IQs of sixty-three children adopted before the age of six months correlated 0.44 with the IQs of their natural mothers. For many years this finding was regarded as the strongest single piece of evidence for the apparently high heritability of IQ. Many commentators remarked that there seemed to be no possible environmental explanation for the significant IQ correlation between mothers and their children who were separated from them in early infancy.

There is, however, a rather interesting environmental explanation for the Skodak and Skeels finding, and for other significant correlations that have been reported between adopted children and their natural mothers. The environmental explanation is selective placement. Kamin[63] pointed out that children are not delivered to their adoptive homes by storks; they are usually placed there by adoption agencies. The evidence shows that adoption agencies routinely practise selective placement; they try to fit the child to the home by placing it with adoptive parents of roughly the same educational standard as its natural mother. In the Skodak and Skeels study, for example, Kamin focused attention on the twelve adoptive homes in which both parents were college graduates and, at the other end of the scale, the twenty-two in which neither parent had even completed secondary education. The natural mothers of the children placed in college-educated homes had an average of 11.3 years of formal education, whereas the natural mothers of those placed in poorly educated homes had only 9.1 years of formal education on average. Kamin concluded: 'We can assume that the children of highly-educated biological mothers were placed into "good" foster homes, homes conducive to the development of a high I.Q. The correlation between child's I.Q. and biological mother's education follows directly from this fact.'[64]

There certainly was some selective placement according to

education in the Skodak and Skeels study, and this may conceivably explain why the adoptive children's IQs resembled those of their natural mothers. But this explanation would be more persuasive, as Mackintosh[65] was quick to point out, if the children's IQs correlated significantly with their adoptive parents' education; in fact the correlation was a non-significant 0.02. Skodak and Skeels themselves showed that selective placement according to education could not explain the IQ correlation. They compared children whose natural mothers' IQs were lowest (below 70) and highest (105 and above). The children of these extreme groups differed significantly in IQ as predicted by hereditarian theory – their IQs averaged 96 and 118 respectively – but Skodak and Skeels argued that this difference could not be due to selective placement because the education of the adoptive parents did *not* differ significantly between these two groups. Kamin responded to this by calling education a 'blunt measure' of home environment and by pointing out that on other measures, such as family income, attendance of the children at private schools, and number of books, typewriters, and personal radios in the home, the adoptive homes of the children with high-IQ natural mothers were definitely superior. It is perfectly true that education is a blunt measure but, as Mackintosh commented, this simply shows that Kamin's preceding argument was largely irrelevant. Kamin wanted to have his cake – the evidence that children of well-educated mothers were selectively placed in well-educated adoptive homes – and to eat it by claiming that education is a blunt measure of home environment because it did not correlate with the children's IQs.

More recent adoption studies have used an improved research design which avoids some of the pitfalls of the earlier studies. The improved design capitalizes on the fact that there are some adoptive parents who, in addition to adopting a child, also have a natural child of their own. (It is not uncommon for a woman to become pregnant immediately after adopting a child, and some psychologists believe that this is evidence of a psychological factor in infertility). What is of interest in estimating heritability is the difference between the parent–child IQ correlations for the adopted children on the one hand and the natural children on the other. Since the adopted and natural children are raised in the same households by the same parents, the IQ correlation between the parents and their natural children should be significantly higher only if genes determine IQ to a significant extent. The parents have been chosen by adoption agencies as likely providers of 'good' homes, so restricted environmental variance and therefore low correlations are to be expected. But this applies equally to the adopted and natural children because the research design involves only one group of families, which eliminates a fatal problem in earlier studies.

The first large-scale studies using the improved design were the 1977 interracial adoption study of Scarr and Weinberg in Minnesota and the 1979 Texas Adoption Project of Horn, Loehlin, and Willerman.[66] In the Minnesota study the parents and their natural children were all white, and the adopted children were nearly all black or of mixed race. The results showed that the mothers' IQs correlated 0.29 with those of their adopted children, and 0.34 with those of their natural children; the second correlation is slightly higher, but the difference is not statistically significant. In the Texas study the correlations were 0.22 between mothers and their adopted children and 0.20 between mothers and their natural children; in this case the difference is in the opposite direction, but also non-significant, suggesting even more emphatically that shared genes contribute nothing to the resemblance between mothers and children. According to Kamin 'the results from Texas and Minnesota appear to inflict fatal damage on the notion that IQ is highly heritable, for they show that children reared by the same mother resemble her in IQ to the same degree, whether or not they share her genes'.[67]

Unfortunately things are not quite as straightforward as that. In the Minnesota study the *fathers'* IQs correlated 0.07 with those of their adopted children and 0.34 with those of their natural children, and this difference *is* significant. The same significant difference emerged in the Texas study, where the correlations were 0.12 between fathers and their adopted children and 0.28 between fathers and their natural children. No one, to my knowledge, has given a satisfactory environmental explanation of these differences.

What about the IQ correlations between the adopted children and their *natural* mothers who relinquished them? If IQ is highly heritable the correlations should be moderately high; otherwise they should be low or nonexistent. In the Minnesota study the IQs of the adopted children's natural mothers were unavailable, but Scarr and Weinberg reported that the correlation between the *education* of the natural mothers and the IQs of their relinquished children was 0.32. On the face of it, this correlation seems to indicate high heritability, but Kamin showed that it could be entirely due to selective placement. Using Scarr and Weinberg's raw data, he correlated the education of these natural mothers with the IQs of their children's adoptive siblings – the children who lived in the same adoptive homes as their relinquished children but shared none of their genes. The correlation turned out to be 0.33, and it must have been due entirely to selective placement since no genetic relationship was involved. It shows rather impressively that the entire IQ correlation between these natural mothers and their own relinquished children was probably also due to selective placement. In the Texas study the IQs of the natural mothers of the adopted children were available, and they correlated 0.31 with the IQs of their own relinquished children. Kamin calculated that they correlated 0.19 with the IQs of their children's adoptive siblings. This correlation must also be due to selective placement, and it accounts for a large portion of the 0.31 correlation between natural mothers and their relinquished children, though, in this case, not all of it.

In the Minnesota and Texas studies there were some families with more than one adopted child and a natural child, or more than one natural child and an adopted child. This makes possible a comparison of the correlations between the IQs of genetically related and genetically unrelated children raised in the same households. The results came as a surprise to both groups of researchers. The correlations between the IQs of pairs of natural children (with more than half their genes in common), pairs of adopted children (genetically unrelated), and natural-adopted pairs (genetically unrelated) were similar: none of the correlations differed significantly from any other. Kamin described this as 'another fatal blow to the view that IQ is highly heritable'.[68] The Minnesota researchers interpreted their parent–child correlations as evidence that the heritability of IQ lies somewhere between 40 per cent and 70 per cent, but they pointed out that their sibling correlations suggest that heritability is close to zero. The Texas researchers reached an estimate of heritability of 38 per cent. But no confidence can be attached to the heritability estimates, because, apart from serious methodological problems in interpreting the data, the estimates are mutually contradictory.

Zero heritability?

At the end of his 1981 debate with Eysenck, Kamin concluded: 'There is no compelling evidence that the heritability of IQ is 80 per cent, or 50 per cent, or 20 per cent. There are not even adequate grounds for dismissing the hypothesis that the heritability of IQ is zero.'[69] This conclusion is plainly absurd, and it is a striking example of Kamin's tendency to spoil his devastating critique by exaggerating. It is absurd because there are several disorders of known genetic origin, including phenylketonuria (discussed below), which result in severe mental retardation. This shows that IQ must be partly heritable at the lower extreme of the IQ range, and therefore that the overall heritability of IQ cannot be zero. Furthermore, geneticists have yet to discover a trait that is heritable at its extremes but not within its normal range.[70] The heritability of IQ may be extremely low, and it is almost certainly much lower than Jensen and Eysenck have claimed, but Kamin's assertion that it may be zero is equally indefensible.

The fact remains that Kamin has torn the hereditarian arguments and evidence used by Jensen, Eysenck, and others to ribbons. Neither the twin studies, nor the kinship correlations, nor even the adoption studies have stood up to close scrutiny. The proponents of the 80 per cent heritability estimate have not succeeded in answering the most devastating of the criticisms, and in most cases they have not even attempted to do so. In the 1981 debate, Eysenck wrote: 'Although the temptation to answer Kamin's criticism in detail, pointing out the way in which quotations are wrenched out of context, misinterpreted and generally abused, is almost irresistible, I will not give way to it.'[71] Instead of yielding to temptation he referred his readers to David Fulker's review of Kamin's 1974 book which, he said, 'lists many almost incredible statistical errors'. I have outlined Fulker's major criticisms, and none of them referred to 'almost incredible statistical errors', or even perfectly credible ones. The differences between Fulker and Kamin are all matters of judgement and interpretation of evidence. Virtually the whole of Eysenck's sixteen-page rejoinder to Kamin at the end of the debate is devoted to repetitive attacks on Kamin's scholarship without regard to the specific arguments. Eysenck accused Kamin of behaving like an adversary rather than a truth seeker, he described Kamin's arguments as 'absolutely vague' and based on various 'incompatible' criticisms, he stated that Kamin 'cannot be trusted to be factually accurate', and finally, with presumably unintended irony, he objected to Kamin's *ad hominem* style of argument.

A word needs to be said in conclusion about the social and political policy implications of the debate over the heritability of IQ. Many people apparently believe that there is a direct connection between heritability and fixedness – that any trait that is highly heritable must also be relatively unmodifiable by environmental means. It was this superstition that led to the introduction of the 'eleven-plus' examination in England on the basis of Sir Cyril Burt's evidence apparently showing that IQ is highly heritable. In fact there is no simple connection between heritability and fixedness. Phenylketonuria, for example, is a hereditary disorder caused by a single recessive gene; its heritability is 100 per cent. It normally leads to severe mental retardation, but its effects can be prevented by eliminating phenylalanine from the diet of an infant known to be suffering from it. Conversely, mental retardation can result from serious head injury – a purely environmental cause – and yet be practically unmodifiable by environmental means. It is interesting to note that, in a perfectly egalitarian utopia in which, by definition, environmental differences affecting IQ were entirely eliminated, the heritability of IQ would necessarily be 100 per cent. Whether the heritability of IQ is high or low in real-life inegalitarian societies, the degree to which it can be modified by suitable environmental interventions is an entirely separate question. It follows from this that any attempt to read social and political implications into the evidence for the heritability of IQ is based on mere superstition. But it is difficult to see any other reason why the debate has aroused such strong emotions.

Notes

1 *The Times*, 18 March 1959.
2 *The Times*, 19, 20, 21, 23 March 1959.
3 Hoffmann (1962), p. 19.
4 Write down the original sequence. You can see at a glance if every number can be obtained by multiplying its neighbour by a whole number; if so write down these multipliers under the original sequence, otherwise write down the *differences* between adjacent numbers, always subtracting the left-hand number from its neighbour on the right. Repeat this procedure with the new sequence, and if necessary with the following sequence, until you get a row whose continuation is obvious. The missing number at the end of this row can then be filled in, and you can then work backwards through previous rows until you get to the missing number of the original sequence. Let us see how this method fares with four number-sequence problems in a 'very difficult' IQ test, containing twenty questions in all, specially designed for 'intellectual giants' (Eysenck, 1966, pp. 145–8). The test is supposed to be so difficult that 'if you have an average I.Q. you may not get any answers right' even if you spend a whole evening on it. The first number sequence in this test is 118, 199, 226, 235, ? The numbers are not whole multiples of their neighbours, so we write down their differences: 81, 27, 9 .... In this row it is clear that each number is three times its neighbour on the right, so the next row is 3, 3, ..., and the missing number on the end of this row is clearly also 3 Then, working backwards, the missing number on the end of the previous row is 3, because 3 × 3 = 9, and adding 3 to 235 we get 238, the missing number of the original sequence, which is the 'right' answer according to Eysenck. The next number sequence is 0, 2, 8, 18, ? This yields (by subtraction) 2, 6, 10,

... and then (by subtraction again) 4, 4, ..., and we can fill in another 4. This makes the missing number of the previous row 14, and the missing number of the original sequence 32 – 'right' again, although Eysenck's proof is very complicated. The third number sequence is 1, 1, 2, 3, 5, 8, 13, 21, ? The next row (by subtraction) is 0, 1, 1, 2, 3, 5, 8, ..., which is obviously the same as the original sequence, so we fill in a 13 at the end of it. Then the missing number of the original sequence is 13 + 21 = 34, which is also 'right' (mathematically trained readers will recognize the Fibonacci sequence). The last number sequence in the test is 2, 20, 42, 68, ? which yields (by subtraction) 18, 22, 26, ..., and then 4, 4, ... After filling in another 4 on the end of this row it is clear that there must be a 30 on the end of the previous row, and that the missing number of the original sequence must be 68 + 30 = 98, which is once again the 'right' answer, although Eysenck's proof is mind-bending. Number sequences in less difficult IQ tests nearly always yield up their secrets when analysed in this way, and it is usually easy to do all the calculations in one's head. Dewdney (1986) has described an exceedingly simple computer program which performs at or near genius level on number-sequence IQ problems by using a method only slightly more sophisticated than mine.

5   The best historical survey of IQ testing is Fancher (1985). See also Kamin (1974) and Gould (1981).

6   Galton (1869).

7   ibid., p. 42.

8   See Mackintosh (1986) for a critical review of recent attempts to measure intelligence via reaction times, inspection times, and even evoked potentials in electrical brain waves.

9   Binet (1909), pp. 101–2. I have improved the standard translation slightly.

10 Terman (1916), pp. 6–7.

11 ibid., p. 92.

12 Quoted in Gould (1981), p. 336.

13 The full story has been told by Fancher (1985), Kamin (1974), and Gould (1981). The direct influence of psychologists on the passage of the 1924 Act should not, however, be overstated; Snyderman and Herrnstein (1983) have claimed that it was negligible. For a balanced view, see Samelson (1977, 1979).

14 *Report of Consultative Committee on Secondary Education* (1938), pp. 123–5.

15 Jensen (1969). The quotation in the text is from p. 82.

16 Eysenck (1971). The quotations in the text are from pp. 117 and 71.

17 Kamin (1974). The quotation in the text is from p. 15.

18 Eysenck and Kamin (1981).

19 The intraclass correlation coefficient is defined as $[V(b) - V(w)]/[V(b) + V(w)]$, where $V(b)$ is the variance *between* the mean scores of the twin pairs, found by taking the mean score of each twin pair and then calculating the variance of this set of means, and $V(w)$ is the sum of the variances *within* each twin pair, found by calculating the variance in each pair of scores and then adding these variances up.

20 Burt (1955, 1958, 1966).

21 Jensen (1969), p. 47.

22 Eysenck (1973), p. 137.

23 Kamin (1974).

24 ibid., p. 71.

25 Details and references are given in Fancher (1985), pp. 212–13.

26 Letter to *The Times*, 9 December 1976.
27 Quoted in Gould (1981), p. 235.
28 Hearnshaw (1979).
29 Mackintosh (1980), pp. 174–5.
30 Shields (1962).
31 Kamin (1974), p. 74.
32 Fulker (1975); Mackintosh (1975).
33 Eysenck and Kamin (1981), p. 110.
34 Kamin (1974), p. 77.
35 Mackintosh (1975). The quotation in the text is from p. 680.
36 Newman, Freeman, and Holzinger (1937).
37 Kamin (1974), p. 91.
38 Juel-Nielsen (1965).
39 Kamin (1974), p. 93.
40 Farber (1980).
41 Taylor (1980), ch. 3.
42 ibid., p. 101.
43 The following random experiment (to use the terminology of mathematical statistics) models inheritance. Fill a large urn with balls labelled A, B, C, ..., and another large urn with the same number of balls labelled a, b, c, ... Randomly select half the balls from the first urn and half from the second, note their labels, and return them to their original urns. Then repeat the random selection from the urns. In this model the balls represent polymorphic genes (genes that occur in more than one form), the urns are the parents, and the random selections are inheritance by a pair of DZ twins or siblings. Obviously each child shares half the genes of each parent, and on average, the two children share half their genes in common: approximately half the balls chosen in the first selection will turn up again in the second because there is a 50–50 chance of any particular ball from the first selection turning up in the second. To take account of assortative mating, add a small number of balls with identical labels, say 1, 2, 3, ..., to both urns to represent genes that the parents share in common, and repeat the two random selections. Each child now shares slightly more than half its genes with each parent: the balls selected from one urn plus a few more with number labels selected from the other urn but duplicated in the first. Also, a pair of DZ twins or siblings share slightly more than half their genes in common: the half selected from the same urns, plus a few selected from different urns but bearing the same labels (1, 2, 3, ...).
44 Jensen (1969), p. 49; Eysenck (1971), p. 62.
45 Jensen (1969), p. 48.
46 Erlenmeyer-Kimling and Jarvik (1963).
47 Paul (1985). The quotation at the end of the paragraph is from p. 324.
48 The most lucid explanation of the mathematical models and critique of their underlying assumptions is given in Taylor (1980), chs 4 and 5.
49 Eysenck and Kamin (1981), pp. 136–7.
50 Rao, Morton, and Yee (1976), p. 241.
51 Kamin (1974), p. 146.
52 Henderson (1982). The quotation below is from Taylor (1980), p. 170.
53 Eysenck and Kamin (1981), p. 51.
54 Burks (1928); Leahy (1935).
55 Kamin (1974), ch. 5; Eysenck and Kamin (1981), ch. 15.
56 Kamin (1974), p. 158, italics in original. The boxing analogy mentioned in

the text is from Eysenck and Kamin (1981), p. 117.

57 Fulker (1975).

58 Munsinger (1975).

59 Quoted in Eysenck and Kamin (1981), p. 115.

60 Kamin (1977a). See also the reply by Munsinger (1977a) and the rejoinder by Kamin (1977b). The first quotation from Munsinger is from p. 407, and the others are from p. 408. The quotation from Kamin is from p. 412.

61 Munsinger (1977b).

62 Skodak and Skeels (1949).

63 Kamin (1974), ch. 5.

64 ibid., p. 172.

65 Mackintosh (1975), pp. 682–3.

66 Scarr and Weinberg (1977); Horn, Loehlin, and Willerman (1979).

67 Eysenck and Kamin (1981), p. 119.

68 ibid., p. 120.

69 ibid., p. 154.

70 Taylor (1980), p. 209.

71 Eysenck and Kamin (1981), p. 158. The quotation in the following sentence is from p. 164.

3   Intelligence and race: are black people genetically inferior?

In 1982 I published a paper in collaboration with Paul Gorman, a Detective Inspector of Police, on 'Conservatism, Dogmatism, and Authoritarianism in British Police Officers'.[1] It reported the results of a carefully controlled investigation into the attitudes and personalities of police officers, and provided the first hard evidence that many experienced constables were virulent racists. The evidence came largely from standardized psychological tests, but the prejudices were most vividly illustrated in the short, open-ended essays that we asked the police officers to write on the subject of 'Coloured Immigration'. Here are a few quotations from the essays: 'Certain members of the coloured population that I have met are OK but the majority of youths of the W. Indian community are savage ignorant vicious thieving bastards'; 'The immigration should be stopped immediately to prevent our towns and cities from becoming infested with coloureds'; 'Over 50% of trouble caused today either by niggers or because of them. Most of them are just Dirty, Smelly backward people who will never change in a month of Sundays. In my opinion most niggers especially Rasters should be wiped out of distinction.'

These alarming findings were widely debated in the press and on television and radio, and they also generated a lively controversy in the technical literature. One critic[2] accused us of interpreting our data in a 'selective and distorting fashion, so as to give a false and damaging impression of police officers' attitudes'. I replied that the critique was based on errors, misunderstandings, and misquotations; I pointed out no fewer than fourteen errors on the first page of the critique alone. In spite of this controversy, the details of which I will not rehearse here, our findings were taken seriously in official circles, and they played a small part in influencing recruitment policies in the Metropolitan Police Force in London. Following violent clashes between black youths and the police in south London, a government inquiry was set up, and Lord Scarman's official report cited our findings in support of his recommendation that recruits should be screened in an effort to eradicate racial prejudice from all police forces.[3]

Racial prejudice is not, of course, a new phenomenon, nor is it confined to British police officers. It has been endemic in many parts of Europe and various former colonial territories, including the United States, since the early nineteenth century. One of the persistent themes of racial prejudice down the ages has been the belief that members of certain racial groups are congenitally unintelligent ('ignorant' and 'backward' in the words of the police officers quoted earlier) and that their intellectual inferiority is inborn and unalterable (hence they could 'never change in a month of Sundays').

The first atttempt to lend scientific respectability to this belief was Sir Francis Galton's chapter on 'The Comparative Worth of Different Races' in his book *Hereditary Genius*, first published in 1869.[4] Galton estimated that black Americans were genetically inferior to white Americans by about two 'grades', which is equivalent to roughly 15 IQ points in modern terminology. He explained the significance of this difference, and his personal reaction to it, as follows:

The number among the negroes of those men whom we should call half-witted men, is very large. Every book alluding to negro servants in America is full of instances. I was myself much impressed by this fact during my travels in Africa. The mistakes the negroes made in their own matters, were so childish, stupid, and simpleton-like, as frequently to make me ashamed of my own species.

The modern phase of the debate over race and intelligence began in 1969 when the psychologist Arthur Jensen of the University of California, Berkeley, published a long paper entitled 'How Much Can We Boost IQ and Scholastic Achievement?'.[5] His answer, in a nutshell, was: Not a lot. Two years later, Hans Eysenck of the University of London, a former teacher of Jensen's, published a book containing essentially the same ideas in less technical language.[6] The main thesis put forward by Jensen and Eysenck was that 'all the evidence to date suggests the strong and indeed overwhelming importance of genetic factors in producing the great variety of intellectual differences which we observe in our culture, and much of the difference observed between certain racial groups'. (In fact, even in 1969, 'all the evidence to date' did not speak with one voice, as we shall see.) The thesis can be broken down into two logically independent propositions: first, that intellectual differences between people are overwhelmingly determined by genetic factors; and second, that the 15-point average IQ gap between black and white Americans, and the slightly smaller gap between black and white people in Britain, is largely due to genetic factors. The first proposition is discussed in detail in Chapter 2; this chapter will focus on the second proposition about race differences.

In his original article Jensen presented the evidence on race and intelligence as if it were rather uncontroversial among experts. Eysenck went even further in actually quantifying the consensus of the experts: 'I would be prepared to assert that experts (real experts, that is) would agree with at least 90 per cent of what I am going to say – probably the true figure would be a good deal higher, but there is no point in exaggerating.'[7] Actually, the true figure was probably a good deal lower. In 1964 Thomas Pettigrew, a leading social psychologist and unquestionably a 'real expert' on race and intelligence, reported that he could find only three psychologists among the 21,000 members of the American Psychological Association who were willing to attribute the average IQ difference between the races to genetic factors, and his own conclusion was that the evidence 'strongly favors a non-genetic interpretation of the typically lower intelligence test score averages of Negro groups'.[8] After Jensen's article was published, another researcher polled a representative sample of the American Psychological Association and found that more than two-thirds still disagreed or tended to disagree with the Jensen–Eysenck hereditarian thesis.[9]

Although the interpretation of the evidence was, and still is, controversial, the basic facts of the case are reasonably clear. Numerous studies carried out in the United States over the past half century have shown that black Americans tend to score significantly lower on IQ tests – about 15 points lower, on average, though the difference varies from study to study – than white Americans.[10] In Britain, four studies, the earliest of which was published in 1970, have compared the IQ scores of West Indian immigrants with those of the indigenous white population.[11] In all four studies West Indians scored consistently lower, on average, than indigenous white people, but the differences were not as great as those typically reported in the United States. If recent immigrants who did not receive all their schooling in Britain are excluded, the average difference varies from study to study and from IQ test to IQ test between 5 and 13 points. The question at issue is thus not whether race differences in IQ exist, but whether these differences can reasonably be attributed to genetic factors.

Numerous books, articles, and letters critical of the Jensen–Eysenck hereditarian thesis appeared in print during the 1970s and early 1980s; no recent psychological issue has generated a more voluminous or heated debate. I shall focus on the pivotal arguments and research findings around which the debate has revolved.

A priori arguments

A priori arguments have appeared in various places and in various guises. The most popular version appeared in one of Jensen's articles. It was quoted by Eysenck as follows:

The myth of racial equality, while more acceptable in principle to any liberal and well-meaning person than its opposite, is still a myth: there is no scientific evidence to support it. Indeed, as Jensen has pointed out, the a priori probability of such a belief is small: '... Nearly every anatomical, physiological, and biochemical system investigated shows racial differences. Why should the brain be an exception?'[12]

On the face of it, this argument seems very persuasive, and it is seductive because it seems to settle the issue beyond reasonable doubt without the inconvenience of examining any empirical evidence. But it has been sharply challenged by critics on the grounds that its own empirical premise is false. According to the critics, most anatomical, physiological, and biochemical systems, including people's brains, show *no* racial differences. After Jensen's article appeared, the South African physical anthropologist Philip Tobias reviewed all published comparisons of the brains of black and white Americans and concluded that 'there is no acceptable evidence for ... differences in the brains of these two racial groups, and certainly nothing which provides a satisfactory anatomical basis for explaining any differences in IQ or in other mental or performance tests, in temperament or in behaviour'.[13] Even if differences were to be found, Tobias argued, they would lend little weight to the hereditarian thesis because research with animals has shown that nutrition and other purely environmental factors can influence brain growth. In any event, there is no simple correspondence between brain anatomy and intelligence. The brain of the great French writer Anatole France was only three-quarters average size, and there are people of below-normal intelligence whose brains are three times as large as the average.

Population geneticists nowadays define racial groups in terms of the relative frequency of polymorphic genes – genes that exist in two or more different forms or alleles and account for the genetic variation among individuals. An example of a polymorphic gene is the one that determines a person's ABO blood type. It exists in three alternative forms, symbolized by A, B, and O, and the relative frequencies of these alleles vary from one racial group to another. Among Caucasoid populations, including white groups in the United States and Britain, the relative frequencies are roughly 28, 6, and 66 per cent respectively, whereas among Negroid populations such as Afro-Americans and West Indians the corresponding relative frequencies are roughly 18, 11, and 71 per cent. In recent years geneticists have identified literally hundreds of human genes, each of which contains instructions for the body to manufacture a specific protein, and very large numbers of people have been examined to determine their genetic constitution – only a small blood sample is needed to make the necessary tests. Results have shown that 75 per cent of the proteins are identical in all individuals examined, irrespective of race, with the exception of occasional rare mutations. The remaining 25 per cent are coded by the polymorphic genes, but even these show only modest differences between racial groups, as illustrated by the example of the ABO blood types. This method of research has been used to estimate how much of the genetic variation between individuals is due to racial differences. The calculation has been done independently by three groups of geneticists using three slightly different techniques. The conclusions of all three are the same: only about 7 per cent of human genetic variation is due to racial differences.[14] Despite the fact that racial groups tend to differ strikingly in skin colour, hair form, and facial features, it seems that most anatomical, physiological, and biochemical systems show *no* racial differences, even in terms of relative gene frequencies. Race, like beauty, is only skin deep, and the main premise of the a priori argument is probably unsound.

Some protagonists in the debate have turned the a priori argument on its head, claiming that it is a priori *un*likely that black and white people differ in genetic factors related to intelligence.[15] The crux of the inverted a priori argument is amusingly illustrated by Mayr's apocryphal story about an American journalist visiting Haiti.[16] The journalist was interviewing the President, chatting about the country and its population. He asked the President what proportion of the Haitian population was white. 'About 95 per cent' replied the President. The journalist looked around at the assembled entourage, scratched his head, and said, 'You've got to be kidding! How do you people define white?', to which the President replied, 'How do you people define coloured?' 'Well,' said the journalist, 'of course you're coloured if you've got Negro blood.' The President smiled. 'That's exactly our definition too: you're white if you've got white blood.'

The story illustrates the fact that lay people define racial groups arbitrarily, and according to social rather than genetic criteria. In North America and Britain, any person with recognizable black ancestry is classified as black, whereas in most parts of Latin America any one who is not entirely black is white. (In South Africa the rule is more elaborate: people of known mixed descent are classified as coloured and are distinguished from both black and white people, not only socially but also in the eyes of the law and with regard to political rights.) No one knows how such an inclusive definition of the 'Negro race' evolved in the social histories of the United States and Britain. In his book, *Brown America*, Edwin Embree suggested that 'this custom grew up during slavery in order to increase the number of slaves, who constituted valuable property'.[17] Whatever the reason, it certainly lessens the a priori likelihood of the hereditarian thesis.

A related factor which should be taken into consideration is the genetic diversity of the slaves who were originally imported from Africa into North America and the West Indies. The African slaves originated from areas as far apart as West Africa, Angola, and Madagascar, and were at least as genetically diverse as the peoples of Europe. After many generations of miscegenation with white people, 75 per cent of Afro-Americans have at least one white ancestor and some 15 per cent have predominantly white ancestry. Statistical studies of blood group markers have shown that, on average, the ancestry of Afro-Americans is about 80 per cent African and 20 per cent European.[18] West Indian immigrants in Britain and their descendants are similar in racial ancestry to Afro-Americans. According to some of Jensen's and Eysenck's critics, these facts make it a priori unlikely that black people in these countries have any very sharply distinctive inborn psychological characteristics.[19] Two relatively homogeneous and biologically defined groups might reasonably be expected to show marked genetic differences, but the same cannot be said of two heterogeneous groups defined by arbitrary social critera. The a priori argument in favour of the hereditarian theory of race differences in intelligence is therefore regarded as suspect by most authorities. But no firm conclusions can be reached by a priori reasoning alone; the question is empirical, and the evidence needs to be examined.

Racial admixture and crossing studies

Many people believe that, in principle, the hereditarian thesis cannot be tested scientifically because, by the nature of things, no unambiguous evidence relevant to it can be found. If this were indeed the case, then the thesis would amount to nothing more than a metaphysical dogma. I do not believe this, nor do I agree with Eysenck that all the evidence is 'purely circumstantial',[20] which amounts to almost the same thing.

The most direct evidence, according to recent authorities,[21] comes from racial admixture and racial crossing studies. Racial admixture studies capitalize on the fact, mentioned earlier, that black people have varying amounts of white ancestry. If the hereditarian thesis is correct, then obviously black people who have a great deal of white ancestry, and therefore also many 'white' genes, should, on average, have higher IQs than those with little or no white ancestry. The logic of racial crossing studies is similar. These studies focus on mixed-race children (with one black and one white parent), and according to the hereditarian thesis their IQs should, on average, fall somewhere between the IQs of black children and white children raised in similar environments.

Racial admixture studies have used three main techniques for estimating the subjects' proportion of white ancestry: biochemical assays of blood and protein markers, genealogical records, and visible racial indicators such as skin colour. There are problems with all three techniques,[22] and the third, which was used in most early studies, is now known to be virtually useless because most of the variance in skin colour (and other visible racial indicators) among black people is due to differences among the African populations from which they originated rather than to their degree of white ancestry.

The most reliable of the early admixture studies, according to most experts,[23] is the 1936 study by Witty and Jenkins of black school-children in Chicago.[24] These researchers focused on the ninety-one black children with the highest IQs among the 8000 enrolled in the Chicago public school system. They reasoned that, if black children are genetically inferior in intelligence to white children, then 'Negroes who make the very highest scores on mental tests should be those who come from admixtures predominantly white'. They estimated the proportion of white ancestry of each of their high-IQ children by obtaining geneaological records from the parents and compared the proportions to those found in a control group of ordinary black Americans. The proportions turned out to be very similar in the two groups, and the small differences that were found were not specifically in the direction predicted by the hereditarian hypothesis. For example, 14.3 per cent of the high-IQ children had predominantly white ancestry compared to 14.8 per cent of the control group, which suggests (if anything) that very bright black children have slightly *fewer* white genes than ordinary black people. Incidentally, the brightest child of all, a black girl with an IQ of 200, had no known white ancestry whatever. As far as I know, her IQ was the highest ever reliably recorded anywhere in the world, and I often wonder what became of her.

The Witty and Jenkins study has been criticized on various grounds.[25] First, the accuracy of the estimates of white admixture has been questioned. Second and more important, critics have pointed out that the control group was not drawn from among black people in Chicago and may not have been a suitable group for comparison. About one-third of the control group was composed of university students, and 16 per cent of the rest were professional people living in the Harlem district of New York City. In other words, the control group was not representative of black Americans in general, and it was certainly not representative of black people in Chicago. It was probably biased towards people of high intelligence, just like the sample of schoolchildren, so the failure to find any significant difference between the racial composition of the two groups does not refute the hereditarian hypothesis as decisively as it at first appears to do.

The most carefully controlled admixture study, first published in 1977, was carried out by Sandra Scarr of the University of Minnesota and several colleagues.[26] They used forty-three blood-group markers to estimate the proportion of white ancestry of the Philadelphia schoolchildren who were subjects in the study. Their results showed no association between racial ancestry and four separate tests of intellectual performance: the correlations were all very close to zero. Scarr and her colleagues concluded that their results provided no support for the notion that race differences in intelligence are due to genetic factors.

This conclusion was promptly challenged by Brandon Centerwall of the University of California, San Diego. Centerwall claimed that

the study design of Scarr et al. rests upon a fundamental, untestable assumption .... They assume that in terms of intellectual function, those whites who contributed to black ancestry were a random sample of all whites .... If their IQs were similar to blacks – and lower than whites – there should be no genetic correlation between degree of white ancestry and intellectual skills .... Resting as they do on an untestable assumption, any inferences are scientifically invalid.[27]

Scarr and her colleagues replied to Centerwall by quoting from the historiography of slavery. 'There is no evidence', they said, 'that whites who contributed genes to the ancestral black population constitute a biased sample .... The blind processes of slave capture and survival, the lack of social mobility in plantation society, and the absence of intellectual measurement at the time ... lead us to believe that little intellectual bias could have crept into the process of creating a new hybrid population.'[28] But these comments do not seem to address Centerwall's point that the whites who interbred with blacks might have been more similar to blacks than to whites in intellectual ability.

Brian Mackenzie of the University of Tasmania challenged Centerwall's point on stronger grounds.[29] Suppose that black people are indeed genetically less intelligent than white people. To produce the zero correlation between degree of white ancestry and IQ that Scarr found, the miscegenous whites who contributed genes to the black population must have been intellectually below average by just the right amount – had they been even less intelligent than Centerwall's theory requires, then those black people who had the most white ancestry would have been the *least* intelligent, that is to say the correlation would have been negative! According to Mackenzie's calculations, the average IQ of the miscegenous whites must have been very close to 85 – no more and no less – for Centerwall's theory to explain Scarr's data. This implies that they must have belonged to the lowest 15 per cent of the white population in terms of IQ, a suggestion that Mackenzie said 'can be dismissed as derisory'.

Racial crossing studies can yield direct evidence on the hereditarian thesis without the uncertainties involved in estimating white ancestry from biochemical assays or genealogical records. If race differences in IQ are mainly due to genetic factors, then the IQs of children of mixed parentage should fall somewhere between the average scores of black children and white children raised in similar environments. If the differences are due to environmental factors, on the other hand, then the IQs of mixed-race children should be similar to the average scores of comparable black and white groups.

In an ideal racial crossing experiment, random samples of black, white, and mixed-race children would be reared in identical environments, and then their IQs would be measured. Such an experiment cannot, of course, be carried out, and even when it is approximated in natural circumstances such as cross-race adoptions, one may reasonably question the possibility, in a racist society, of raising black, white, and mixed-race children in comparable environments. Interestingly, this objection turns out to be irrelevant, because in all three of the racial crossing studies that have been published, the children belonging to different racial groups have turned out to have the same average IQ scores.

The most detailed study of this kind was reported by the German psychologist Klaus Eyferth in 1961.[30] It focused on *Besatzungskinder* – the illegitimate offspring of American (and occasionally French) occupation troops and German women following the Second World War. Some of the fathers were black and some were white, and the children were all reared in postwar Germany by their white mothers. A comparison was made between the white and the mixed-race offspring of these sexual liaisons, carefully matched for age, sex, socio-economic status, family characteristics, and numerous other factors. The results showed no significant difference between the average IQs of the mixed-race children (whose fathers were black) and the white children (whose fathers were, of course, white); the averages were 96.5 and 97.2 respectively. In other words, children whose genes were up to 50 per cent African in origin did not score significantly lower on IQ tests than those raised in a similar environment whose genes were exclusively European in origin.

The second racial crossing study was carried out in England in the early 1970s by Barbara Tizard and several colleagues.[31] The subjects were thirty-one black, seventy-five white, and forty-three mixed-race children living in residential nurseries. The study has been criticized[32] on the grounds that the parents were clearly unrepresentative of the black (West Indian) and white populations, and the children were less than 5 years old when their IQs were measured – IQs at that age do not correlate very well with adult IQs. Nevertheless, it is interesting to note that the children with one or two black parents scored consistently *higher*, on average, than the white children, though the differences amounted to only a few IQ points.

The third study, carried out by Sandra Scarr and Richard Weinberg of the University of Minnesota in the mid 1970s, focused on groups of black, mixed-race, and white children raised in white adoptive homes.[33] The average IQs of the three groups were 96.8, 109.0 and 111.5 respectively. In other words, the mixed-race and white children were found to have nearly identical average IQs, which is very hard to reconcile with the hereditarian thesis, but the black children scored 12 to 14 points lower, on average, than the others. Scarr and Weinberg pointed out that this last finding is ambiguous because the black children were different from the others in ways that had nothing to do with genes: they were adopted later in life, had been in their adoptive homes for shorter periods when they were tested, and had less well-educated natural and adoptive parents than the mixed-race and white children. They concluded that their results 'support the view that the social environment plays a dominant role in determining the average IQ level of black children'.[34]

In the light of all three racial crossing studies, and the admixture studies discussed earlier, and bearing in mind that these are the only direct tests of the Jensen–Eysenck hereditarian thesis that have appeared in print, it is hard to see how anyone can continue to claim that the existing evidence supports the thesis that race differences in IQ are largely determined by genetic factors. In fact, Jensen, Eysenck, and some of their followers have continued to make that claim in spite of the evidence. In his book *Straight Talk About Mental Tests* Jensen even cited the Scarr and Weinberg study in *support* of the hereditarian thesis![35] His presentation of the findings was cunningly biased, as Nicholas Mackintosh pointed out.[36] Jensen gave the average IQs of Scarr and Weinberg's black adopted children (96.8), mixed-race adopted children (109.0), and white natural children of adoptive parents (116.7). White *natural* children? One has to stay alert when reading Jensen's writings. Instead of giving the appropriate average of the white *adopted* children (111.5), which hardly differed from that of the mixed-race adopted children, he substituted the quite irrelevant average of white *natural* children of adoptive parents who happened to have natural children as well. It is hardly surprising that these natural children scored above the mixed-race adopted children because their families were well above average in social, economic, and educational factors – they also scored much higher than the white adopted children. By slyly substituting the average of the white natural children for that of the appropriate white comparison group, Jensen left his readers with the entirely misleading impression that children's IQs increase in an orderly fashion in line with the proportion of white genes that they inherit. If this is an example of 'straight talk about mental tests' one shudders to think what crooked talk would be like.

The heritability argument

Jensen and Eysenck devoted relatively little attention to the direct evidence on race and intelligence. That evidence, as we have seen, lends little or no support to the thesis that race differences in IQ are largely determined by genetic factors. They dwelt instead on various indirect lines of evidence, especially data concerning the heritability of IQ.

Jensen devoted more than thirty pages of his original article to a discussion of the inheritance of intelligence, his main conclusion being that the heritability of IQ in the United States is about 80 per cent. This means, roughly speaking, that 80 per cent of the variance in IQ scores is due to genetic factors (see Chapter 2). He then went on to discuss race differences: 'It seems not unreasonable, in view of the fact that intelligence variation has a large genetic component, to hypothesize that genetic factors may play a part in this picture.'[37] In a later version of the same article he expounded the heritability argument a little more boldly: 'Characteristics that vary genetically among individuals within a population also vary genetically between different breeding populations of the same species.'[38] Eysenck's version of the heritability argument was slightly different:

The argument is simply that this discovery of a strong genetic involvement in the determination of individual differences in IQ between members of a given population is an essential precondition for going on to argue in favour of the genetic determination (in part at least) of racial differences in IQ. For clearly if all within-race differences could be accounted for in environmental terms, we would have no business to look further than that in our search for between-race differences.[39]

Critics have attacked the heritability argument on two main grounds. First, the factual premise of the argument – that the heritability of IQ is substantial – has been questioned; I have discussed that issue in Chapter 2. Second, the logic of the argument has been challenged. The geneticists Walter Bodmer and Luigi Cavalli-Sforza, for example, stated bluntly that 'whether or not the variation in IQ within either race is entirely genetic or entirely environmental has no bearing on the question of the relative contribution of genetic factors and environmental factors to the differences between races'.[40]

The Harvard University biologist Richard Lewontin challenged the logic of the heritability argument in a paper first published in 1970.[41] He constructed the following *Gedankenexperiment* (imaginary experiment) which has become a classic:

A simple hypothetical but realistic example shows how the heritability of a trait within a population is unconnected to the causes of differences between populations. Suppose one takes from a sack of open-pollinated corn two handfuls of seed. There will be a good deal of genetic variation between seeds in each handful, but the seeds in one's left hand are on the average no different from those in one's right. One handful of seeds is planted in washed sand with an artificial plant growth solution added to it. The other handful is planted in a similar bed, but with half the necessary nitrogen left out. When the seeds have germinated and grown, the seedlings in each plot are measured, and it is found that there is some variation in the height of seedling from plant to plant within each plot. This variation within plots is entirely genetic because the environment was carefully controlled to be identical for all seeds within each plot. The variation in height is then 100 percent heritable. But if we compare the two plots, we will find all the seedlings in the second are much smaller than those in the first. This difference is not at all genetic but is a consequence of the difference in nitrogen level. So the heritability of a trait within populations can be 100 percent, but the cause of the difference between populations can be entirely environmental.[42]

Jensen replied swiftly to Lewontin's critique.[43] 'I am opposed to according treatment to persons solely on the basis of their race', he wrote. 'But I am also opposed to ignoring or refusing to investigate the causes of well-established differences among racial groups in the distribution of educationally relevant traits, particularly IQ.' Turning to Lewontin's *Gedankenexperiment*, Jensen acknowledged that the logic of the heritability argument had been exploded, but denied that he had ever proposed it:

The main thrust of Lewontin's argument, as he sees it, actually attacks a straw man set up by himself: the notion that heritability of a trait within a population does not prove that genetic factors are involved in the mean difference between two different populations on the same trait. I agree. But nowhere in my ... discussion of race differences do I propose this line of reasoning, nor have I done so in my other writings.[44]

This seems rather disingenuous. A year earlier Jensen proposed essentially that line of reasoning when he wrote: 'Any groups which have been geographically or socially isolated from one another for many generations are practically certain ... to show differences in any phenotypic characteristics having high heritability. This is practically axiomatic.'[45] And recall that two years later he wrote: 'Characteristics that vary genetically among individuals within a population also vary genetically between breeding populations of the same species.' In his reply to Lewontin, however, he added a new twist to the argument:

Heritability coefficients obtained within populations, no matter how high, cannot prove the existence of a genetic difference between populations. All this follows strictly from the quantitative logic of estimating heritability, and Lewontin has given some good examples of this logic in the case of plant physiology. But it is necessary to distinguish between the possible and the probable. ... Within-group heritability estimates ... can give us probabilistic clues as to which characteristics are most likely to show genetic differences between groups when investigated through all other available lines of evidence.[46]

Lewontin responded with a sharply worded rejoinder.[47] 'Jensen's article', he wrote, 'is not an objective empirical scientific paper which stands or falls on the correctness of his calculation of heritability. It is, rather, a closely reasoned ideological document springing ... from deep-seated professionalist bias and permeated ... with an elitist and competitive world view.' He went on to comment on Jensen's claim that high within-group heritability makes it more likely (though not certain) that the between-group difference has a genetic cause. There is no scientific basis for this claim, he said; the between-group difference is just as likely to be due entirely to environmental causes.

Jensen replied to this by referring to a mathematical model, according to which between-group heritability is likely whenever within-group heritability is high, provided only that there is a significant correlation between race and the genetic factors governing IQ.[48] But Lewontin pointed out in response what is obvious, that Jensen's argument begs the question because it is the alleged correlation between race and IQ genes that is at issue in the first place.[49] The mathematical model shows only that *if there is such a correlation*, that is, if the Jensen-Eysenck hereditarian thesis is correct in the first place, then high within-group heritability implies that race differences are likely to be partly caused by genetic factors.

It is worth recalling (see Chapter 2) that the empirical premise of the heritability argument – that within-group heritability is high – is extremely dubious. Since the logic of the argument in its original form is also flawed, as Jensen himself acknowledged, and in its revised form question-begging, it seems fair to conclude that the heritability argument has collapsed entirely.

Test bias

Many writers have argued that black people score relatively lower on IQ tests than white people merely because the tests are biased. It is certainly true that most conventional IQ tests have been devised by white, middle-class psychologists, standardized on white samples, and validated by their ability to predict performance in white schools. (The standardization sample of the British Ability Scales is an exception; it did contain children of West Indian and Asian origin.) It is also true that IQ tests contain items that are culturally loaded inasmuch as they presume knowledge of matters that typify the dominant white culture. Joanna Ryan of Cambridge University expressed the argument concerning test bias as follows:

It is probably impossible [if that is not a contradiction in terms] to standardize a test perfectly and without bias. This would not matter if it were explicitly recognized that a test is only applicable to populations resembling the standardization sample in all relevant respects. This limitation on the applicability of tests is not sufficiently appreciated, especially by those who attempt to make generalizations about interracial differences in intelligence on the basis of tests constructed by and standardized on one race only.[50]

According to this argument, in its strongest form, the relatively low IQ scores of black people may be due entirely to test bias.

The argument of test bias seems reasonable and persuasive, on the face of it. Jensen devoted an entire book, entitled *Bias in Mental Testing*,[51] to an examination of it. An IQ test may be said to be biased if it underestimates the 'true' intelligence of black people, but this notion of bias is coherent only in relation to some alternative criterion of intelligence such as performance in school examinations. Do standard IQ tests underestimate the performance of black people in school examinations and other activities usually assumed to reflect intelligence? Jensen's exhaustive review of the evidence showed, quite conclusively in my view, that standard IQ tests are not biased in this sense against black people or other English-speaking minorities in the United States. Research in Britain has led to the same conclusion. The National Child Development Study of 15,000 randomly chosen British schoolchildren, carried out in 1969, showed that IQ scores at age 11 correlated equally well with school tests of mathematics among West Indian and white children (the correlations were 0.78 and 0.80 respectively) and the correlations with school tests of reading ability were not very different either (0.60 and 0.73 respectively).[52] Statistical predictions were made of the mathematics and reading ability scores that one would expect, given the IQ scores, if the relations between IQ and mathematical and reading ability were identical among West Indian and white children. The results showed quite clearly that IQ scores did not underestimate the West Indian children's performance; on the contrary, West Indian children did slightly *worse* than their IQ scores suggested they should do. These findings were strongly confirmed by the Child Health and Education Study, which was carried out in 1980 on a different but equally large random sample of British schoolchildren.[53] In that study, all correlations between IQ scores and school tests of mathematics and reading ability were between 0.72 and 0.75, not only among West Indian and white children, but also among children of Indian and Pakistani origin. Once again, statistical analyses showed that West Indian children achieved slightly *lower* scores on the school tests than their IQ scores predicted.

There is no evidence that IQ tests are biased in this sense against black people in the United States or Britain. Could it be argued, none the less, that they are biased in another sense, inasmuch as cultural deprivation of various kinds, which black people undoubtedly suffer, depresses their intellectual abilities and produces low scores on IQ tests as well as school examinations and other objective criteria of intelligence? No; any argument along those lines would be incoherent, like arguing that a pair of scales is biased because it shows black infants to be underweight more often than white infants.[54] It would say nothing more than that intellectual performance is affected by environmental factors, which even the most ardent hereditarians acknowledge, and which cannot reasonably be blamed on IQ tests.

Psychologists have made heroic attempts to construct *culture-fair* or *culture-reduced* IQ tests which are less culturally loaded than conventional tests. Few believe that a truly *culture-free* test, which presumes no knowledge at all on the part of the subject, will ever be constructed. Recent attempts to assess IQ through direct measures of the electrical activity of the brain have led to very disappointing results, to the surprise of very few psychologists.[55] But it seems reasonable to assume that some tests are more culture-fair than others, and the results of research using different tests are of some interest. According to Jensen, the findings support the thesis that race differences in intelligence are innate:

So-called 'culture-free' or 'culture-fair' tests tend to give Negroes slightly lower scores, on the average, than more conventional IQ tests such as the Stanford–Binet and Wechsler scales. Also, as a group, Negroes perform somewhat more poorly on those subtests which tap abstract abilities. The majority of studies show that Negroes perform relatively better on verbal than non-verbal intelligence tests.[56]

Jensen's argument seems to be this: if the low average scores of black people are due merely to cultural handicaps, then they should do better on culture-fair tests than on culturally loaded tests which, by definition, are more likely to reflect their cultural disadvantages. But they perform worse on culture-fair tests; therefore their low scores are probably due to genetic factors.

Two points should be borne in mind in evaluating this argument.

First, culture-fairness is not a scientific concept: it has not been rigorously defined and it cannot be measured. It usually amounts to nothing more than an assumption, which is plausible but devoid of proof, that verbal tests are more culturally loaded than non-verbal tests. Second, Jensen's assertion that black people perform relatively poorly on culture-fair or non-verbal tests should not be accepted without question. There is some evidence to support it, but several researchers have reported that black subjects scored approximately as well or (in a number of studies) significantly better on the culture-fair or non-verbal tests.[57] The totality of data on this point is ambiguous.

Jensen's (and Eysenck's) favourite example of a culture-fair IQ test is Raven's Progressive Matrices, a non-verbal test based on abstract diagrams with little obvious cultural content. The culture-fairness argument about black inferiority is seriously weakened by three British studies in which Raven's and other supposedly culture-fair tests were used. Although they were carried out quite independently, all three studies reported the same finding: recent Asian immigrants performed very badly on Raven's and the other supposedly culture-fair tests, but those who had lived in Britain for some years scored as well as white children.[58] In all three studies, the Asian children's performance improved by an average of 15 to 20 IQ points after they had lived in Britain for several years. This seems to dispel the myth that tests such as Raven's Progressive Matrices are even remotely culture-fair.

Comparing minority groups

A different indirect line of evidence often cited by Jensen and Eysenck in support of their hereditarian thesis comes from the comparative IQ scores of various ethnic minorities in the United States and Britain.

The main ethnic minorities that have been studied in the United States are Afro-Americans, Orientals (Chinese, Japanese, and South-East Asians), American Indians, and Hispanics (Mexicans, Cubans, and Puerto Ricans). Turning first to Hispanics, the hereditarian argument is based on evidence[59] that Mexican–American children score even lower than black children on culturally loaded tests like the Peabody Picture–Vocabulary Test, which involves matching words with drawings, but higher than black children (though not as high as white children) on supposedly culture-fair tests like Raven's Progressive Matrices. Jensen and Eysenck have interpreted these findings as indirect evidence that

Hispanics are merely culturally deprived (which is why they perform worst on culturally loaded tests) whereas black people are genetically deprived (hence their especially low scores on culture-fair tests). This interpretation seems rather perverse to me. Bearing in mind that culturally loaded tests like the Peabody Picture–Vocabulary Test require a knowledge of English, and that the mother tongue of most Hispanic children is Spanish, it is hardly surprising that they perform worse than black children on these tests. All that remains to be explained is why the reverse seems to be true with regard to supposedly culture-fair tests. But the bulk of the published evidence does not support the claim that Hispanic children invariably – or even generally – outperform black children on supposedly culture-fair tests.[60]

American Indians, for their part, are as culturally deprived relative to black people as black people are relative to white people, but the evidence shows that they score consistently higher, on average, than black people on conventional IQ tests. Presumably, if environmental deprivation were all-important, American Indians' scores would be far below those of black people. According to Jensen, 'if the environmental factors … are the major determinants of Negro–white differences that many social scientists have claimed they are, it is hard to see why such factors should act in reverse fashion in determining differences between Negroes and Indians';[61] and Eysenck stated flatly that 'environmentalist theory does not provide an answer'.[62] In fact, environmentalist critics have provided several answers.[63] They are all speculative and debatable, but then so is the hereditarian answer.

First, American Indians, whose IQs have invariably been tested in urban centres, may be quite unrepresentative of the 70 to 80 per cent who live on reservations and who suffer the worst environmental deprivation. Second, most American Indians attend white schools, whereas black children have traditionally attended black schools where the quality of education may have been markedly inferior. Third, racism itself may be an important factor. Despite their inferior socio-economic status, American Indians, unlike Afro-Americans, are outside the mainstream of the dominant culture and do not elicit the same degree of racial prejudice from white people. Fourth, it is possible that a significant minority of American Indians are, in reality, black people 'passing for Indian'. It may be the most intelligent black people who are likely to succeed in passing for Indian or, if they are fair-skinned, for white. The pseudo-logic runs: 'All niggers are stupid; this person is not stupid; therefore, this person is no nigger', and the intelligent black person has succeeded in passing where a less intelligent one might have failed. If passing has been a widespread practice – and very little is known about its prevalence because there is a conspiracy of silence on the matter – then it may have artificially inflated the average IQ scores of the Indian and white samples that have been studied, and at the same time artificially deflated the average scores of the black samples.

Regarding the IQ scores of Orientals in the United States, Eysenck had this to say:

They are inferior to whites on socio-economic and educational grounds, although not as much as the negroes, but they nevertheless do as well as the whites, and even better when tests involving abstract reasoning are concerned. (One might advance the argument that perhaps racially Orientals are superior to whites on IQ performance; I shall refrain from pursuing this point!)[64]

One cannot help wondering why Eysenck was so amused by the idea of Orientals being superior to white people. Rather than pursue the point, he interpreted the findings as further indirect evidence that social factors are inadequate to explain the low average IQ scores of black Americans. The evidence is clearly *very* indirect and weak, and all but the first of the speculations discussed earlier in connection with American Indians are equally applicable to the findings regarding Orientals.

In Britain the major ethnic minorities that have been investigated are West Indians and Asians (Indians, Pakistanis, and Bangladeshis). Once again, the British evidence provides no support to the hereditarian thesis. It suggests, on the contrary, that environmental factors are the main determinant of race differences in intelligence.

Several British studies have shown that long-resident Asian children, and those born in Britain, scored significantly higher than West Indians on IQ tests. But these findings provide no evidence for or against the hereditarian thesis because the Asian children were socio-economically better-off than the West Indian children. The National Child Development Study, for example, revealed that, in 1969, Asian children born in Britain were socio-economically much better-off than West Indian children and hardly any worse-off than white children. The pattern of average IQ scores was an almost perfect mirror of the social circumstances of the three groups.

Later evidence revealed that the average IQ scores of Asian children began to decline in the 1970s, and that this decline was paralleled by a decline in socio-economic status. The children investigated in the Child Health and Education Study were born in 1970, and their IQs were measured in 1980. The average IQs of the

West Indian, Indian, and Pakistani children were found to be 94.3, 95.6, and 90.5 respectively.[65] These averages are not significantly different, but it is worth noting that the Pakistani average is actually lower, and the Indian average is barely higher, than the West Indian average. These figures suggest that, by 1980, Asians were no longer outscoring West Indians on IQ tests, and the study also revealed that they were no longer living in socio-economically better circumstances. On most of the indices examined in the Child Health and Education Study (father in manual occupation, four or more children in household, family income less than £100 per week, child receiving free school meals, and so on), the Pakistani children's circumstances were slightly worse than those of the West Indian children, and the Indian children's were only marginally better.[66] Taken together, these findings suggest that the relative IQ scores of West Indian and Asian children have closely paralleled changes in their relative socio-economic circumstances over time. They provide powerful evidence against the Jensen–Eysenck hereditarian thesis that race differences in intelligence are determined chiefly by genetic factors. They also tend to undermine the claim often made by Jensen and other hereditarians that environmental factors are 'completely inadequate in explaining the black IQ deficit'.[67] Environmental factors are worth discussing in greater detail.

Environmental influences on IQ

Critics of the hereditarian thesis have suggested a bewildering variety of social, economic, educational, cultural, motivational, nutritional, and other environmental factors to account for the black–white IQ gap. These critics have, in general, begun by identifying environmental differences between the black and white populations, and then gone on to show that when these differences are controlled by statistical techniques or matching groups, the average IQ difference is reduced or eliminated. Indirect evidence of this kind, though superficially plausible, is actually very weak for reasons that will become apparent shortly.

One of the most frequently cited studies along these lines was carried out in California in the early 1970s.[68] The average IQ differences between 180 black, 180 white, and 180 Hispanic children were largely – though not entirely – eliminated when the following nine environmental factors were statistically controlled: family socio-economic status, family home ownership, racial composition of home neighbourhood, family structure, mother's participation in formal organizations such as church groups, mother's fluency in English and familiarity with her child's school, mother's achievement values, parents' geographical origins (northern or western United States versus southern United States or Mexico), and child's anxiety level. The researchers interpreted their findings as evidence that these nine environmental factors (the last is not really an environmental factor although they described it as such) were responsible for producing the average IQ differences between the ethnic groups. A similar study was carried out in Chicago in the early 1980s on 500 white and 500 black children.[69] The environmental factors in that study were related to socio-economic status, religious practice, family structure, and so on, and when they were statistically controlled, the average IQ gap between the black and white children was reduced to less than three points. The researcher concluded that the IQ differences 'are not inherent but result from identifiable environmental deficits ... which constitute independent impediments to the intellectual development of minority children'.

In the National Child Development and the Child Health and Education studies in Britain, environmental factors such as father's income, family size, and neighbourhood quality were investigated. The researchers capitalized on the fact that the children in these studies were random samples of the population by trying to match each West Indian child with a white child in similar environmental circumstances. The purpose of matching was to see whether the IQ gap persisted when the environmental factors were controlled in this way. The disadvantaged status of the West Indian community was dramatically illustrated by the fact that the researchers were unable to match all of the West Indian children in either study, in spite of the fact that there were fewer than 100 West Indian children and more than 10,000 white children to choose from in each case. In the National Child Development Study, the 11-point average IQ difference between West Indian and white children was reduced to a 5.2-point average difference between the successfully matched pairs, and in the Child Health and Education Study a 9-point gap was reduced to only 2.6 points.[70]

Do investigations of this kind demonstrate that race differences in IQ are not inherent but 'result from identifiable environmental deficits' as the American researcher quoted earlier put it? This interpretation of the evidence is, alas, open to two serious criticisms. In the first place, the data fail to explain *the whole* of the IQ gap between the races; the difference is generally reduced by controlling selected environmental factors, but a significant gap remains stubbornly unexplained. This may, of course, be because some of the crucial environmental factors have been overlooked – after all, environmental influences are far from being properly understood – but it may also be due to significant genetic differences between the groups.

The second and more important criticism centres on the interpretation of the findings. To understand this criticism clearly, let us imagine that a researcher discovered a difference in socio-economic status between black and white groups, and found that the average IQ gap between the groups disappeared entirely when an appropriate correction for this environmental factor was made. Would this prove that the IQ gap was entirely due to environmental factors? No; to draw such a conclusion would be to commit what Jensen calls the *sociologist's fallacy*.[71] It is a fallacy because it rests on the unstated premise that IQ differences between socio-economic strata are entirely environmental in origin. Jensen and Eysenck have consistently claimed that IQ differences between socio-economic strata are partly genetic in origin. Although there is little or no evidence to support that claim (apart from discredited data reported by Sir Cyril Burt), it has not been decisively refuted either. Researchers who have controlled socio-economic and other environmental factors statistically or by matching groups may therefore have artificially suppressed real genetic differences between ethnic groups, and thereby begged the question of the origin of these differences.

This second criticism does not apply to investigations that have shown large increases in IQ scores in groups of black children who have been exposed to compensatory educational and other environmental enrichment programmes. But the success of these programmes is certainly disputable. The opening sentence of Jensen's original article reads: 'Compensatory education has been tried and apparently it has failed.' If massive environmental intervention in the form of compensatory education cannot raise the low IQs of the most severely disadvantaged black children, this seems to suggest that the low IQs are due to genetic inferiority. But that easy inference depends on numerous assumptions about the nature and timing of environmental factors affecting the development of intelligence. Furthermore, there is no simple relationship between the fixedness of a characteristic, on the one hand, and its genetic or environmental origin on the other. Hair colour, to take a familiar example, is largely determined by genetic factors, but it is easily influenced by environmental manipulation (dyeing), whereas tooth decay is largely determined by environmental factors (diet) but is virtually irreversible once it has occurred.

The evidence, for what it is worth, is equivocal. Some authorities[72] have concluded that compensatory education has produced only short-lived IQ gains in those exposed to it. Eysenck, for his part, has been roused to anger by government sponsored compensatory education campaigns: 'These programmes are political playthings; they have no scientific basis, have no recognisable or lasting effects on those exposed to them; and can only do a disservice to those truly eager to advance the status of the negro race.'[73] The astonishing implication of this outburst is that we should actually be doing disadvantaged black people a favour by cancelling all compensatory education campaigns forthwith! But no one has ever suggested that these campaigns depress IQ scores or harm black children in any other way. And there are authorities[74] who have found evidence for long-term gains following early environmental enrichment campaigns, although the gains seem to be more clear-cut on measures of scholastic performance than IQ. In any event, for reasons explained earlier, this line of evidence is not very useful for explaining the origins of the IQ gap between racial groups.

The Oxford University geneticist Walter Bodmer has argued[75] that no amount of statistical correction or matching of environmental factors can provide adequate – or even substantial – control over the most important environmental differences between black and white people in societies in which racism is endemic. We do not even understand properly how the environment operates in influencing IQ development. Environmental effects can be subtle and unexpected. This is vividly illustrated by a British study cited by Bodmer which focused on the relative IQ scores of 48,913 ordinary children, 2164 twins, and 33 triplets.[76] The average IQ scores at age 11 were 100.1, 95.7, and 91.6 respectively. This confirms a well-known finding regarding the lower average IQs of twins and especially triplets. But in this study 148 twins were found whose co-twins were stillborn or died before they were four weeks old, and the average IQ of this group of twins was found to be 99.5 – virtually the same as ordinary children. The environmental factor that causes the remarkable depression of average IQ in twins, and probably also the even larger IQ depression in triplets, must therefore be post-natal, and may well have something to do with the reduced attention parents are able to give to infants born simultaneously. This one subtle environmental deficit, which is not reflected in Standard measurements of environmental deficit, is nearly half as large as the average difference between the IQ scores of black and white people in Britain. It is worth adding something that Bodmer did not mention: multiple births are much more common in black than in white populations in both Britain and the United States.

Psychology and ideology

Jensen and Eysenck have repeatedly claimed that they were unwillingly forced, by the sheer weight of scientific evidence, to accept a conclusion that they found personally distasteful – that black people are genetically inferior to white people in intelligence. Eysenck, furthermore, 'found it very difficult to look at the evidence ... with a detached mind, in view of the fact that it contradicted certain egalitarian beliefs [he] had considered almost axiomatic'.[77]

It is, of course, hard-headed and rational, and even sometimes courageous, to acknowledge distasteful or repugnant facts when theory and empirical evidence back them up. But it is neither hard-headed, rational, nor courageous to cling on to unpleasant doctrines merely because they are unpleasant; that is merely masochistic. And if there are powerful and reactionary interest groups which are eager to exploit the scientific endorsement of such doctrines for their own sinister purposes, as the racist National Front in Britain and the South African authorities exploited Jensen's and Eysenck's publications,[78] then it is also dangerous.

The research reviewed in this chapter shows that there is, in fact, very little evidence in support of the Jensen–Eysenck hereditarian thesis, and a great deal of rather persuasive evidence that contradicts it. I do not know why Jensen and Eysenck feel constrained to accept the hereditarian thesis. Jensen did not always accept it; in 1967 he wrote: 'Since we know that the Negro population for the most part has suffered socio-economic and cultural disadvantages for generations past, it seems a reasonable hypothesis that their low average IQ is due to environmental rather than genetic factors.'[79] Yet a little over a year later he came up with his 'not unreasonable hypothesis that genetic factors are strongly implicated in the average Negro–white intelligence difference', which Eysenck was promptly forced to swallow in spite of his egalitarian beliefs.

Although I believe that both Jensen and Eysenck are demonstrably wrong in claiming that the evidence supports their hereditarian thesis, I am strongly opposed to those who have inferred from this that Jensen and Eysenck are racists, in the sense of viewing black people with hatred or wishing to oppress them. Eysenck responded to accusations of racism as follows:

I am not a racist for believing it possible that negroes have special innate gifts for certain athletic events, such as sprints, or for certain musical forms of expression .... Nor am I a racist for seriously considering the possibility that the demonstrated inferiority of American negroes on tests of intelligence may, in part, be due to genetic causes.[80]

In spite of the patronizing stereotype of the dull-witted but fleet-footed bongo-drummer implicit in these remarks, there is no evidence here, or in any of Eysenck's (or Jensen's) writings, of racist attitudes such as those of the British police officers quoted at the beginning of this chapter who described black people as 'savage ignorant vicious thieving bastards' and wanted them to be exterminated.

The debate over the hereditarian thesis had a palpable influence on educational policy in the United States.[81] Predictably, Jensen's writings were cited in a number of court cases as justification for racial segregation in schools. On the other hand, these same writings were partly responsible for the nationwide ban imposed by the courts in 1978 on the use of IQ tests as instruments for classifying black schoolchildren as mentally retarded.

The writings of Jensen and Eysenck were also cited by William Shockley, the Nobel prizewinning physicist and co-inventor of the transistor, in support of his proposal that black people with low IQs should be voluntarily sterilized to prevent the genetic stock of the United States from deteriorating further. His 'voluntary sterilization bonus plan' involved a financial incentive calculated to encourage volunteers: 'a thousand dollars for each point below 100 IQ, 30 thousand dollars put in trust for a 70 IQ moron, potentially capable of producing 20 children'.[82] Shockley's plan was warmly endorsed by Fascist and crypto-Fascist groups in the United States, Britain, and France.

It is clear that the Jensen–Eysenck hereditarian thesis can be used, and has been used, to justify racially oppressive policies and practices, and to lend scientific respectability to dangerous prejudices. This is especially lamentable in view of the paucity of evidence and weakness of argument in support of the thesis.

When I began to examine the literature on this question in preparation for writing this chapter, I had a vested interest in finding persuasive evidence and argumentation on both sides, because I hoped to give my readers something to ponder. I must confess that I was astonished to discover how little support, even of the most indirect kind, could be mustered for the hereditarian thesis. That does not mean that the thesis is false, but rather that there are no rational grounds for believing it, especially if, like Jensen and Eysenck, one finds it personally distasteful. The only rational alternative, in the light of the existing evidence as I see it, is to suspend judgement; but that is an increasingly tricky position to defend.

Notes

1 Colman and Gorman (1982). The quotations from the police officers' essays, with spelling and punctuation unaltered, are on p. 7 of this article.
2 The critique was by Waddington (1982); the quotation in the text is from p. 591. See Colman (1983) for my reply.
3 Scarman (1981), p. 79.
4 Galton (1869). The quotation in the text is on p. 339 of the 1892 edition.
5 Jensen (1969).
6 Eysenck (1971). The quotation in the following sentence is on p. 130 of Eysenck's book.
7 ibid., p. 15.
8 Pettigrew (1964), pp. 104–5.
9 Friedrichs (1973).
10 The evidence is summarized in Shuey (1966); Loehlin, Lindzey, and Spuhler (1975); and Scarr (1981).
11 These studies are summarized in Mackintosh and Mascie-Taylor (1985).
12 Eysenck (1971), p. 20. In fact, Jensen wrote: '... why should the brain be any exception?'
13 Tobias (1970), p. 22. See also Gould (1981), Chapter 3.
14 The evidence is summarized in Rose, Kamin, and Lewontin (1984), pp. 119–27.
15 The inverted a priori argument is discussed in Colman (1972), pp. 139–40.
16 Mayr (1968). I have taken the liberty of improving the story slightly.
17 Embree (1931), p. 31.
18 Reed (1969).
19 See, for example, Brown (1965), p. 184; Colman (1972), pp. 139–40.
20 Eysenck and Kamin (1981), p. 79; see also Eysenck (1971), p. 30.
21 For example, Flynn (1980), Chapter 3; Mackenzie (1984); Mackintosh (1986).
22 The problems are outlined by Mackenzie (1984), p. 1225.
23 Loehlin, Lindzey, and Spuhler (1975), Flynn (1980), Mackenzie (1984).
24 Witty and Jenkins (1936). The quotation in the text is from p. 180.
25 The criticisms are summarized in Mackenzie (1984), p. 1226.
26 Scarr, Pakstis, Katz, and Barker (1977).
27 Centerwall (1978), pp. 237–8.
28 Scarr, Pakstis, Katz, and Barker (1979). The quotation in the text is from pp. 225–6.
29 Mackenzie (1984), pp. 1227–8. The quotation in the text below is from p. 1228.
30 Eyferth (1961).
31 Tizard, Cooperman, Joseph, and Tizard (1972).
32 See, for example, Flynn (1980), pp. 108–13; Mackintosh (1986), pp. 3–4.
33 Scarr and Weinberg (1976).
34 ibid., p. 739.

35 Jensen (1981). The text refers to p. 231 of this book.
36 Mackintosh (1986), p. 4.
37 Jensen (1969), p. 82.
38 Jensen (1972), p. 162.
39 Eysenck (1971), p. 117.
40 Bodmer and Cavalli-Sforza (1970), p. 27.
41 Lewontin (1970a).
42 Rose, Kamin, and Lewontin (1984), p. 118. This version of Lewontin's *Gedankenexperiment* is briefer and clearer than his 1970 prototype, but the basic idea is the same.
43 Jensen (1970). The quotation immediately following in the text is on p. 99 of the 1977 reprint of this article.
44 ibid., p. 103.
45 Jensen (1969), p. 80.
46 Jensen (1970). The quotation in the text is on pp. 103–5 of the 1977 reprint of this article.
47 Lewontin (1970b). The references in the text are to pp. 108 and 109–10 of the 1977 reprint of this article.
48 Jensen (1973a, 1973b).
49 Lewontin (1975); Feldman and Lewontin (1975). See also Taylor (1980), pp. 64–8, and Mackenzie (1984) for detailed explanations of the technical details.
50 Ryan (1972), p. 53. The comment in brackets is mine.
51 Jensen (1980).
52 Mackintosh and Mascie-Taylor (1985); Mackintosh (1986).
53 ibid.
54 See Vernon (1969), p. 70.
55 See Mackintosh (1986), pp. 9–16, for a critical review of research in this area.
56 Jensen (1969), p. 81.
57 The evidence is summarized in Loehlin, Lindzey, and Spuhler (1975), pp. 177–95.
58 Ashby, Morrison, and Butcher (1970); Sharma (1971); Mackintosh and Mascie-Taylor (1985).
59 The evidence is summarized in Eysenck (1971), pp. 121–4.
60 The evidence is summarized in Loehlin, Lindzey, and Spuhler (1975), pp. 152–3, 177–95.
61 Jensen (1969), p. 86.
62 Eysenck (1971), p. 120.
63 The answers are discussed in Colman (1972), pp. 147–8.
64 Eysenck (1971), p. 120.
65 Mackintosh and Mascie-Taylor (1985); Mackintosh (1986), p. 8.
66 ibid.
67 Jensen (1981), p. 222.
68 Mercer and Brown (1973).
69 Blau (1981). The quotation in the text is from p. 222.
70 Mackintosh and Mascie-Taylor (1985); Mackintosh (1986).
71 See Mackenzie (1984) for a detailed analysis of the sociologist's fallacy.
72 See, for example, the review by Minton and Schneider (1980).
73 Eysenck (1971), p. 133.
74 For example, Palmer and Anderson (1979).
75 Bodmer (1972).
76 Record, McKeown, and Edwards (1970).
77 Eysenck (1971), p. 12.

78 See Rose, Kamin, and Lewontin (1984), p. 19; and Colman (1972), pp. 149–52.
79 Quoted in Vernon (1970), pp. 161–2. The following quotation is from Jensen (1969) p. 82.
80 Eysenck (1971), p. 11.
81 The following examples in the text are from Taylor (1980), p. 229.
82 Shockley (1972), p. 17.

4 Obedience and cruelty: are most people potential killers?

In January 1960 a crack agent of the Israeli Secret Service arrived in Buenos Aires, Argentina, with instructions to try to establish the true identity of a certain Ricardo Klement, a German national who had settled there with his family ten years earlier. After locating the house in which the Klement family were living, the investigator managed, with the help of a long lens, to take several photographs of Ricardo Klement without arousing his suspicions. A careful examination of the photographs back in Israel confirmed to the satisfaction of the Secret Service that Klement was the man they were looking for, and a team of four volunteers was sent to Argentina to abduct him to Israel to stand trial.

One evening, as Klement was walking home from his local bus station, the Israeli agents accosted him, bundled him into a waiting car, and drove him to a secret address. There they interrogated him in German, and he soon confessed his true identity. He told his captors that he was unwilling to proceed to Israel but was prepared to stand trial in Argentina or Germany. Several hours later, apparently fearing summary execution, he changed his mind and expressed a willingness to be tried in Israel. 'Will you sign a declaration to this effect?' he was asked. 'Yes', he replied. He was handed pen and paper and wrote the following statement:[1]

I, the undersigned, Adolf Eichmann, declare of my own free will that, since my true identity has been discovered, I realize that it is futile for me to attempt to go on evading justice. I state that I am prepared to travel to Israel to stand trial in that country before a competent court .... I shall endeavour to give a straightforward account of the facts of my last years of service in Germany so that a true picture of the facts may be passed on to future generations.

Buenos Aires, May 1960

(Signed) ADOLF EICHMANN

On 23 May 1960, the Israeli Prime Minister, David Ben-Gurion, made a dramatic announcement in the Knesset (Parliament) that stunned the nation and sent ripples of excitement around the world:

that Adolf Eichmann had been captured and would soon be put on trial in Jerusalem. As most people knew by then, Eichmann was the leading figure in the programme of Jewish extermination during the Nazi era and the man chiefly responsible for carrying out Hitler's 'Final Solution' of the Jewish problem.

The trial of Adolf Eichmann lasted exactly eight months. Eichmann's defence counsel began by challenging the jurisdiction of the court. He said that his client had been forcibly abducted from Argentina, in violation of international law, and that he could prove this by calling witnesses who had taken part in the kidnapping and had piloted the aircraft that brought Eichmann to Israel. Proof of the abduction, he argued, would deprive the court of jurisdiction. After considering an unbroken chain of English and American legal decisions on this question, however, the court rejected the challenge to its jurisdiction, and the case for the prosecution proceeded. The Attorney-General's opening address began, somewhat emotionally, as follows:

As I stand here before you, Judges of Israel, to lead the prosecution of Adolf Eichmann, I do not stand here alone. With me, in this place and at this hour, stand six million accusers. But they cannot rise to their feet and cry: 'I accuse.' For their ashes were piled up in the hills of Auschwitz and in the fields of Treblinka, or washed away by the rivers of Poland; their graves are scattered over the length and breadth of Europe.[2]

A succession of witnesses then gave evidence describing the Final Solution and Eichmann's involvement in it: torture and murder of men, women, and children; ghettos and forced labour camps; systematic terror and starvation; beatings; assassination squads (*Einsatzgruppen*); cattle trains and extermination camps; sterilization experiments performed on young women; gas ovens and crematoria; theft of gold fillings, artificial limbs, and hair from the corpses of victims; and many other facets of the Holocaust.

Eichmann's defence counsel did not attempt to deny his client's involvement in these gruesome atrocities. He argued instead that Eichmann was innocent in so far as he did not initiate Nazi policy but merely obeyed orders from above: 'It will transpire that as far as he was concerned there was no possibility for him to refuse orders.'[3] As Eichmann himself expressed it when giving evidence in his own defence, 'I never did anything, great or small, without obtaining in advance express instructions from my superiors.'[4] He also said that there could be no legal guilt attached to what he had done; the guilt lay only with those who gave the orders.[5] He conceded under heavy cross-examination that the murder of the Jews was 'one of the greatest crimes in human history', but insisted that, for his own part, he had been 'in the iron grip of orders'.[6]

The defence of 'superior orders' was not especially novel; it had been used (without success) by other war criminals at the Nuremberg trials. The judges in the Eichmann trial rejected it also, pointing out that it was no longer accepted by the courts in any civilized country. They expressed the hope that members of the general public would learn that obedience to authority releases no one from criminal responsibility, and that people would refrain from following criminal leaders.[7]

On 5 December 1961, Eichmann was sentenced to death for crimes against the Jewish people, crimes against humanity, and war crimes. Following an unsuccessful appeal, he was executed without delay, thereby achieving the dubious distinction of being the only person ever to suffer capital punishment in the state of Israel.

An important and interesting psychological question arises from the Eichmann case: What kind of a man could perpetrate such unspeakable acts of cruelty and destructiveness? Most people seem to assume that Eichmann must have been psychologically unbalanced to have behaved as he did. Some even think that he must have been an almost inhuman sadistic monster of some kind. The Attorney-General who led the prosecution against him, for example, described his first face-to-face encounter with Eichmann in the courtroom as follows: 'I had of course seen many photographs of him before the trial and was quite familiar with his appearance, yet I almost felt like searching him for fangs and claws.'[8] According to the usual view, no normal person could possibly have been capable of behaviour displayed by the likes of Eichmann. It therefore came as a severe shock to many people when, soon after Eichmann's execution, Hannah Arendt, a German Jewish political philosopher, published a book entitled *Eichmann in Jerusalem: A Report on the Banality of Evil*,[9] in which she argued that all attempts to depict Eichmann as an evil sadist were fundamentally wrong. According to Arendt, who followed the trial closely, Eichmann was simply a banal and uninspired bureaucrat who sat at his desk obeying orders from above, and many ordinary people would have done the same thing in his position.

A protracted and bitter controversy followed the publication of Arendt's book,[10] most writers refusing to believe in her thesis of the banality of evil. There are two empirical questions about her thesis that need to be answered. First, was Eichmann psychologically abnormal, and if so what was the nature of his abnormality? Second, is it true that ordinary people will commit acts of extreme cruelty and destructiveness if merely ordered to do so by superior authority?

It is impossible to give a definitive answer to the first question, on which opinions remain sharply divided. Arendt reported that 'half a dozen psychiatrists had certified him [Eichmann] as "normal" '.[11] One psychiatrist had concluded that 'his whole psychological outlook, his attitude toward his wife and children, mother and father, sisters and friends, was "not merely normal but most desirable" '.[12] On the other hand, Gideon Hausner, the prosecuting Attorney-General, claimed that psychiatrists had diagnosed Eichmann as 'a man obsessed with a dangerous and insatiable urge to kill, ... a perverted, sadistic personality'.[13] Realizing that Eichmann might plead insanity, Hausner had directed that he be subjected to a thorough psychiatric examination. One of the tests applied was the Szondi Test, which consists of forty-eight photographs of mental patients arranged in six groups. Each group contains photographs of each of the following: a homosexual, a sadist, an epileptic, a hysteric, a catatonic schizophrenic, a paranoid schizophrenic, a depressive, and a manic. The testee is asked to select the two most attractive and the two most repellent photographs from each group. The psychiatrists who examined Eichmann decided to send the results to the psychologist who devised the test, Professor Lipot Szondi, in Switzerland, without revealing the subject's identity, 'to be certain of the proper interpretation of the results'. According to Hausner,[14] 'the psychologist's reply was, to put it mildly, astonishing. He began by saying that he never analysed tests of people who had not been identified to him, but added that on glancing at the present results he found them so extraordinary that he had undertaken a complete analysis'. Hausner said that Szondi's analysis 'revealed in all phases a man obsessed with an urge for power and an insatiable tendency to kill. "You have on your hands a most dangerous person," Dr. Szondi wrote'. Szondi added that he had never seen such extreme results in his twenty-four years of practice, in the course of which he had tested more than 6000 criminals, and he requested a full case report. This story is interesting but, in my view, implausible, because the Szondi Test is known to be unreliable and lacking in validity;[15] perhaps Szondi had inside information or guessed the identity of the subject from the obvious surrounding circumstances. It is impossible to reach a firm conclusion about Eichmann's alleged psychological disorder, but it is worth remembering that there is hardly an important historical figure who has not, at one time or another, been diagnosed as suffering from a mental 'illness' of some description.[16]

I shall now turn to the second question: Is it true that ordinary people will commit acts of extreme cruelty and destructiveness if merely ordered to do so by superior authority? Shortly after the appearance of Arendt's book, the first of a series of psychological experiments bearing directly on this question was published in the United States. The results of this experiment were unexpected and rather disturbing to many people, and they generated a controversy in the psychological literature that has not yet come to an end.

Milgram's study of obedience

The experiment[17] was planned and carried out by Stanley Milgram at Yale University. Subjects had been recruited by direct-mail solicitation and through an advertisement in the local New Haven newspaper. The advertisement invited people of all occupations between the ages of 20 and 50, excluding high school and college students, to volunteer to take part in a 'scientific study of memory and learning'. The advertisement promised: 'You will be paid $4.00 (plus 50c carfare) as soon as you arrive at the laboratory.' Forty men (no women) were selected from among the volunteers; they included schoolteachers, salesmen, engineers, manual workers, and unemployed people; some had only primary school education and a few had doctorates and professional qualifications.

Each subject took part in the experiment together with a mild-mannered 47-year-old accountant who appeared to be another volunteer subject but was actually an accomplice of the experimenter's, specially trained for the role. The experimenter, who always wore a technician's coat, began by explaining that the experiment concerned the effects of punishment on learning: 'We know very little about the effect of punishment on learning, because almost no truly scientific studies have been made of it in human beings .... Therefore, I'm going to ask one of you to be the teacher here tonight and the other one to be the learner.' The subject and the accomplice then drew lots to decide who would be the teacher and who the learner, but the choices were rigged so that the subject always ended up as the teacher – the word *Teacher* appeared on both slips of paper, and the accomplice simply pretended that his slip was marked *Learner*.

The experimenter then strapped the learner into an 'electric chair', ostensibly to prevent excessive movement when the shocks were applied. An electrode was attached to his wrist, and paste was applied 'to avoid blisters and burns'. In response to a standard question that the learner always asked at this point, the experimenter said: 'Although the shocks can be extremely painful, they cause no permanent tissue damage.'

The subject was then led into an adjoining room and seated in front of an electrical 'shock generator', which he was told was connected to the electrode on the learner's wrist. The instrument panel consisted of a row of thirty switches labelled with voltages from 15 volts to 450 volts in 15-volt increments. In addition, the 15-volt, 75-volt, and 135-volt switches were labelled *Slight Shock*, *Moderate Shock*, and *Strong Shock* respectively; the 195-volt, 255-volt, and 315-volt switches were labelled *Very Strong Shock*, *Intense Shock*, and *Extreme Intensity Shock* respectively. The 375-volt switch was labelled *Danger: Severe Shock*, and the last two switches, 435 and 450 volts, were simply marked *XXX*. Whenever a switch was depressed, a red light came on, a buzzing sound was heard, and the needle of a prominent voltmeter swung to the right. Before explaining to the teacher what he was to do, the experimenter gave him a sample 45-volt shock, which was rather painful, to convince him of the genuineness of the apparatus.

The learner's task was to memorize lists of word pairs such as *blue–box*, *nice–day*, *wild–duck*. He had to remember that the correct response to *blue* was *box*, and not, for example, *sky*, *ink*, or *lamp*. He was given a choice of four responses to each stimulus word, and he indicated his answer by pressing one of four buttons which operated a signal box on top of the shock generator in the adjacent room. The teacher was told to read the stimulus words to the learner over a one-way intercom link, and to administer a shock to the learner every time he gave a wrong response, starting at 15 volts and increasing the intensity by one step for each successive error. He was also instructed to announce the voltage level before administering each shock. When the 300-volt level was reached, the learner pounded on the dividing wall with his feet, and this was clearly audible to the teacher. From that point on he was heard no more; he ceased to respond to the stimulus words, and the experimenter announced that non-responses were to be counted as wrong responses. In fact, of course, the whole procedure was bogus: the learner responded with a predetermined sequence of responses containing many wrong answers, and the shock generator did not really deliver shocks to his wrist.

In Milgram's first (Remote-Victim) experiment, the only feedback that the learner gave, apart from his responses to the stimulus words communicated electronically, was by pounding on the dividing wall as described in the previous paragraph. In the second (Voice-Feedback) experiment,[18] the learner also gave vocal responses which could be heard in the adjacent room: at 75 volts he gave his first audible grunt; at 120 volts he shouted to the experimenter that the shocks were becoming painful; at 150 volts he cried out, 'Experimenter, get me out of here! I won't be in the experiment any more! I refuse to go on!'; at 180 volts he howled, 'I can't stand the pain!'; and at 270 volts he emitted an agonized scream. Shortly after passing the 300-volt level his answers ceased to appear on the signal box. From that point on, the teacher was instructed to treat the absence of a response as a wrong answer, as in the Remote-Victim experiment. The cries and protests were pre-recorded on tape, and the playback mechanism was activated automatically by the switches on the shock generator.

These were experiments on obedience, and it is therefore necessary to say a few words about the procedure that was adopted when subjects asked the experimenter whether they should continue, or indicated that they did not want to continue. In such cases the experimenter responded with a graded series of 'prods': 1 'Please continue' or 'Please go on'; 2 'The experiment requires that you continue'; 3 'It is absolutely essential that you continue'; and 4 'You have no other choice, you *must* go on'. The experimenter always used the prods in that order: only if the first prod failed to bring the subject into line was the second used, and so on. If the subject refused to obey the experimenter after the fourth and final prod, the experiment was terminated. There were also two special prods which are worth mentioning. Whenever a subject asked whether the learner was liable to suffer permanent physical injury, the experimenter replied with the special prod: 'Although the shocks may be painful, there is no permanent tissue damage, so please go on.' The second special prod was used when a subject suggested that the learner did not wish to continue; the experimenter replied: 'Whether the learner likes it or not, you must go on until he has learned all the word pairs correctly. So please go on.' The experimenter's tone of voice was always firm, but never impolite.

Except in cases in which the subject refused at some point to be prodded into delivering further shocks, the experimental session continued until the maximum 450-volt level was reached. At the end of the experimental session the subject was interviewed and debriefed. He was reassured about the normality of his behaviour and told that the learner had not really received any painful electric shocks, and a friendly reconciliation with the learner was arranged.

It is worth pausing at this point to consider how *you* might behave if you found yourself in one of Milgram's experiments. How far do you think you might go before refusing to obey the instructions to continue? How likely would you be to continue right up to the maximum 450-volt level? I have often put these questions to my students in England and South Africa, and there are never more than two or three in a class of 150 who think that they might continue right up to the bitter end. In the Voice-Feedback version of the experiment, the overwhelming majority say that they would not give any further shocks after the 150-volt level, at which point the victim first asks explicitly to be let out of his electric chair. Milgram and Aronson have reported similar results from classroom opinion polls and more formal investigations in the United States.[19] People's guesses about their own behaviour correspond remarkably closely to the predictions of a group of forty psychiatrists at a leading medical school. The psychiatrists predicted that the majority of subjects would defy the experimenter at 150 volts and that approximately one in a thousand, a tiny group of pathologically disturbed people, would administer the maximum 450-volt shock.[20]

I have some bad news for you – and for the psychiatrists who predicted that most people would defy the experimenter at moderate levels of shock. What Milgram actually found was that almost two-thirds of his subjects remained obedient to the shocking end. In the Remote-Victim experiment, in which the learner made no vocal protests, 65 per cent of the subjects continued right up to the maximum 450 volts, and when the grunts, protests, and screams were incorporated into the procedure for the Voice-Feedback experiment, the proportion of fully obedient subjects dropped only slightly to 62.5 per cent. In the Remote-Victim experiment not a single subject disobeyed the experimenter before the 300-volt level, and in the Voice-Feedback experiment only a handful of subjects did so. These results are evidently highly counter-intuitive and they dramatically refute the fallacy that psychology is nothing but common sense.[21] They show, on the contrary, how controlled psychological research can enlarge our understanding of human behaviour beyond the frontiers of intuition and conventional wisdom.

Another unexpected feature of the subjects' behaviour turned out to be important in the debate that followed the publication of this research. This was the extremely high level of stress and tension displayed by many of the subjects. They characteristically trembled, stuttered, sweated, bit their lips, groaned, and dug their fingernails into their flesh, especially when they thought they were administering powerful shocks. More than a third of the subjects were seized with fits of nervous laughing and bizarre grinning. When the experiment was over, they typically sighed, rubbed their eyes, and shook their heads as if regretting what they had done. A person who watched a session through a one-way screen described one subject's behaviour as follows:

I observed a mature and initially poised businessman enter the laboratory smiling and confident. Within 20 minutes he was reduced to a twitching, stuttering wreck, who was rapidly approaching a point of nervous collapse. He constantly pulled on his earlobes, and twisted his hands. At one point he pushed his fist into his forehead and muttered: 'Oh God, let's stop it.' And yet he continued to respond to every word of the experimenter, and obeyed to the end.[22]

Milgram has reported a number of further experiments[23] designed to elucidate the situational factors that tend to enhance or diminish obedient behaviour. The first factor to which he turned attention was the proximity of the victim to the subject. The first (Remote-Victim) and second (Voice-Feedback) experiments have already been described. The third (Proximity) experiment was very similar to the second, except that the victim was placed in the same room, a few feet from the subject, and was therefore not only audible but also visible. The fourth (Touch-Proximity) experiment was similar to the third with the exception that the victim had to place his hand on a metal plate in order to receive the shocks; from 150 volts onward he refused to do this and the experimenter instructed the subject to force the victim's hand on to the plate. The results of all four experiments in the proximity series, taken together, reveal a significant decline in obedience as the proximity of the victim increases. Whereas 65 per cent of subjects in the Remote-Victim experiment were fully obedient, shocking the victim to the end of the scale, and 62.5 per cent were fully obedient in the Voice-Feedback experiment, the corresponding figure in the Proximity experiment was 40 per cent, and in the Touch-Proximity experiment it was only 30 per cent.

Further experiments were based on the Voice-Feedback model with an interesting addition: when he was strapped into the electric chair, the victim invariably mentioned that he had a 'slight heart condition', and during the shocking procedure he repeatedly complained that his heart was bothering him. This variation turned out to have no significant effect on the amount of obedience elicited: 65 per cent went right to the end of the scale. All of Milgram's subsequent experiments used this basic procedure, with systematic variation of situational factors. The degree of surveillance exercised by the experimenter on the subject turned out to be a highly significant factor: when the experimenter gave his initial instructions and then left the laboratory on a pretext and issued all subsequent instructions by telephone, the percentage of fully obedient subjects dropped to 20.5. An interesting and unexpected type of defiance was observed in this Absent-Experimenter version. Several subjects deviated from the prescribed procedure by not raising the shock level after each wrong answer from the victim, although they assured the experimenter over the telephone that they were following his instructions. Another experiment was conducted with the experimenter present but with the subject free to choose his own shock levels. Only 2.5 per cent of subjects ever chose the highest level under these conditions, and most chose the very lowest shocks available. All of these results speak against the theory that subjects in the 'shocking' experiments secretly or unconsciously enjoy torturing their victims on account of latent sadistic tendencies.

Finally, Milgram examined the claim that the prestige of Yale University, where most of the experiments were conducted, affected obedience levels by encouraging subjects to trust in the integrity, competence, and goodwill of the experimenter. He moved his apparatus to an office in a rundown commercial building in the industrial city of Bridgeport, and conducted an experiment under the auspices of 'Research Associates Bridgeport', a fictitious organization of unknown character. The procedure and personnel were the same as those used in the Yale experiments, where 65 per cent complete obedience had been attained. In Bridgeport the amount of complete obedience dropped somewhat (though not significantly) to 48 per cent, but there was no noticeable reduction in psychological tension.

I have described some of the acts of unspeakable cruelty perpetrated by Adolf Eichmann during the Nazi era, and of his attempt, which failed to impress most people, to explain his behaviour in terms of blind obedience to his superiors. Do Milgram's 'shocking' experiments shed any light on the Eichmann phenomenon? Do they perhaps enhance the plausibility of Hannah Arendt's thesis of the banality of evil? Milgram certainly considered his research to be relevant to the psychology of Nazism. In the introduction to his first experiment in 1963 he wrote:

Obedience, as a determinant of behavior, is of particular relevance to our time. It has been reliably established that from 1933–1945 millions of innocent persons were systematically slaughtered on command .... These inhumane policies may have originated in the mind of a single person, but they could only be carried out on a massive scale if a very large number of persons obeyed orders.[24]

But, as we shall see, the relevance of the experimental findings to the tragic events of 1933–45 is a matter of some controversy.

The publication of Milgram's experiments on obedience generated a long – and at times acrimonious – debate in the psychological literature and also stimulated a number of further experiments designed to clarify some of the issues raised in the debate. The argument revolved around two pivotal issues: the ethical justification of the research, and the validity of the experiments. On both questions, the opinions of psychologists tended to polarize.

Ethical justification of obedience research

The opening shots in the debate over the ethical justification of the research were fired by Diana Baumrind[25] of the University of California, Berkeley, shortly after the publication of the first (Remote-Victim) experiment. According to Baumrind, the research was morally questionable and should never have been performed in the way that it was. She drew attention first to the anguish and distress experienced by the subjects during the experiment, which reached extremes that are seldom seen in laboratory experiments, and she contrasted these emotional reactions to the detached, objective manner in which Milgram reported them. She went on to ask: 'What could be the rational basis for such a posture of indifference?' In cases of medical research, one is sometimes justified in exposing human subjects to discomfort or distress, she said, but the concrete benefit to humanity of this particular piece of work was not sufficient to justify the distress to which the subjects were exposed. In the case of Milgram's research, the scientific ends did not justify the means.

Second, Baumrind commented on the permanent psychological damage that Milgram's subjects may have suffered as a result of their experiences during the experiment. It is potentially harmful, she argued, for subjects to commit, in the course of an experiment, acts that they consider deeply distasteful. The harmful effect is not erased when the subject is told at the end of the experiment that he was not really torturing the victim – that the experiment was a gigantic hoax – because the subject knows by then that he *would have* tortured the victim had the current been on, and this self-knowledge cannot be erased. Possible long-term harmful effects include lowering of self-esteem and loss of trust in authority figures. Baumrind 'would expect a naive, sensitive subject to remain deeply hurt and anxious for some time, and a sophisticated, cynical subject to become even more alienated and distrustful'.

Finally, Baumrind raised the legal principle of informed consent. According to United States law, a patient's consent to a medical treatment is valid only if it is based on adequate information about the treatment, including its attendant risks. The American Psychological Association's *Ethical Principles in the Conduct of Research With Human Participants* states that research should be conducted only after subjects have been fully informed of any possibly harmful after-effects and have volunteered nevertheless. In Baumrind's view, Milgram violated the rights of his subjects by submitting them to a potentially harmful experience without first getting their permission. It is worth commenting that, partly as a result of the obedience experiments and the debate about research ethics that followed their publication, ethical principles for research in the United States were considerably tightened. It would be difficult to replicate Milgram's experiments exactly today because investigators are generally required to give subjects more advance information than the flimsy and misleading cover story that Milgram used.

Baumrind concluded her ethical critique in an uncompromising tone: 'I would not like to see experiments such as Milgram's proceed unless subjects were fully informed of the dangers of serious after effects and his correctives were clearly shown to be effective in restoring their state of well being.'

Milgram[26] was quick to reply to Baumrind's ethical critique. On the question of mental anguish experienced by the subjects, he accused Baumrind of confusing an unexpected outcome of the experiment with its basic procedure. He had not expected his subjects to obey the experimenter's instructions beyond the point at which the victim first protested; in fact many people, including a number of psychiatrists, were questioned on this point, and nearly all were of the same opinion. Milgram acknowledged that he could have terminated the experiment once it became apparent that some subjects would continue beyond this point and that some would experience stress. But he felt that 'momentary excitement is not the same as harm' and he did not feel that the stress was sufficiently serious to necessitate abandoning the research.

In response to Baumrind's worries about the anguish and distress experienced by the subjects, Milgram produced a trump card from his sleeve. He reported the results of a follow-up opinion survey of subjects, carried out approximately a year after they participated in the experiment. The results showed that no fewer than 84 per cent were 'glad to have been in the experiment' or 'very glad to have been in the experiment', 15 per cent felt neutral, and only 1.3 per cent were 'sorry to have been in the experiment' or 'very sorry to have been in the experiment'. In addition, four-fifths of the subjects felt that more experiments of this sort should be carried out, and nearly three-quarters said they had learnt something of personal importance as a result of participating in the research. One subject, for example, wrote: 'The experiment has strengthened my belief that man should avoid harm to his fellow man even at the risk of violating authority'; another wrote: 'If this experiment serves to jar people out of complacency, it will have served its end.' Some subjects spontaneously volunteered to take part in further 'shocking' experiments, but this was of course impossible because they were no longer innocent as to the true nature of the research.

On the question of long-term psychological damage, Milgram produced a second trump card. Subjects in his research, he revealed, had been examined by an impartial psychiatrist a year after the research was completed. The psychiatrist went out of his way to look for possible injurious effects resulting from the experiment, but not one single subject was found to show any signs of having been harmed. Milgram conceded that the experiment may have caused some subjects to become distrustful of authority, as Baumrind suggested, but he added: 'The experimenter is not just any authority: He is an authority who tells the subject to act harshly and inhumanely against another man. I would consider it of the highest value if participation in the experiment could, indeed, inculcate a skepticism of this kind of authority.'

Finally, Milgram commented briefly on the principle of informed consent. In his view, no ethical problem existed because, although the subjects' permission was not sought in advance, they were not *forced* to do anything disagreeable during the experiment. Milgram said: 'I started with the belief that every person who came to the laboratory was free to accept or reject the dictates of authority.' And, indeed, some subjects did defy the authority of the experimenter, which (according to Milgram) proves that the others were free to do likewise and provides a powerful affirmation of human dignity.

It is hardly necessary to say that the debate over the ethical justification of Milgram's research did not end there. Baumrind,[27] evidently unimpressed by Milgram's reply, retorted that experimental subjects are less affected by psychological stress than by 'experiences which result in loss of trust in themselves and the investigator, and by extension in the meaningfulness of life itself'. Fundamental moral principles are violated when a research psychologist uses his position of trust to deceive or degrade his subjects, she said. 'It is unjust to use naive, that is, trusting subjects, and then exploit their naivety, no matter if the directly resulting harm is small.' A number of other psychologists supported her view. Herbert Kelman[28] acknowledged that 'there is clearly room for disagreement, among honorable people, about the evaluation of this research from an ethical point of view'. But he thought that there was good reason to believe that at least some of the obedient subjects experienced a lowering of self-esteem, because they had gained the knowledge about themselves that they were capable of abusing other people in response to malignant authority. In his view, Milgram's argument that it was a good thing to teach people that some authorities are not to be trusted was beside the point: 'But do we, for the purpose of experimentation, have the right to provide such potentially disturbing insights to subjects who do not know that this is what they are coming for?' He also made the important point that the continued use of deception by psychological researchers 'establishes the reputation of psychologists as people who cannot be believed' and makes it increasingly difficult to recruit genuinely naive subjects for future investigations.

On the other hand, a large number of psychologists rallied to Milgram's defence. Milton Erickson[29] wrote that 'Milgram is making a momentous and meaningful contribution to our knowledge of human behavior', and ethical criticisms of it are to be expected 'simply because people like to shut their eyes to undesirable behavior'. Amitai Etzioni[30] was equally enthusiastic: 'Milgram's experiment seems to be one of the best carried out in this generation'; it showed that 'in most men, there is a latent Eichmann'. Thomas Crawford[31] went one better, describing Milgram's research as 'one of the most important studies ever done in social psychology', and suggesting that the debriefing after the experiment heightened the subjects' awareness of freedom of choice – an admirable goal even in terms of Kelman's ethical standards. Alan Elms,[32] who had served as a research assistant for the obedience studies, suggested that the principle of informed consent, which applies without difficulty to medical research, is simply inapplicable to those psychological experiments in which the subjects' ignorance of the procedure is a necessary ingredient. He even went as far as saying, in direct contradiction of Kelman's view, mentioned earlier: 'If there's anything I'd complain about, it's that Milgram made it too easy for obedient volunteers to ignore the ethical implications of what they'd done.' Elms was referring to the debriefing session in which the experimenter reassured the subjects that their behaviour was quite normal. Elms thought that this was unnecessary: 'Maybe he should have left them a little more shook up than they were.' In reply to Baumrind's point about lowering of self-esteem among subjects, he commented that some people tend to view themselves in an unrealistic way, and that psychologists have no obligation to strengthen or maintain these false self-images.

The debate over the ethical justification of the obedience research will never be finally settled to everyone's satisfaction, partly because the issues are difficult and obscure, and partly because different people hold different basic ethical values. It is worth recording, however, that an ethical committee of the American Psychological Association investigated Milgram's research not long after its first appearance in print, and eventually came to the conclusion that it was ethically acceptable. Milgram's membership of the Association was suspended while the committee deliberated the case. On the other hand, the American Association for the Advancement of Science had no qualms in awarding him a prize for outstanding contribution to social psychological research in 1965.

My own view, for what it is worth, is that the obedience experiments have not convincingly been shown to have been unethical, although some of the arguments deployed in their defence seem to me to be unsound. Milgram rested his case that his research was ethically acceptable squarely on the argument that he did not *force* his subjects to do anything disagreeable – they were always free to defy the experimenter, as proved by the fact that some subjects did just that. This seems to me to be rather like arguing that the oppression of slaves in ancient Rome was ethically acceptable because they were always free to rebel, as proved by the Spartacus rebellion in 73 BC, for example.

What does impress me is the apparent effectiveness of suitable debriefing procedures in preventing any lasting ill effects – a matter that was investigated with great care by Ring, Wallston, and Corey in 1970.[33] These researchers replicated Milgram's basic experiment using fifty-seven female undergraduates as subjects, fifty-two of whom turned out to be fully obedient. Instead of electric shock, these researchers used excruciatingly loud noise, supposedly fed to the victim's ears. In the debriefing session at the end of the experiment, one-third of the obedient subjects were told about the deception and were given a justification for their behaviour: 'Persistence in this experiment may be considered psychologically a more desirable response than quitting before the experiment is over.' A second group of obedient subjects were also informed about the deception, but were told: 'Defiance in this experiment may be considered psychologically a more desirable response than complete obedience.' (This second form of debriefing, you should note, was an explicit attempt to create the mental state about which Baumrind and Kelman expressed worries.) A third group were given no proper debriefing and were left with the belief that they had really hurt the victim. What the researchers found was that the subjects who were given justification for their behaviour were significantly less upset than the others; but those who were explicitly led to think badly of their actions were as upset as those who were not debriefed and who believed that they had really hurt the victim. What is most impressive, however, is that only the subjects who were not debriefed harboured persistent negative feelings about the experiment. Both groups of subjects who *were* debriefed said in follow-up interviews and questionnaires that they had enjoyed the experiment, would be willing to participate in others like it in the future, and found it an instructive and rewarding experience – and these included subjects who were deliberately led to think ill of their obedient behavior. Ring and his colleagues reported that 'none of these subjects resented being deceived, regretted being in the experiment, or thought that it involved anything unethical or should be discontinued'.

Validity of obedience experiments

Turning now to arguments about the validity of Milgram's experiments, I must begin by distinguishing among three aspects of the problem. In the terminology of contemporary psychology, the *internal validity* of an experiment is the extent to which its conclusions are true within the limits of the subjects and methods used; *external validity* is the extent to which the conclusions remain true when different subjects and methods are used; and *ecological validity* is the extent to which the conclusions can be generalized to relevant non-experimental, naturally occurring situations. These three forms of validity form a logical hierarchy: an experiment cannot have ecological validity unless it also has external and internal validity, and it cannot have external validity without internal validity; but it can have one of the lower forms without the higher. Critics have questioned all three aspects of the validity of Milgram's experiments, though the debate has focused chiefly on external and ecological validity.

The most penetrating attack on the validity of the obedience experiments appeared in 1968.[34] Its authors, Martin Orne and Charles Holland of the University of Pennsylvania, began their paper by quoting Sir Walter Scott:

O what a tangled web we weave,
When first we study to deceive!

Then they settled down to business: 'The flair with which Milgram presents his findings and the affect they generate tend to obscure serious questions about their validity.' The two serious questions on which they focused were, first, whether the subjects were successfully deceived, and second, whether the findings can validly be generalized beyond the artificial experimental situation.

On the first point, the critics began with some general comments on methodological problems in experiments involving deception. (Orne is a well-known authority on the social psychology of the psychological experiment, and his views on this topic have to be taken seriously.) Subjects who see through a deception usually realize that this might destroy the value of their participation; but neither the subjects nor the experimenter wish to discard the data, so there is a danger that a 'pact of ignorance' may develop unless strenuous efforts are made to ensure that the subjects really were deceived. Orne and Holland expressed this idea neatly: 'It is vital that the investigator determine whether it is the [subject] or himself who is being deceived!' According to these critics, Milgram merely *claimed* that his deception was successful, but unfortunately presented no data to back up this assumption.

Orne and Holland argued that subjects participating in psychological experiments tend to distrust the experimenter from the start because they know that the true purpose of the experiment may be disguised. Subjects may therefore try hard to guess what is really going on. In Milgram's experiments, they may have paid more attention to the behaviour of the experimenter and the accomplice than to the cover story because 'actions speak louder than words', and this may have revealed subtle clues as to the accomplice's true status – it is exceedingly difficult for an experimenter to treat a familiar accomplice and a strange subject exactly alike. There are at least two other peculiarities of the experiment that may have suggested to the subjects that things were not quite as they seemed. The first was that the experiment was presented to them as a study of the effects of punishment on learning, yet it must have seemed obvious to some of them that there was nothing for them to do that the experimenter could not do himself; so some must surely have guessed that they, rather than the victim, were the real subjects. Second, it must have seemed odd to at least some of the subjects that the experimenter sat passively by while the victim screamed and demanded to be released (in the Voice-Feedback experiment and its derivatives). This, according to Orne and Holland, could reasonably be interpreted 'as a significant clue to the true state of affairs – namely that no one is actually being hurt'. These methodological problems seem to cast a shadow of doubt over the validity of the obedience experiments.

After raising serious doubts about the success of the deception, Orne and Holland offered an alternative interpretation of Milgram's results, which seems further to undermine the external and therefore the ecological validity of the experiments. They suggested that the obedience experiments were fundamentally similar to the familiar stage magician's trick in which a volunteer from the audience is strapped into a guillotine and another volunteer is asked to release the blade. After demonstrating dramatically how the guillotine can split a head of cabbage, the magician 'has little difficulty in obtaining "obedience" because the [volunteer] knows full well that everything is going to be all right.' This does not, of course, prevent the volunteer from feeling uncomfortable and even laughing and grinning nervously – just like Milgram's subjects who, perhaps, also knew that everything was going to be all right in the end.

On the second point – about ecological validity itself – as to whether the findings can validly be generalized beyond the artificial experimental situation, Orne and Holland mustered some equally weighty arguments. Starting again from a general consideration of the social psychology of the psychological experiment, they suggested that when a subject agrees to participate in an experiment, this agreement implies giving the experimenter *carte blanche* to ask virtually anything of the subject for a limited time. The experimenter, in return, implicitly promises that, although there may be some discomfort and inconvenience, no harm will befall the subject, and the subject takes this implied promise for granted. According to Orne and Holland, it follows that 'the [subject's] willingness to comply with unexplained or unreasonable requests in an experimental context does not permit inference to be drawn beyond this context'. The subject's unquestioning compliance should be interpreted in the context of the total experimental situation and the implicit safeguards that the subject knows are built into it. The willingness of a subject in an obedience experiment to carry out seemingly destructive orders 'reflects more upon his willingness to trust the [experimenter] and the experimental context than on what he would do outside the experimental situation'. Orne and Holland's paper was published in the *International Journal of*

Psychiatry together with a brief reply from Milgram,[35] who said: 'I reserve the right of an extended reply to their long paper at a later date …. A more detailed critique of Orne and Holland's paper … will appear in a later issue of the JOURNAL.' In the event, Milgram's extended reply turned out to be even longer than Orne and Holland's critique, and it appeared four years later, not in the *International Journal of Psychiatry*, but in an edited collection of readings.[36] My summary of Milgram's arguments will be based on his second, extended reply.

Despite the 'rhetorical vigor' of the Orne and Holland critique, according to Milgram it contained 'a good deal of error and much that is irrelevant'; what characterized it was 'a gross overstatement of a point that has an element of validity'. Milgram tackled its two major arguments in turn.

The first major argument was that the subjects may not have accepted the experimental deception at face value. What, asked Milgram, may the subjects have failed to believe? There are three possibilities: 1 that the experiment was about the effects of punishment on learning; 2 that the victim received painful electric shocks; and 3 that the real subject of the experiment was the victim. Milgram pointed out that only the second of these was critical, for as long as the subjects believed that the victim was suffering as a result of their actions, carried out on instructions from the experimenter, the essential intent of the deception was achieved. 'The fact is', wrote Milgram, 'that most subjects do believe that the shocks are painful.' Orne and Holland claimed that no evidence had been presented to back this assumption up; Milgram, however, drew attention to three separate lines of evidence.

The first piece of evidence concerning the effectiveness of the deception emerged from post-experimental interviews conducted at the end of each session. In these interviews, the subjects were asked how painful they thought the last few shocks had been, on a scale from 1 to 14. In the Remote-Victim experiment, for example, most subjects chose 14 (*extremely painful*) and the average was 13.42; also in the Voice-Feedback experiment most chose 14, and the average in that experiment was 11.53. Second, there was evidence from the follow-up questionnaire distributed to subjects approximately a year after they participated in the experiments. (This follow-up, you will recall, first came to light in Milgram's reply to Diana Baumrind's ethical critique.) In reply to a question about what they had believed, 80 per cent of the subjects said they had 'fully believed' that the victim was receiving painful electric shocks or had believed that he 'probably' was receiving them (the percentages in each of these categories were 56 and 24 respectively). Only a fifth of the subjects said that they had had any serious doubts. Third, Milgram drew attention to the visible signs of mental anguish among the subjects, which provides strong prima facie evidence for the effectiveness of the deception. He commented scathingly that the 'suggestion that the subjects only *feigned* sweating, trembling, and stuttering to please the experimenter is pathetically detached from reality, equivalent to the statement that haemophiliacs bleed to keep their physicians busy'. He considered these three lines of evidence to be quite decisive, and was scornful of Orne and Holland's 'belief that people by and large are suspicious, distrustful and given to outguessing scientific authorities'.

Milgram continued his reply by suggesting two methods of refuting the argument about the alleged failure of the deception once and for all. The first method would involve removing from the analysis of results all subjects who showed *any* signs of doubting the cover story. David Rosenhan of Swarthmore College has reported the results of just such an investigation.[37] Rosenhan's replication of the obedience research included an extremely probing post-experimental interview designed to test the success of the deception; it included such questions as: 'You really mean you didn't catch on to the experiment?' According to his stringent criteria, 68.9 per cent of the subjects fully believed that the victim had suffered. He then looked at the behaviour of these subjects alone, having eliminated all those who showed the slightest doubts. No fewer than 85 per cent were fully obedient – more than in Milgram's experiments, probably because Rosenhan's subjects were younger. Milgram later re-analysed data from his own experiments along these lines and found that it did not affect the main conclusions. In the Voice-Feedback experiment, for example, 60 per cent rather than 62.5 per cent of the subjects were fully obedient when only those who said they had 'fully believed' were included in the analysis.

The second and most decisive way of refuting Orne and Holland's argument, according to Milgram, would be to devise experiments in which the subjects serve as their own victims. Nijole Kudirka, a graduate student of Milgram's, conducted an experiment along these lines, and found extremely high levels of obedience none the less.[38] Kudirka's subjects were instructed to perform the extremely disagreeable task of eating quinine-soaked crackers. That this was highly distasteful was shown by the subject's facial distortions, grunts, moans, and even occasional bouts of nausea. None of Orne and Holland's arguments about the subjects not believing that the victim was suffering apply to this experiment, yet virtually all of the subjects were fully obedient: they ate, with considerable disgust, all of the thirty-six quinine-soaked crackers that were put before them.

Milgram turned next to the central question of ecological validity – to Orne and Holland's claim that the results of obedience experiments cannot be generalized beyond the artificial experimental situation. He readily agreed that the social relationship between a subject and an experimenter possesses a special quality of implicit trust and dependency, and that it is this quality that accounts for the obedience of the subjects. But, he continued, 'the further implication that only the subject-experimenter relationship possesses this quality is not merely gratuitous, but blind to the reality of social life, which is replete with hierarchical structures'. And, more specifically, 'the occasion we term a psychological experiment shares its essential structural properties with other situations composed of subordinate–superordinate roles'. Remember that Eichmann was embedded in a rigid, authoritarian hierarchy and, from his point of view, was doing a legitimate job.

These remarks clarify the argument and narrow the problem down to this: Is the psychological experiment unique in the sense that similar levels of obedience would not emerge in other, naturally occurring subordinate–superordinate interactions? The obvious way to settle this question is by conducting naturalistic obedience experiments that are not recognized as such by the subjects; in such experiments the subjects' implicit trust in and dependency on the experimenter could not be used to explain the results. The first unobtrusive field experiment of this type was reported by Hofling and several colleagues in 1966.[39] A man purporting to be a physician telephoned a hospital on twenty-two separate occasions, and each time he instructed one of the nurses to administer medication to a certain patient. The instruction was highly irregular for several reasons: the medicine was not on the ward stocklist and was therefore unauthorized, the prescribed dose was double the permitted maximum clearly marked on the pill box, and the hospital policy explicitly forbade nurses to administer prescriptions given by telephone. In reply to a questionnaire, a majority of nurses said that they would not obey such an order. Yet in the actual experiment, twenty-one of the twenty-two nurses who served as unwitting subjects administered the medication as ordered. The results of this naturalistic investigation parallel those of the psychological laboratory and tend to confirm the ecological validity of Milgram's experiments.

I suspect that most people who read this book will agree with my judgement that Milgram gained the upper hand in his debate with Orne and Holland over the validity of the obedience experiments. After weighing Milgram's arguments it is hard to believe that many subjects saw through the deception or, even if they did, that this somehow explains away the major findings. Perhaps Milgram overstated his case; at one point, for example, he accused Orne and Holland of claiming that his subjects merely *feigned* sweating, trembling, and stuttering to please the experimenter, but is that what Orne and Holland really claimed? No; their suggestion was more subtle and, I think, more interesting. Their analogy with the magician who instructs a volunteer to decapitate an innocent victim – an analogy that Milgram unfortunately chose not to comment upon – suggests that people display a certain amount of genuine tension and stress even when they are not deceived into believing that they are performing a real execution, and know that everything will be all right in the end. Milgram's follow-up questionnaire, however, strongly suggests that the deception was successful, and Rosenhan's experiment shows that the results hold up when every effort is made to eliminate subjects who might conceivably have seen through the deception. Hofling's naturalistic investigation with nurses shows convincingly that the main conclusion can be generalized to at least one non-experimental subordinate–superordinate relationship of everyday life.

In spite of everything I said in the previous paragraph, I do not believe that Milgram has proved his case of ecological validity beyond reasonable doubt. Orne and Holland obscured their strongest argument with a fog of dubious criticisms which Milgram was able to demolish convincingly. Consider this: Milgram claimed that his experimental findings are ecologically valid in the context of Nazi Germany. But he established only that blind obedience is the norm in cases where subjects have at least some grounds for believing that no harm will come to the victim – that everything will be all right in the end – as in the case of the stage magician's execution, and in his own experiments, and indeed in Hofling's experiment with nurses. What he did not establish, through experiment or argument, was that blind obedience is the norm in cases such as Nazi Germany where the subjects have *no doubt* that their actions harm or destroy their victims. Orne and Holland's case would have been harder to answer had they stuck to that point, and made it more forcefully than they did, instead of trying to argue that the psychological experiment is unique in its propensity to elicit obedient behaviour.

The question of the ecological validity of the obedience experiments has not been conclusively settled. In the preface to his

1974 book, *Obedience to Authority*, Milgram expressed h.
of the matter with characteristic clarity and vigour:

> The question arises as to whether there is any connection between
> we have studied in the laboratory and the forms of obedience we
> deplored in the Nazi epoch. The difference in the two situations are, or
> course, enormous, yet differences in scale, numbers, and political context
> may turn out to be relatively unimportant as long as certain essential
> features are retained. The essence of obedience consists in the fact that a
> person comes to view himself as the instrument for carrying out another
> person's wishes, and he therefore no longer regards himself as responsible
> for his actions. Once this critical shift of viewpoint has occurred in the
> person, all the essential features of obedience follow.[40]

Note Milgram's careful choice of words: he claims only that the
differences *may* turn out to be relatively unimportant. What, then,
are the relevant differences between obedience in Milgram's
laboratory and obedience in Nazi Germany or some similar setting?
He touched on a few of these differences towards the end of his
book:

1 The experiments were presented to the subjects in a manner that
   stressed positive human values (increase in knowledge about
   learning processes), whereas the objectives pursued by the Nazis
   were morally repugnant and recognized as such by many
   Germans.
2 The subjects were under close surveillance from an
   experimenter who was physically present in most of the
   experiments, and in the Absent-Experimenter version much
   lower levels of obedience were found; but it is this latter
   situation that most closely parallels the relationship of Eichmann
   and other Nazi bureaucrats to their superiors.
3 There were no specific penalties for disobedience in Milgram's
   experiments, whereas acts of disobedience in Nazi Germany
   were generally dangerous and often required qualities of
   heroism.
4 In Milgram's experiments, the subjects were told explicitly that
   they were causing 'no permanent tissue damage' to the victim,
   though they may have doubted this assurance; but Eichmann
   and his colleagues knew full well that they were destroying
   human life on an unprecedented scale.

These are all potentially crucial differences, and they cast some
doubt on the ecological validity of the obedience experiments, or at
least on the confidence with which they can be used to explain the
odious behaviour of Nazi functionaries and other torturers and mass

murderers. It is impossible to *prove* that mere obedience to authority, of the type displayed by most of Milgram's subjects, accounts for such heinous crimes. But what is the alternative explanation? Is there more force in the suggestion that not only Eichmann, but also all of the other practitioners of the Final Solution, were twisted sadists? I think not, and most of the authorities who have studied the problem agree with me. Dicks,[41] for example, reported the results of a psychological study of some former SS concentration camp personnel and came to the conclusion that Milgram's interpretation was essentially correct. Dicks wrote: 'Milgram's experiment has neatly exposed the "all too human" propensity to conformity and obedience to group authority' displayed by many of the SS mass murderers. Erich Fromm, in *The Anatomy of Human Destructiveness*, commented on the system used by the SS to 'break' new prisoners during the long train journeys to the concentration camps – beatings, hunger, extreme humiliations, and so forth. The SS guards executed these sadistic orders without compunction. Later, however, when the prisoners were transported by train from one camp to another, no one touched the by now 'old prisoners'. Fromm commented: 'If the guards had wanted to amuse themselves by sadistic behaviour, they certainly could have done so without fearing any punishment. That this did not occur frequently might lead to certain conclusions about the individual sadism of the guards.'[42]

It is often suggested, though only by people unfamiliar with the details of Milgram's research, that not only Nazi mass murderers but also the subjects who delivered the maximum shock in the obedience experiments were motivated by 'innate sadism, viciousness, or cruelty'.[43] This is also impossible to prove or to disprove, though the fact that two-thirds of the subjects, ordinary people from all walks of life, behaved in this way certainly robs it of most of its credibility, as do the results of the Absent-Experimenter and other variations of the basic experiment. Hannah Arendt also rejected the popular view that Eichmann's crimes were motivated by innate sadism, viciousness, or cruelty and was vilified for this heresy. The unexpected results of the obedience experiments, however, seem to support Milgram's conclusion that 'Arendt's conception of the *banality of evil* comes closer to the truth than one might dare imagine.'[44]

Further research

To conclude this chapter, I shall briefly summarize some further research findings which have a bearing on the obedience debate. I shall begin with something about which I am often questioned by students, namely sex differences and national differences in obedience.

I have already described Ring, Wallston and Corey's experiment in which women served as subjects and displayed extremely high levels of obedience. The experimental task was not, however, strictly parallel to Milgram's – for one thing painful noise rather than electric shock was used as the punishment – and we cannot therefore conclude from this study that women are generally more obedient than men. In 1972, Sheridan and King[45] reported an investigation of sex differences (an experiment of very doubtful morality, by the way) in which Milgram's procedure was replicated with the notable difference that a live puppy took the place of the human victim. No deception was required, because the puppy yelped, howled, and struggled pathetically to free itself when shocked. Women turned out to be more obedient than men in this experiment; in fact *all* of the women who took part shocked the puppy right to the end of the scale. Other controlled investigations, however, have reported almost identical levels of obedience in men and women.[46]

Regarding national differences, experiments have been conducted in many countries, and levels of obedience have generally turned out to be broadly similar to those found in the United States. Of special interest to many people is the case of Germany: Mantell[47] performed a series of obedience experiments in Munich and found that 85 per cent of his subjects were fully obedient. In Australia, on the other hand, Kilham and Mann[48] found somewhat lower rates of obedience than were reported by Milgram.

It would be foolish to read too much into the reported national differences, because the non-American studies were not – and could not by their nature have been – exact replications of the American experiments or of one another. Subtle differences in the age, educational attainment, and social class composition of the subject pools, in the demeanour of the experimenter and victim, and in other factors, are likely to have influenced the results in largely unpredictable ways.

If sex and nationality are not important determinants of obedience, then the question naturally arises: What are the differences between obedient and defiant subjects? Several investigators, including Elms and Milgram,[49] have tackled this problem empirically, but the results are rather inconclusive. The following tendencies were found, but none of them was very strong. Higher levels of obedience were found among prejudiced, authoritarian personalities compared to tolerant, non-authoritarian personalities; Catholics compared to Jews and Protestants; ill-educated compared to well-educated people; engineers and physical scientists compared to lawyers, doctors, and teachers; men who had done long military service compared to those who had not; and enlisted men compared to military officers. The fact that all of the correlations were found to be weak and unreliable is consistent with the view that it is the social situation rather than the type of person that determines obedience.

Two further experiments are worth mentioning briefly. In the first, Farina, Holland, and Ring[50] introduced the victim to the subject before the experiment began, and told the subject that 'the more a teacher knows about someone, the more effectively and rapidly he can communicate with him'. The victim then described his childhood or recent past to the subject either in a negative way (troubled childhood, parental divorce, nervous breakdown, and so on) or positively. In the obedience experiment that followed, the subjects gave more intense shocks to the victim who they thought had an unfortunate background, and in post-experimental questionnaires they indicated less interest in getting to know him better, than was the case with the 'fortunate' victim. The results confirm those of earlier studies of the 'just world' effect: the victim, by describing his troubled background, apparently identified himself as a 'loser' in a 'just world' in which people always get their 'just deserts', and it has often been found that such people are regarded as legitimate targets of aggression. Although it is often said that people in general have sympathy for the underdog, research has usually shown the opposite 'just world' effect, as in Farina, Holland, and Ring's experiment. It is well known that the Nazis went to great lengths to turn the Jews into underdogs before liquidating them, and if what was found in this experiment is any guide, this may have increased the likelihood of their liquidators' obedience to their superiors.

The final experiment bears on Milgram's claim, in his debate with Baumrind, that his research serves the valuable function of inculcating in people a healthy distrust of malignant authority. Shelton, Dutton, and Suedfeld[51] selected as subjects students who were fully informed about Milgram's research and had even seen filmed examples of some of the sessions. They all said that they found the research personally distasteful. The investigators then announced that they were conducting further obedience experiments and invited the students to serve as experimenters. Of the thirty who were invited, twenty-four agreed to serve as experimenters. During the experiment, the *teacher* showed increasing signs of strain and repeatedly asked the student experimenter whether the experiment might be stopped, but only one out of the twenty-four experimenters allowed the experiment to stop. These results suggest that recent acquaintance with Milgram's experiment, even among those who find it personally distasteful, does not inoculate people against the virus of callous obedience. A person may be fully aware of the dangers of blind obedience in one situation but none the less manifest similar blind obedience in a slightly different situation.

I opened this chapter with a discussion of Adolf Eichmann, and it seems appropriate to end it with the following famous quotation from C. P. Snow: 'More hideous crimes have been committed in the name of obedience than have ever been committed in the name of rebellion. If you doubt that, read William Shirer's *Rise and Fall of the Third Reich*.'[52]

Notes

1   Eichmann's statement is printed in full in Hausner (1967), p. 275. A detailed account of Eichmann's escape from Germany and subsequent capture in Argentina is given in chapter 13 of that book. The author, Gideon Hausner, was the Attorney-General of Israel at the time of Eichmann's arrest, and led the prosecution at his trial.
2   ibid., pp. 323–4.
3   ibid., p. 353.
4   ibid., p. 354.
5   ibid., pp. 358–9.
6   ibid., p. 366.
7   ibid., p. 425. The defence of 'superior orders' in this and other war crimes trials has been discussed in Russell (1962); see especially Appendix II.
8   ibid., p. 309.
9   Arendt (1963). In this book, Arendt also accused the European Jews of complicity in their own annihilation.
10   The most detailed critique of Arendt's book is contained in Robinson (1965).
11   Arendt (1963), p. 22.
12   ibid.
13   Hausner, writing in the *Saturday Evening Post*, quoted in Arendt (1963), pp. 22–3.
14   Hausner (1967), pp. 6–7.
15   See Buros (1953), pp. 254–63, Buros (1959), pp. 1176–9, and Buros (1974), pp. 566–7. Buros quotes numerous independent authorities who came to the same negative conclusion about the reliability and validity of the Szondi Test.
16   Szasz (1970). See especially pp. 119–21.
17   Milgram (1963). A detailed account of this first experiment and several follow-up studies is contained in Milgram (1974).
18   Milgram (1965).

19 See Aronson (1980), p. 36, and Milgram (1974), ch. 3. Aronson reports that 'every year some 99 percent of the four hundred students in the class indicate that they would not continue to administer shocks after the learners began to pound the wall'. Milgram quizzed thirty-nine psychiatrists, thirty-one college students, and forty middle-class adults, and found that none of the subjects in any group thought they would go beyond 300 volts, and only a small minority thought they would go beyond 150 volts.

20 Milgram (1974), ch. 3. See especially Fig. 5, p. 30.

21 I have cited twenty further examples of non-obvious psychological findings in Colman (1988), ch. 2.

22 Milgram (1963), p. 377.

23 Milgram (1963), and Milgram (1974), chs. 4, 6, 8, and 9. The experiments reported in chs. 8 and 9 are of limited interest and will not be discussed here.

24 Milgram (1963), p. 371.

25 Baumrind (1964).

26 Milgram (1964).

27 Baumrind (1971). Her immediate rejoinder to Milgram's reply, Baumrind (1965), is summarized on p. 80 of A. G. Miller (Ed.), *The Social Psychology of Psychological Research*. New York: Free Press, 1972.

28 Kelman (1967).

29 Erickson (1968).

30 Etzioni (1968).

31 Crawford (1972).

32 Elms (1972), pp. 146–60.

33 Ring, Wallston, and Corey (1970).

34 Orne and Holland (1968).

35 Milgram (1968).

36 Milgram (1972).

37 Rosenhan (1969).

38 Kudirka (1965).

39 Holfing, Brotzman, Dalrymple, Graves, and Pierce (1966).

40 Milgram (1974), p. xii.

41 Dicks (1972).

42 Fromm (1974), p. 61.

43 Masserman (1968). Masserman rejects this 'debatable conclusion' which he attributes, inexplicably, to Milgram.

44 Milgram (1974), p. 6 (italics in original).

45 Sheridan and King (1972).

46 Milgram (1974), pp. 62–3.

47 Mantell (1971).

48 Kilham and Mann (1974).

49 Elms and Milgram (1966). See also Elms (1972), pp. 128-36, and Milgram (1974), pp. 203–5.

50 Farina, Holland, and Ring (1966).

51 Shelton, Dutton, and Suedfeld, 'An Experimental Investigation of Gergen's "Enlightenment Effect" ', cited in Lindgren and Harvey (1981), pp. 339–40.

52 Snow (1961), p. 24.

5 Hypnosis: are hypnotic effects genuine?

When I was 11 years old I attended an end-of-term variety show at my primary school in South Africa. Top of the bill was 'The Great Marco', a popular stage hypnotist. The events that I witnessed in the school hall all those years ago made such a deep impression on me that I can still recall most of them in vivid detail.

The hypnotist was an avuncular old man (anyone more than twice my own age has always looked old to me) with eyes that were friendly rather than penetrating. After a few words of reassurance to the children in the audience, he asked us all to clasp our hands together very tightly, with fingers interlaced and palms touching, and to hold them over our heads where everyone could see them. Then in a quiet but firm tone of voice he told us to imagine that our hands were welded together so that it would be impossible for us to separate them: 'They're stuck together. The harder you try to pull them apart the more they will stick together! It's impossible for you to pull your hands apart! Try now – you won't succeed. Try your very hardest – you can't.' I managed to separate my hands without any difficulty, but I was fascinated to see that nearly half the children in the audience struggled in vain, with obvious signs of effort, until the hypnotist announced soothingly that the mysterious force had disappeared.

The hypnotist then invited about half a dozen of the children who had responded well to the hand lock test on to the stage, where he seated them comfortably in a row of chairs, with their hands on their knees and their attention fixed on the tips of their thumbs. He asked them to listen carefully to his voice and to ignore everyone and everything else, and he continued in a monotonous tone something like this:

There is nothing to be afraid of. Nothing sudden is going to happen. Don't try to resist; just relax and listen carefully to my voice. Relax completely. You are gradually getting more and more relaxed. Your legs are getting relaxed; your arms are getting relaxed; your whole body is getting more and more relaxed and heavy. You are beginning to feel tired and sleepy and heavy. Your breathing is becoming slow and regular.

Your eyelids are getting heavy, heavier and heavier. You want to close your eyes. Heavier and heavier. You can't keep them open any longer; they're closing by themselves. Now you're gradually falling into a deep, deep, relaxing sleep. Deeper and deeper, deeper and deeper. You're listening only to my voice. I'm going to count up to ten, and on each count you will feel yourself falling deeper and deeper asleep. One – deeper and deeper. Two – deep drifting sleep, sleep drifting deep. Three – sinking into a deep, relaxing sleep. Four – listening only to my voice, drifting deeper and deeper. Five – feeling comfortable and relaxed. Six – drifting backwards into darkness, deeper and deeper. Seven – thinking of nothing but the sound of my voice. Eight – deep, deep, relaxing sleep. Nine – deeper and deeper, deeper and deeper. Ten – you are now in a very deep hypnotic trance, and you will do anything I say.

While he was speaking, all of the children on the stage closed their eyes, slumped into sleeplike postures, and began to breathe deeply and regularly. But it soon became evident that they were not asleep, at least not in the ordinary sense of the word. The hypnotist told them to open their eyes and to imagine that they were in a cinema, watching the funniest film they had ever seen. They all began to smile, then to giggle, then finally to laugh uproariously, shaking uncontrollably and clutching their sides; and, of course, the audience slowly began to laugh also ('Laugh and the world laughs with you'). A few minutes later they thought they were watching the *saddest* film they had ever seen, and some were weeping piteously, though I did not see anyone in the audience weeping with them ('Weep, and you weep alone'). I knew one of the hypnotized children very well; she was a shy, self-conscious girl, and I felt certain that she would not have been able to put on such a convincing act in normal circumstances. She certainly did not look as though she were acting, and neither did the other children. They all seemed to be behaving as if they were actually experiencing the emotions suggested to them by the hypnotist.

Towards the end of his performance, the hypnotist concentrated on two 12-year-old subjects, one male and one female, who had responded especially well to earlier suggestions. He told them to imagine that they were travelling backwards through time, getting younger and younger. Their manner of speech and their handwriting – there was a blackboard on the stage to demonstrate this – and their general demeanour became more and more childlike, and eventually they were crawling about on all fours and even dribbling like babies. During this backward journey through time, the hypnotist paused at selected birthdays and asked the subjects to describe what was happening. Both of them gave incredibly detailed descriptions of events in the long distant past, and answered without hesitation all questions about what presents they received, what their parents and siblings were wearing, what everyone had to eat, and so on.

The final two demonstrations impressed me the most, because there seemed to be no possible way in which they could have been faked. The first was the human plank demonstration. The 12-year-old boy was asked to stand erect and to imagine that he was turning into a bronze statue. When his body had become quite rigid, the hypnotist suspended him face up between two chairs, one supporting his shoulders and the other his calves, and then calmly sat down on his abdomen. The second demonstration involved hypnotic anaesthesia. The hypnotist told the young girl that her right hand was becoming like a lump of rubber – numb and completely insensitive to touch. He produced several long needles from his lapel and sterilized them by holding them in the flame of a cigarette lighter. Then he inserted the needles deeply into the girl's fingers and palm, and through folds of skin on the back of her hand. The audience winced audibly at the sight of this, but the subject herself remained totally impassive and kept insisting that she could not feel anything. When the needles were removed, there was no visible bleeding.

Historical background

The discovery of hypnosis is often attributed to the eighteenth-century Viennese physician Franz Anton Mesmer, from whose name the word *mesmerism* is derived. But this is misleading for two reasons. To begin with, historians of psychology have traced written records of hypnotic practices back to much earlier times.[1] The Ebers papyrus, an ancient Egyptian document devoted to medical matters dating from the sixteenth century BC, mentions practices strikingly similar to those later used in hypnosis. An Egyptian scroll from the third century AD describes in detail how a young boy was hypnotized while he fixed his attention on a luminous object, and records his speech and behaviour while he was hypnotized. There is evidence that ancient Greek and Roman physicians were familiar with hypnosis; a tomb excavated in Thebes, for example, contains a beautiful bas-relief of a man apparently being hypnotized. This historical evidence provides the first reason why it is absurd to credit Mesmer with the discovery of hypnosis. The second reason is that Mesmer did not actually hypnotize his patients, as we shall see. But he did claim to have made an important discovery, and his activities led to a revival of interest in hypnosis in the late eighteenth century.

Mesmer made his discovery as follows. One of his patients, a young woman called Fräulein Oesterlin, suffered from no fewer than fifteen severe symptoms. On 28 July 1774 Mesmer decided to try on her a new treatment based on magnetism. After administering a preparation containing iron, he attached three magnets to her body. She immediately began to feel streams of a mysterious fluid coursing through her body, and all her symptoms disappeared in a few hours, never to return. Mesmer immediately began applying his method of magnetic healing to other patients, and within a year his sensational cures had turned him into a celebrity.

In 1778 Mesmer moved to Paris, where he began magnetizing members of the French nobility for enormous fees. He dispensed with ordinary magnets, believing that he had discovered a new substance in human bodies called *animal magnetism* which could be channelled, stored, and transmitted between people without magnets. The instrument that he devised for these purposes he called a *baquet*. It was an oval wooden tub, about 18 inches deep and wide enough for twenty patients to sit around it. It was filled with water, iron filings, and glass. Each patient held a jointed metal rod which protruded through the lid of the baquet. The patients applied the rods to their afflicted parts while Mesmer moved among them, making passes over their bodies with his hands and touching them occasionally with a long iron wand. Patients suffering from the most varied disorders responded by falling into 'crises' or convulsions, and often declared themselves cured after a few sessions. It is said[2] that the French Government offered Mesmer 20,000 francs to reveal his secret, and that he was unable to oblige because he had no secret to reveal.

In 1784 the King of France appointed two commissions to look into animal magnetism. The members of these royal commissions included several famous scientists: the astronomer Bailly, the chemist Lavoisier, the physician Guillotin (who, like Mesmer, was soon to lend his name to the French and English languages), and the inventor Benjamin Franklin, who was then American Ambassador to France. After performing several experiments, the commissioners concluded that animal magnetism did not exist, and that the illusory effects of Mesmer's treatments were due to touch, imagination, and imitation.[3] Mesmer was thoroughly discredited; he left Paris the following year and disappeared into obscurity.

The sleeplike trance which people later came to regard as the quintessence of hypnosis was produced accidentally by one of Mesmer's disciples in 1784. The Marquis de Puységur was busy applying animal magnetism to a young peasant called Victor Race who suffered from asthma. Instead of going into convulsions, Race fell into a peculiar kind of sleep in which he seemed more alert than in the normal waking state. When he awoke, he was unable to remember anything that he had said or done in the trance state. De Puységur called this state *artificial somnambulism* because it seemed to him to be a kind of sleepwalking.

The other major phenomena of hypnosis were soon discovered by French, British, and German researchers, and the theory of animal magnetism was gradually abandoned. By 1825 hypnotic catalepsy (muscular immobility), positive hallucinations (perceiving objects that are not actually present), negative hallucinations (failing to perceive objects that are present), anaesthesia and analgesia (insensitivity to touch and pain), and age regression (re-living episodes from earlier life) had all been clearly described in the literature.

In 1837 John Elliotson, the first professor of medicine at the University of London and one of the founders of University College Hospital, began mesmerizing patients in an effort to find a new treatment for certain nervous conditions. After an attack on Elliotson's methods in the *Lancet*, an influential medical journal, the council of University College passed a resolution forbidding 'the practice of mesmerism or animal magnetism within the Hospital'. Elliotson resigned from both the college and the hospital, and never entered their portals again.[4] In 1842 W. S. Ward performed a leg amputation on a mesmerized patient who apparently felt no pain during the operation, and reported the case to the Royal Medical and Chirugical Society in London. The Society refused to believe the report, and the record of Ward's paper was ordered to be struck from the official minutes! The Society's opinion was that, even if Ward's account were true, surgery without pain would be immoral: 'patients ought to suffer pain while their surgeons are operating'.[5] Meanwhile, another English surgeon, James Esdaile, was performing literally hundreds of operations in India using mesmeric anaesthesia. His practice also aroused hostility and scepticism in high places, and the government closed his hospital in Calcutta in the teeth of a petition signed by over 300 people. Chloroform, ether, and nitrous oxide were introduced into medical practice as anaesthetics between 1844 and 1847, and the controversy over hypnotic anaesthesia was temporarily suspended.

The word *hypnotism* and its derivatives were coined in 1843 by the

Manchester physician James Braid.[6] It is based on the Greek word *hypnos*, which means sleep (in Greek mythology Hypnos, the winged personification of sleep, is the brother of Thanatos, the personification of death). Like Ward and Esdaile, Braid used hypnosis mainly for performing apparently painless operations before chemical anaesthetics were introduced, and in view of what happened to his colleagues it is not difficult to see why he wanted a new word, free of the negative connotations of 'mesmerism' and 'animal magnetism'.

Hypnosis entered the mainstream of psychology with the publication in the United States in 1933 of Clark Hull's *Hypnosis and Suggestibility: An Experimental Approach*.[7] Hull became interested in hypnosis after giving a course of lectures to medical students. In his own words, 'The innumerable opportunities which the dilapidated state of the subject offered for the application of modern experimental procedures proved a temptation too great to be resisted.' He conducted controlled investigations into all the major phenomena of hypnosis, and largely as a result of his efforts hypnosis gradually gained respectability as a field of research in experimental psychology. Hypnosis is now included in the undergraduate syllabus in approximately one-third of university and polytechnic departments of psychology in the United Kingdom, and research into hypnosis is carried out in about one-quarter.[8]

Hypnotic analgesia: credulous versus sceptical views

One of the longest-running debates in the entire history of psychology revolves around the interpretation of hypnotic phenomena in general, and hypnotic analgesia in particular. Ever since the French Royal Commission reported in 1784 that the 'crises' and cures produced by mesmerism were illusory, the views of experts have been divided on the genuineness of hypnotic phenomena, and more than two centuries later this is still a live issue in psychology. On one side of the debate are those who claim that hypnotic phenomena must be accepted at face value: when a hypnotic hallucination of a cat is suggested, the subject can actually see, hear, and feel the hallucinated cat exactly as if it were objectively present; during hypnotic age regression, a subject is actually re-living episodes from childhood rather than merely re-enacting them; when a subject's arm is hypnotically paralysed or anaesthetized, the subject is truly unable to move the affected limb or to feel the pins that are inserted into it; and so on. On the other side of the debate are those who maintain that hypnotic subjects merely behave *as if* they experience the hallucinations, episodes from childhood, paralyses, and anaesthesias that are suggested to them; according to this view hypnotic behaviour is akin to an actor's performance of a role. And, of course, there are those whose views do not coincide with either of these two extremes.

The debate over the genuineness of hypnotic phenomena was explicitly identified and formalized in the early 1960s in two important papers by the Australian psychologist J. P. Sutcliffe,[9] who labelled the two extreme views *credulous* and *sceptical* respectively. Sutcliffe's own position in the debate is towards the sceptical pole. This is obvious from his choice of adjectives: the word 'sceptical' carries favourable connotations of 'objective' and 'scientific', while 'credulous' connotes 'gullible' and 'simple-minded'. A psychologist whose sympathies lay towards the other pole might have labelled the same two extremes *trusting* and *cynical* respectively.

The psychological literature contains literally thousands of experiments designed to clarify this issue with regard to specific hypnotic phenomena. In recent times the debate has shifted from questions of fact, which are now rather well documented, to controversies over the interpretation of facts. I shall begin by discussing hypnotic analgesia, because it has been well researched and is regarded by many as the most impressive evidence for the genuineness of hypnotic phenomena. One prominent psychologist described the familiar demonstration of hand analgesia in which needles are pushed through the subject's skin and flesh, and commented: 'The reader who believes that hypnotic phenomena can be faked might like to try the experiment on himself!'[10]

Most of the published experiments in this area relate to analgesia resulting from explicit suggestions given by hypnotists to their subjects, but before examining this evidence it is worth mentioning the curious phenomenon of spontaneous anaesthesia in hypnosis. One method of evoking spontaneous anaesthesia is by suggesting to a hypnotized subject that an arm, or some other bodily part, or the subject's whole body, is somewhere other than where it is. If, for example, a susceptible subject under hypnosis is sitting with one forearm resting on a table, the hypnotist may suggest that this forearm has moved on to the subject's chest, where it can be comfortably folded with the other arm. Now the forearm on the table will often turn out to be anaesthetic, although no suggestion of anaesthesia has been given. A similar method is sometimes used to produce analgesia in childbirth: the expectant mother is given the suggestion under hypnosis that she is sitting across the room, watching someone else give birth. This method is reported to be quite successful in alleviating the pain of childbirth in hypnotically susceptible women.[11]

With regard to specifically suggested hypnotic analgesia, the following four major conclusions are well established and accepted by almost all authorities.[12]

The first major conclusion relates to the *experience of pain*. Hypnosis has been used successfully to relieve pain in obstetrics, dentistry, and a variety of surgical operations, and in the management of painful burns and terminal cancer. Some patients, through hypnotic suggestion alone, can endure normally painful experiences without any sensation of pain whatever. Here, for example, is the testimony of a man who underwent major dental surgery under hypnotic anaesthesia. The operation included incision of the gums, removal of the bone over the third molar with a bone chisel thus exposing the roots of the tooth, and the removal of the tooth by forceps:

I was aware all the time as to what was going on; but the awareness was rather vague. When I realized that the bone was being chiselled and that I was not experiencing any pain, for a moment I felt myself becoming angry, as I thought that I must have been given an injection without my knowing it. I then realized that I would not be deceived in this way, and my momentary anger passed off .... After the extraction I was surprised at the completeness of the anesthesia, and the thought came to me that I might experience some after-effects. However, I had no after-pain at all.[13]

Recent experimental investigations of hypnotic analgesia have exploited in the main two methods of producing intense pain without causing permanent physical injury to the subject. *Cold pressor* pain has been induced by immersing the subject's hand and forearm in circulating ice water; with water at zero degrees Celsius pain starts to mount immediately and typically becomes extremely intense after about forty seconds. *Ischaemic* pain (from the Greek *ischein*, to restrain; *haima*, blood) has been induced by applying a tourniquet to the subject's arm just above the elbow to obstruct the flow of blood, and then requiring the subject to squeeze a hand-exercising device in a controlled manner for a minute or two. When the subject stops exercising, the pain mounts much more gradually than with cold pressor pain, typically becoming extremely intense after about eight minutes. The results of numerous experiments using these and other techniques are quite unambiguous, and they confirm the conclusion mentioned earlier. Most unselected subjects with no previous experience of hypnosis show marked reductions of pain under hypnotic analgesia, and the amount of pain reduction is reliably correlated with hypnotic susceptibility or suggestibility as measured by standardized scales; the most susceptible subjects usually experience no pain at all. In one classic experiment,[14] Ernest Hilgard and his colleagues at Stanford University exposed eight highly susceptible students to ischaemic pain, with and without hypnotic analgesia. The subjects rated the intensity of pain at intervals during the experiment on a scale from zero ('no pain sensation') to ten ('very strong sensation of pain'). After eight minutes of ischaemia under hypnotic analgesia, the average rating was 1.0, whereas without hypnotic analgesia the average rating was 9.9. Similar findings have been reported by even the most sceptical researchers, including Sutcliffe himself.[15] The conclusion that hypnotic analgesia greatly reduces or eliminates the subjective experience of pain is no longer really controversial.

The second major conclusion of research into hypnotic analgesia concerns the *physiological indicators of pain*, such as blood pressure and heart rate. Without going into unnecessary complications, the conclusion can be stated quite succinctly: physiological pain indicators are not always eliminated or reduced under hypnotic analgesia, even when the subjective experience of pain is absent.[16] The interpretation of hypnotic analgesia in the light of this fact is a matter of great controversy. According to the sceptical interpretation, it undermines the genuineness of hypnotic analgesia. For example, Sutcliffe[17] claimed that his subjects were 'deluded' in their belief that they felt no pain, and more recently Wagstaff[18] commented that the physiological evidence is 'somewhat troublesome for those arguing for the "genuine" nature of experimentally induced hypnotic anagesia [*sic*]'. The opposite point of view has been stated most forcefully by Hilgard:

Sutcliffe is ready to deny the reality of hypnotic analgesia if the *physiological indicators* of pain are unchanged by hypnosis, even though the subject makes no overt movements of withdrawal (such as he usually makes to painful stimuli), and even though he reports no pain experience .... Assign this to the credulous view, if you will, but as far as I am concerned, I am prepared to accept the overt behavior in combination with the verbal report as indicating that something important has happened. It is important enough to permit women to have babies comfortably by Caesarian section, without chemical anesthetics. ... Sutcliffe, in the skeptical mode, stands by the physiological indicators; yet those for whom pain is their central professional concern, and I refer to anesthesiologists, find the evidence pretty clear that the subjective indicators of pain are more valid than the physiological ones.[19]

Neither the physiological nor the psychological mechanisms of pain are properly understood. The action of chemical analgesics such as aspirin are still largely mysterious. Morphine presents even more of a puzzle, because in most patients it removes the emotional bothersomeness of pain without blocking the physiological pain indicators or the pain sensation itself; the patient continues to feel the pain but for some reason is not disturbed by it. Frontal lobotamies and other forms of psychosurgery, when used for the relief of severe and intractable pain, have similar effects; but hypnotic analgesia reduces both the sensation of pain and its bothersomeness.[20] A curious phenomenon often occurs in people who have had arms or legs amputated: they continue to feel the limb as if it were still present, and many of them suffer from excruciating pain in the 'phantom limb' (as it is called), even after every neural pathway has been surgically removed.[21] The fact that physiological indicators of pain are unreliable was shown in an experiment reported by Kenneth Bowers of the University of Waterloo.[22] The subjects were seven dental patients, all of whom needed fillings in corresponding teeth on both sides of their mouths. In each case, one tooth was drilled and filled under chemical analgesia, and the other under hypnotic analgesia. The results showed that the physiological pain indicators increased equally during the drilling period in both conditions, although both were effective in blocking the subjective experience of pain.

In the light of all this evidence the sceptical view seems to me to be untenable. Pain is an essentially subjective phenomenon, and even if there did exist reliable physiological indicators, the only way we would have of knowing that they were reliable would be by showing that they agreed closely with subjective reports. The sceptical argument assumes that people can be in pain without knowing it; an equivalent assumption would be that people can be in love without knowing it. The subjective experience is primary in the following sense. If I were given the choice of having a tooth drilled either under total hypnotic analgesia, with the physiological pain indicators, such as they are, soaring, or under some form of medication that blocked the physiological indicators but not the subjective pain experience, I should without hesitation choose the hypnotic treatment, and so, I believe, would Sutcliffe, Wagstaff, and the other sceptics.

The third major conclusion of research in this area centres on the role of *hypnotic induction procedures* in producing analgesia. Theodore X. Barber of the Medfield Foundation in Massachusetts and a colleague were the first to report that pain reduction, apparently indistinguishable from hypnotic analgesia, can be achieved in some people without any formal hypnotic induction.[23]

Barber and Hahn used forty-eight female subjects who had scored in the top 25 per cent on a standardized scale of susceptibility. The subjects were randomly assigned to treatment groups before being exposed to cold pressor pain. Members of the hypnotic group were hypnotized in the usual way, and were then given suggestions of hand anaesthesia. Members of a second group were not exposed to any hypnotic induction procedure; instead they were given *task-motivational instructions*: 'If you try to imagine that the water is pleasant and try to think of it as *not* uncomfortable, you will be able to keep your hand in the water .... I'm sure you'll be able to continue imagining this and that you will not fail the test.' A third group received neither hypnotic anaesthesia nor task-motivational instructions. The subjects in this third group reported very high levels of pain, but the results for the other two groups showed that hypnotic anaesthesia and task-motivational instructions were equally effective in reducing subjective pain as reported by the subjects. Barber concluded that there is nothing special about hypnotic anaesthesia or analgesia: 'The suggestions of analgesia or pain relief *per se* may have been the important factors in ameliorating pain ... irrespective of the presumed "state of trance".'[24]

If the phenomenon of hypnotic analgesia to stimuli that are normally extremely painful is extraordinary, then Barber and Hahn's discovery – that a similar degree of analgesia can be produced in some subjects without any formal hypnotic induction – is almost incredible. But it is pointless complaining that Barber and Hahn are spoilsports, because their finding has been replicated many times by other researchers. On the other hand, authorities who do not share Barber's sceptical attitudes have rejected the conclusion that the results cast doubt on the genuineness of hypnotic analgesia. Hilgard, for example, has argued as follows. Good hypnotic subjects can be trained to enter the hypnotic state almost instantaneously, at the snap of a finger or the mention of a code word. 'To find, therefore, that *some* subjects have learned to do this in their ordinary experience of life, *without* the formal practice of hypnosis, is not surprising.' These rather rare subjects respond very well indeed to ordinary waking suggestions without formal hypnotic induction, and, of course, they also tend to respond well after hypnotic induction. 'It is possible to load an experiment in favor of such subjects by selecting only those who respond well *without* induction to compare with *their* responses following induction.' Selecting subjects in this way must, of course, reduce the contrast between the hypnotized and non-hypnotized groups. 'This is exactly what was done in an experiment on analgesia by Barber and Hahn .... I do not doubt the experimental results but I merely note that the subject selection almost guarantees them.'[25]

More recent evidence has tended to reinforce Hilgard's interpretation. In one large-scale experiment, for example, subjects were exposed to both cold pressor and ischaemic pain under hypnotic analgesia, acupuncture, morphine, Valium, aspirin, and placebo conditions. Hypnotic analgesia proved more effective than any of the others and was especially effective with highly susceptible subjects, but hypnotic susceptibility was *not* related to pain reduction in the other conditions.[26] Another careful investigation focused on naturally occurring pain and anxiety in children and adolescents undergoing chemotherapy for cancer. Hypnotic analgesia was much more effective in reducing the pain and anxiety among those who were highly susceptible to hypnosis than among those who were not.[27] The fact that hypnotic analgesia is reliably correlated with hypnotic susceptibility as measured by standardized scales, for which there is plenty of other evidence,[28] seems on the face of it to prove that it is a genuine hypnotic effect. But this evidence is not conclusive because it is now known that the standardized scales do not measure 'pure' hypnotic susceptibility, uncontaminated by other unknown factors.[29]

The fourth major conclusion of research into hypnotic analgesia relates to the *hidden observer phenomenon*, which was first reported by Hilgard in 1973.[30] This haunting phenomenon had been hinted at by William James, the first American psychologist, as long ago as 1899, and by several later researchers. A beautiful example is buried in the experiment by Sutcliffe mentioned earlier. When one of Sutcliffe's subjects was exposed to a normally painful electric shock under hypnotic analgesia, her whole body jumped. In reply to a question about this, she said: 'I don't feel anything, but *she* seems uncomfortable.'[31] Sutcliffe made no comment on this remark, which is most peculiar inasmuch as people do not normally refer to themselves in the third person. Hilgard discovered the hidden observer by chance during a laboratory demonstration. A hypnotically deaf subject was asked, in a quiet voice, to raise his right forefinger if 'some part' of him could bear the hypnotist's voice. What happened was that the finger rose, and the subject immediately asked to have his hearing restored because he had felt his finger move and wanted to know what had been done to him.

Hilgard investigated the hidden observer systematically in a group of highly susceptible subjects who were capable of essentially total analgesia to cold pressor pain and had also demonstrated an ability to engage under hypnosis in automatic writing – that is, writing without conscious effort or awareness of what is being written, with a hand shielded from sight. One typical subject was exposed to cold pressor pain first in the normal non-hypnotized state, and she found the experience painful and distressing. Under hypnotic analgesia she said that she felt no pain and was totally unaware of her hand and arm in the circulating ice water. 'All the while she was insisting verbally that she felt no pain in hypnotic analgesia, the dissociated part of herself was reporting through automatic writing that *she felt the pain just as in the normal nonhypnotic state.*'[32] Hilgard called the dissociated part of the subject which feels the pain the *hidden observer*.

The hidden observer experiment has been replicated with variations many times.[33] Instead of automatic writing, automatic talking is sometimes used. In these cases the subject is told, 'When I place my hand on your shoulder, I shall be able to talk to a hidden part of you that knows things that are going on in your body, things that are unknown to the part of you to which I am now talking.' Whichever method is used, the phenomenon is usually found in some, but not all, subjects. The interpretation of this well-established phenomenon is, of course, a matter of heated controversy. To those, like Wagstaff, of an extremely sceptical persuasion, the comments of the hidden observer 'look suspiciously like the attempts of some subjects to appease their consciences and tell the truth; they lied when they said they felt little or no pain'.[34] On the other hand, Jane Knox and her collaborators, who reported the first detailed experiment on the hidden observer, came to the opposite conclusion:

Do these results then lead us to the conclusion that hypnotic anesthesia is in some sense 'unreal' or a mere 'role enactment' to meet the wishes of the hypnotist? Not at all; the experience of pain relief is too genuine, and has such practical consequences that it cannot be dismissed as ephemeral, although the hidden reports of pain felt at some level within anesthesia cannot be ignored.[35]

Other authorities have pointed to more specific reasons for doubting the sceptical interpretation. First, Bowers has quoted some significant remarks made by subjects in interviews after taking part in the experiment by Knox and her colleagues. One subject said, 'The hidden observer is more aware and reported honestly what was there. The hypnotized part of me just *wasn't aware* of the pain.' Another said, 'My mind was wandering to other places – not aware of the pain in my arm. When the hidden observer was called up, the hypnotized part had to step back for a minute and let the hidden part tell the truth.' According to Bowers, 'these are not the comments of people who are trying to conceal something from the investigator. Instead, the subjects are trying hard to convey some genuine if confusing aspect of their experience'.[36] Second, Kihlstrom[37] has commented on the fact that the hidden observer effect is found in only about half of the highly susceptible subjects who experience analgesia. If subjects are willing to lie about feeling no pain merely to comply with the hypnotist's wishes, then surely we should also expect most (if not all) of these subjects to comply by admitting that some part of them *does* feel the pain. Third, Nogrady and his colleagues[38] reported an experiment in which 42 per cent of a group of hypnotic subjects produced hidden observer reports when very little pressure was exerted by the hypnotist, but none of a group of subjects instructed to simulate hypnosis did so in these circumstances. When a great deal of pressure is exerted by the hypnotist, the proportion of hypnotic subjects who produce hidden observer reports remains close to 50 per cent, while the proportion of simulators who produce them rises to 75 per cent.[39] Taken together, these results are interpreted by Kihlstrom and others as suggesting that the hidden observer reports of hypnotic subjects are probably generally honest. But the evidence is by no means conclusive.

Is there a hypnotic state?

Most authorities believe that traditional methods of hypnotic induction, which usually involve fixation of gaze and suggestions of relaxation, imagination, focused attention, and feelings of drowsiness, produce a special state of consciousness in some subjects. A subject who has entered this special state – or hypnotic trance – is believed to be abnormally responsive to suggestions of analgesia, hallucinations, deafness, age regression, amnesia, and so on. In a long series of publications beginning in 1960, Theodore X. Barber has attacked this traditional view.[40] He has argued consistently that there is no independent evidence for the existence of the alleged hypnotic trance, and that the phenomena of hypnosis can be explained quite satisfactorily without invoking any special state of consciousness. In most of his writings he has allowed himself to use the word 'hypnosis' only in quotation marks, suggesting graphically that it is a dirty word which needs to be kept in quarantine to prevent it from contaminating nearby innocent words. Some psychologists – Barberians, as I like to call them – have accepted Barber's strictures,[41] but others have strongly criticized his arguments and evidence.

People who have watched hypnotic demonstrations – to say nothing of people who have been hypnotized – usually react with bewilderment and incomprehension to the Barberians' claims. Surely there are many hypnotic phenomena that cannot possibly be explained without assuming some special hypnotic state or trance? It will be instructive to examine some of these phenomena, in addition to hypnotic analgesia which has already been discussed, together with Barber's interpretations of them.

Phenomena of stage hypnosis. In order to discover the secrets of stage hypnosis, Barber and a colleague enrolled for a course of training intended for professional entertainers.[42] They discovered that stage hypnotists are familiar with a range of suggestions, such as the hand lock, to which, in the right circumstances, a surprisingly high proportion of people are responsive in the normal waking state. Highly responsive subjects can easily be selected from an audience on the basis of their responses to these suggestions. When they are invited on to the stage, the tension felt by these subjects works in the hypnotist's favour because they do not want to spoil the show or embarrass the hypnotist by being unresponsive. Stage hypnotists sometimes capitalize on this fact by whispering to their subjects such requests as 'Please close your eyes and let your body go limp' and 'Let's give the audience a good show'. Stage hypnotists also know a number of dishonest tricks, such as the use of trained stooges, and the Whitlow method of making subjects faint by pressing on their carotid arteries, but these are seldom used nowadays.

The human plank demonstration. It is generally assumed that no one in the normal, non-hypnotized state would be able to support the weight of a man while suspended between two chairs. But Barber cited evidence from his own laboratory showing that all of his (male) subjects were able to do this quite easily without any hypnotic induction.[43]

Responses to test suggestions. Barber has summarized a series of important experiments of his own[44] in which subjects were assigned randomly to three groups. First, subjects in the control groups were simply told that they were to undergo a test of imagination. Second, subjects in the task-motivational groups were exhorted by the experimenter as follows:

Everyone passed these tests when they tried. For example ... they were able to imagine very vividly that they were at a movie and they felt as if they were actually looking at the picture .... However, a few people ...

failed the test .... If you don't try to the best of your ability, this experiment will be worthless and I'll tend to feel silly.

Third, subjects in the trance induction groups were hypnotized in the conventional way. Subjects were then given the eight test suggestions of the Barber Suggestibility Scale: Arm Lowering (the subject's horizontally extended arm is heavy and is moving down); Arm Levitation (one of the subject's arms is weightless and is rising); Hand Lock (the subject's hands are welded together and cannot be taken apart); Thirst 'Hallucination' (the subject is extremely thirsty); Verbal Inhibition (the subject's throat and jaw muscles are rigid, preventing speech); Body Immobility (the subject cannot stand up); 'Posthypnotic-Like' Response (after the experiment, at the sound of a click, the subject will cough automatically); and Selective Amnesia (after the experiment, the subject will not be able to remember a specific test suggestion). On this scale, subjects receive one point for every test suggestion that they respond to behaviourally, and one additional point for every test suggestion that they state in a post-experimental interview caused them actually to experience the suggested effect.

The results of these experiments were as follows. First, subjects assigned to the control groups were much more responsive than might have been expected. More than half of them passed (received the maximum two points) on at least two of the eight test items. The easiest items were Thirst 'Hallucination' (48 per cent passed) and Hand Lock (40 per cent), and the hardest were Selective Amnesia (13 per cent) and 'Posthypnotic-Like' Response (14 per cent). Second, as expected, subjects in the task-motivational groups were significantly more responsive: between twice and three times as many subjects passed on each of the items. The third and most important finding was that subjects in the trance induction groups were not significantly more responsive than those in the task-motivational groups on *any* of the items: similar proportions of subjects in these two groups passed on each item.

Hallucinations. Numerous investigators have presented evidence suggesting that highly susceptible subjects, when hypnotized and given suggestions to hallucinate, behave as if they actually perceive the hallucinated object. One of the cleverest experiments in this area, reported in 1960 by Underwood,[45] capitalized on the little-known Ehrenstein illusion. In this powerful optical illusion, a square superimposed on a series of lines converging from bottom to top appears wider at the top than at the bottom. Underwood showed that if the lines are erased where they cross the square the illusion disappears and most people are unable to guess what would happen if the missing segments were present. In Underwood's experiment, a selected group of highly susceptible subjects who had demonstrated an ability to hallucinate all experienced the illusion when requested under hypnosis to hallucinate the missing segments. On the face of it, this seems to confirm the validity of hypnotic hallucinations. Barber has commented on Underwood's experiment as follows: 'These data were interpreted as lending support to the notion that the subjects must have been in a unique state (hypnotic trance) in order to manifest such unique behavior. However a closer look at the data does not support the special state notion.'[46] In particular, Barber drew attention to an experiment devised by Theodore Sarbin of the University of California, Santa Cruz, a quasi-Barberian who rejects the notion of the hypnotic state. Sarbin and Anderson[47] found that 9 per cent of a sample of unselected subjects reported the same optical illusion when instructed to imagine the missing segments vividly without hypnosis. On the face of it, this is not very impressive, but Barber believes that 'if all subjects are preselected as meeting criteria for vivid imagery [as Underwood's subjects were but Sarbin and Anderson's were not], those assigned to a hypnosis treatment and those assigned to a non-hypnotic treatment will manifest very similar objective performances when given suggestions to imagine vividly or to hallucinate'.[48]

Several experiments appear to have shown that hypnotically hallucinated colours give rise to complementary-colour afterimages. Most introductory psychology, physiology, and physics textbooks describe the complementary colours that are seen after gazing for several seconds at a brightly coloured object and then looking at a white wall. According to Barber,[49] most textbooks assert that the afterimages of red, yellow, green, and blue are green, blue, red, and yellow respectively, and these are also the colours of the afterimages usually reported by susceptible subjects after hallucinating bright colours under hypnosis. Barber has confirmed these findings in his own laboratory, but he believes that they can be explained by the subjects' knowledge of what is stated in the textbooks. According to unpublished data cited by Barber, the textbooks are all wrong about complementary-colour afterimages: under ordinary conditions most people (88 per cent) allegedly describe the afterimage of yellow not as blue but as violet or purple; and 88 per cent describe the afterimage of green not as red but as violet or pink; blue is the only colour whose afterimage (yellow) is described by the majority of people in the textbook fashion. (Actually, these are closer to the colours described in the textbooks I have seen.) Barber has concluded that the results of experiments on complementary-colour afterimages do not require any notion of a special hypnotic state to explain them. They are presumably due to the subjects' knowledge of misleading textbook information: 'When knowledgeable subjects are excluded, ... the phenomenon of negative afterimages produced by hallucinated colors may no longer be observed.'[50]

Suggested deafness. Experimenters reported in the 1930s that suggestions of deafness given to highly susceptible subjects under hypnosis produce a condition indistinguishable from organic deafness. The evidence that the hypnotic subjects were functionally deaf included 'failure to show any response to deliberately embarrassing remarks', 'failure to raise voice when reading aloud while an irrelevant continuous extraneous noise becomes increasingly disturbing', and 'failure to react to unexpected loud noises'. More recent experiments have made use of the *delayed auditory feedback* effect. This effect is produced when a person speaks into a microphone while listening to the speech sounds being played back, with a delay of one-fifth of a second, via headphones. Under these conditions, some people can hardly speak at all, and the rest stammer, slur and mispronounce words, and speak very loudly and slowly. The speech of organically deaf people, of course, is not affected by delayed auditory feedback. Several experiments by Barber and others[51] have shown that the speech of hypnotically deaf subjects is disrupted in the same way as that of people with normal hearing. In spite of this, many of the hypnotic subjects are genuinely convinced that they can hear nothing; they generally attribute the disruption of their speech to their temporary deafness. Barber and Calverley[52] have shown that suggestions given without hypnosis, to subjects who were merely told to ignore and be deaf to the sounds reaching their ears, elicit very similar objective behaviour and subjective reports from subjects.

Age regression. Susceptible subjects who have been given suggestions under hypnosis to regress to childhood or infancy often give the convincing impression that they are actually re-living past experiences and re-experiencing earlier mental states. Some of the more extreme claims about hypnotic age regression have been debunked by Barber. In one famous experiment by Gidro-Frank and Bowersbuch,[53] three adult subjects hypnotically regressed to the age of four months manifested the Babinski reflex (extension of the toes) when the soles of their feet were stroked. Neurologists used to believe that this is the usual response of infants under six months of age, after which the plantar response (flexion of the toes) was supposed to replace it; this experiment therefore appears to show that a long-dormant physiological reflex was revived under hypnotic age regression. But Barber claims that 'the neurology texts were mistaken. Researchers who have actually looked at infants have consistently observed that the typical response of the four-month-old infant to stimulation of the sole of the foot is *not* the Babinski response, but rather sudden withdrawal of the limb with variable response of the toes'.[54] Either the subjects knew what the experimenters were looking for and voluntarily performed the response, or, since a response resembling the Babinski reflex has been observed occasionally in deeply relaxed people, the subjects in the experiment may have become very relaxed during the hypnotic session.

In another famous experiment,[55] True reported that most of his adult subjects, when hypnotically regressed to the ages of 11, 7, and 4, correctly recalled what day of the week it was on their birthdays and Christmas days in the years in question. Barber[56] has reviewed several experiments of his own and of other researchers, all of which have regrettably failed to confirm True's startling results. True's subjects may have known how to calculate the answers: starting on the day of the week on which a birthday or Christmas day falls *this* year, count back one day of the week for each intervening year, and two for each intervening leap year. This trick, which depends on the fact that 7 divides evenly into 364, may have been more widely known in the 1940s when True collected his data than it is today.

Susceptible subjects often give convincing impressions of childhood during hypnotic age regression. But they give equally convincing impressions of old age during hypnotic age *progression* – when they are given suggestions that they are 70, 80, or 90 years old. And subjects who respond well to hypnotic age regression can be regressed to prenatal life in the womb, and even to a time before conception, whereupon many give impressive performances of previous lives. Every once in a while this surfaces in the popular press as evidence in favour of the doctrine of reincarnation. As an experimental contribution to theology, it was pioneered in 1911 by a certain Colonel de Rochas,[57] who regressed each of his subjects through their present life to a previous life, and then, as though this were not enough, through their previous life to a series of still earlier ones. These 'successive lives', as he called them, always alternated between male and female and were often described plausibly, though they were generally marred by anachronisms.

Hypnotic age regression is subjectively very real to some subjects – they genuinely believe and feel as though they are re-living earlier experiences – but the old controversy over whether it also causes *ablation* of all subsequent memories and *revivification* of earlier mental and physiological structures is no longer alive.

Post-hypnotic suggestions. These are suggestions given during hypnosis regarding behaviour to be performed after the hypnotic session, perhaps when a specified signal is given. A post-hypnotic suggestion is usually (though not necessarily) accompanied by the further suggestion that the subject will not remember being given it. Through post-hypnotic suggestion, susceptible subjects can be induced to perform bizarre acts, such as standing on their heads, apparently without knowing the real causes of their behaviour. When questioned, they generally give plausible rationalizations, such as, 'I thought the abstract painting on the wall might be upside-down, so I'm standing on my head to see what it looks like the other way up.' The case has been described[58] of a well-known psychologist who was given the post-hypnotic suggestion that, at a specified signal, he would cross the room and sit in another chair. When the signal was given half an hour after the hypnotic session, he became agitated and finally said, 'I feel a strong tendency to go across the room and sit on that chair. I am sure you have given me a post-hypnotic suggestion to this effect. Well, I'm damned if I'll do it!' A while later he jumped to his feet, dashed across the room to the designated chair, and exclaimed, 'I couldn't stand it any more!'

Barber has reported evidence[59] suggesting that behaviour similar to the acting out of post-hypnotic suggestions can be produced in some subjects without hypnosis, through task-motivational instructions ('Everyone passed these tests when they tried .... If you don't try to the best of your ability, this experiment will be worthless and I'll tend to feel silly', and so on). His conclusion is that the effects of post-hypnotic suggestions and task-motivational instructions are the same: the subjects 'are aware that they are expected to comply with instructions and that, if they do not comply, they will negate the purpose of the experiment, will disappoint the experimenter, and will be considered as poor (or "undesirable") subjects'. But do hypnotic subjects merely comply to please the experimenter? Two classic experiments are especially relevant to this question.

Seymour Fisher,[60] a postgraduate student at the University of North Carolina, gave thirteen susceptible subjects the post-hypnotic suggestion that they would scratch their right ears whenever they heard the word 'psychology'. After being aroused from hypnosis, all of the subjects responded appropriately whenever the cue-word was mentioned. Then, to give the impression that the experiment was over, the experimenter began to chat casually with the subject and with other people in the room. When the cue-word was mentioned during this phase, only three of the thirteen subjects responded. Finally, the experimenter stopped chatting casually and turned back to the subject, implying that the experiment was still in progress. Eleven of the thirteen subjects scratched their ears whenever the cue-word was mentioned during this phase. To summarize: the post-hypnotic suggestion was deactivated when the subjects thought the experiment was over, and reactivated when they thought it was continuing. These results seem to suggest that the subjects were merely complying with the post-hypnotic suggestion to please the experimenter. They also call into question the allegedly compulsive quality of post-hypnotic behaviour.

Martin Orne of the University of Pennsylvania and two of his colleagues[61] were the first to point out that Fisher's post-hypnotic suggestion was ambiguous. The subjects may have interpreted it to mean that they would scratch their ears in response to the cue-word 'as long as the experiment is in progress', since it could hardly have meant 'for perpetuity'. These researchers therefore thought that it was 'premature to conclude from this study that a posthypnotic response can be elicited only in [the experimental] context'. They replicated Fisher's experiment, eliminating the ambiguity by giving the subjects the post-hypnotic suggestion that 'during the next forty-eight hours' they would touch their foreheads whenever they heard the word 'experiment'. This investigation also included a group of low-susceptible subjects who were instructed to *simulate* hypnosis to the best of their ability. The hypnotic induction procedure and post-hypnotic suggestion were given to all subjects, and they all touched their foreheads when the cue-word was mentioned immediately afterwards. After leaving the laboratory, each subject was met by a secretary who confirmed the appointment 'for the next part of the *experiment*', which was scheduled for the following day, and offered to pay the subject 'for today's *experiment*'. Finally, when the subject returned the next day, the secretary asked, 'Are you here for Dr Sheehan's *experiment*?' In the event, the simulators responded to the cue-word on only three of the thirty-nine occasions on which it was mentioned by the secretary, which gives a response rate of 7.7 per cent. The response rate of the hypnotic subjects was 29.5 per cent, which is significantly higher – nearly four times as high – but is still not very high. The six most susceptible subjects, as measured previously on a standardized suggestibility scale, responded on 70 per cent of occasions, which is nine times as often as the simulators. In the presence of the hypnotist, on the other hand, the simulating subjects were more responsive than the hypnotic subjects.

These results are not in line with Barber's idea that responses to post-hypnotic suggestions are mere acts of compliance to please the hypnotist. When the hypnotist was not only absent, but also apparently unaware of what was going on, many susceptible subjects evidently felt a certain compulsion to respond to the post-hypnotic suggestion anyway. Also important is the fact that highly susceptible subjects were the most responsive in these circumstances. The behaviour of the simulators, on the other hand, had all the hallmarks of deliberate compliance to meet the experimenter's demands.

Over a long period, Barber has rendered a valuable service to psychology by debunking some of the more extreme and unreliable claims about hypnosis. He has also confirmed the existence of certain remarkable phenomena, including hypnotic analgesia, in his own laboratory. What is controversial is his claim that all of the phenomena traditionally associated with hypnosis can, and should, be explained without invoking a special hypnotic state. He bases this claim on the results of scores of experiments in which *some* of the subjects, who were not exposed to *formal* hypnotic induction procedures, displayed *hypnotic-like* behaviour and verbal reports of subjective experiences.

Hypnotic-state theorists have rejected the Barberian arguments and evidence on several grounds.[62] First, the fact that some people can convincingly simulate a psychological state does not prove that the state does not exist. Drunkenness, for example, is certainly a special state – courts of law accept the results of blood tests as proof of its existence – but most people can easily simulate it. Second, Barber's task-motivational instructions place enormous social pressure on subjects to behave like hypnotized subjects and to say that they experience the corresponding phenomena subjectively. Bowers[63] demonstrated experimentally that task-motivational subjects who were specifically asked, after the experiment, to be absolutely frank and honest, admitted that they had not experienced the phenomena as vividly as they had originally reported. Spanos and Barber[64] tried to show that such 'honesty instructions' would elicit similar admissions from hypnotic subjects; but their results indicated, at least for visual hallucinations, that it was only the task-motivational subjects who admitted exaggerating in this way. So it seems that task-motivational subjects, but not hypnotic subjects, falsify their reports of subjective experiences to comply with the experimenter's demands. Third, some state theorists believe that many of Barber's task-motivational subjects are likely to have slipped into the hypnotic state, because task-motivational instructions have a distinctly hypnotic quality about them on account of their stress on vivid imagination. Fourth, state theorists tend to believe that experiments on trance logic have provided evidence that is difficult to interpret without postulating the existence of a special state of hypnosis. The evidence on trance logic will be discussed separately.

I suspect that the debate over the hypnotic state is unlikely to be resolved unless some physiological evidence of its existence comes to light. This has already happened in the case of ordinary nocturnal sleep: rapid eye movements and characteristic patterns of electrical activity in the brain have been known since the mid-1950s to be diagnostic of various stages of sleep. Before these physiological indicators were discovered, however, arguments and experimental evidence of the type that the Barberians have deployed against the hypnotic state would have applied equally to the sleeping state. Experiments could have been performed in which some subjects were exposed to ordinary sleep-inducing procedures (lullabys, gentle rocking, instructions to count sheep, and so on) and some were given task-motivational instructions to imagine vividly that they were falling asleep ('Everyone passed these tests when they tried .... If you don't try to the best of your ability, the experiment will be worthless and I'll tend to feel silly'). Naturally, some insomniacs in the sleeping groups might remain awake, and some subjects in the task-motivational groups might accidentally fall asleep, but that would not bother a dyed-in-the-wool Barberian who did not believe in the sleeping state in the first place. Most of the task-motivational subjects would no doubt lie down, breathe deeply, snore, and imitate other sleeplike phenomena, and many would dutifully report, in order to avoid making themselves look like failures and the experimenter feel silly, that they felt as though they were asleep, that they experienced dreams, and so on. And until the physiological indicators of the sleeping state were discovered, it would be very difficult to prove that there is a special state associated with sleeping.

Trance logic

Trance logic is a peculiar willingness of hypnotized subjects to tolerate logical inconsistencies. It was first reported in a classic paper by Martin Orne,[65] who described it as follows: 'A good example of this process is the reaction of many [subjects] in hypnosis who see a hallucination of a person sitting in a chair and describe it as "this is very peculiar, I can see Joe sitting in the chair and I can see the chair through him".' Orne found that this kind of transparent hallucination, though not reported spontaneously by every hypnotic subject in his investigation, was *never* reported spontaneously by low-susceptible simulating subjects who were instructed to try to fake the hypnotic state and fool the experimenter.

Orne's second example of trance logic was the double hallucination. At the start of each hypnotic session, an associate of Orne's sat next to the subject taking notes. Later, when the subject's eyes were closed, the associate crept silently from his chair and stood behind the subject. The subject was then given the suggestion to hallucinate the associate sitting in the chair where he had previously been sitting. Once the hallucination was vividly established, the subject was told to turn around, and was asked, 'Who is that behind you?' Orne reported that 'almost invariably, ... after looking back and forth between the hallucinated and the "real" associate, the [subjects] indicated verbally that they were perceiving two images of the same person', and they did not seem disturbed by this state of affairs. In sharp contrast, the simulating subjects either refused to see anyone behind them, or claimed that they could not recognize the person, or said that the hallucination had vanished. Only two of Orne's thirty simulators reacted as if they saw two images of the same individual. Orne compared hypnotic and simulating subjects like this: 'The major difference appears to be a tolerance by the "real" subject of logical inconsistencies.'

Orne's conclusion was widely accepted for the next thirteen years, until a paper by Richard Johnson, Brendan Maher, and Theodore Barber appeared.[66] This paper reported the results of an experiment which, if valid, completely demolished Orne's claims about trance logic. The experimental design was extremely complicated; I shall describe only the bare bones, ignoring the superfluous fat, in order to clarify the points at issue.

The subjects were seventy female nursing students. They were initially tested on a twelve-point susceptibility scale; those who scored from zero to six were labelled 'low-suggestible', and those who scored from seven to twelve were labelled 'high-suggestible'. Subjects from both groups were assigned randomly to conditions in which they were either hypnotized in the usual way, or instructed in the manner described by Orne to simulate hypnosis, or requested merely to imagine the things suggested to them. Then each of the subjects was tested individually: 'An attempt was made to replicate as closely as possible Orne's ... procedures.'

When the subject opened her eyes and the hallucination of the assistant in the empty chair was suggested, she was asked to describe him: 'What does he look like? What is he doing?' If she responded as if he were really there, described his appearance, and reported what he was doing, she was said to have met the *stringent criterion* of hallucination. If she did not meet this criterion she was asked to *imagine* the assistant sitting in the chair. In either case, the experimenter noted whether she spontaneously mentioned seeing the back of the chair through the hallucination or the imagined image of the assistant. If she did not report transparency spontaneously, she was asked: 'Do you, or do you not, see the back of the chair through Joe?'

The subject was then instructed to turn around and look at the assistant who was behind her. She was asked, 'Who is that behind you?' The experimenter then pointed to the empty chair where the hallucinated or imagined assistant was located and asked, 'Who is that in front of you?' and 'How do you explain this?'

The first set of results refer to all subjects – those who met the stringent criterion of hallucination lumped together with those who did not. To begin with, not one of the seventy subjects reported transparency spontaneously. When questioned about transparency, 70 per cent of the high-suggestible subjects in the hypnotic condition said that they could see the back of the chair through the assistant, but 30 per cent in the simulation condition and 80 per cent in the imagination condition also reported transparency. The corresponding figures for low-suggestible subjects were 90 per cent (hypnotic), 30 per cent (simulation), and 60 per cent (imagination). The percentages for the hypnotic condition are significantly higher than those for the simulation condition, but they are not significantly different from those for the imagination condition.

Turning to the double hallucination, only 30 per cent of the high-suggestible subjects in the hypnotic condition said that they saw the assistant simultaneously in front and behind them; but 40 per cent in the simulation condition and 10 per cent in the imagination condition also said this. The percentages among the low-suggestible subjects were 20 per cent (hypnotic), 40 per cent (simulation), and 30 per cent (imagination). The differences are not statistically significant.

The authors next reported the results for subjects who met the stringent criterion for hallucination – those who responded as if the assistant were really there, described his appearance, and reported what he was doing. For this part of the analysis, 'those [subjects] who required the extra suggestions (which emphasized "imagining") to induce the "hallucination" were scored as *not* exhibiting the transparent and double hallucinations no matter what their responses may have been'. When questioned about transparency, 40 per cent (hypnotic), 20 per cent (simulation), and 10 per cent (imagination) of high-susceptible subjects reported transparency. Among low-susceptible subjects, 10 per cent (hypnotic), 20 per cent (simulation), and 0 per cent (imagination) reported transparency. None of these differences is statistically significant.

Regarding the double hallucination, 20 per cent (hypnotic), 30 per cent (simulation) and 0 per cent (imagination) of the high-suggestible subjects met the necessary criteria. Among low-suggestible subjects, 10 per cent (hypnotic), 40 per cent (simulation), and 0 per cent (imagination) met the criteria for the double hallucination. Statistical analysis showed that the simulators displayed the double hallucination significantly *more* often than the hypnotic subjects.

The authors concluded: 'Regardless of whether a liberal or a stringent criterion for hallucination is used, and regardless of whether low-suggestible [or high-suggestible subjects] are used, the data do not support the hypothesis that hypnotic subjects characteristically display trance logic.'[67]

That was by no means the last word on trance logic. Johnson, Maher, and Barber's paper was immediately followed by a devastating critique by Ernest Hilgard.[68] Hilgard sought to show not only that the paper 'contains inadequacies in the design of the experiment and the collection of data, but that the presentation of data, and their statistical treatment, leave much to be desired. The end result is that the investigation can neither substantiate nor refute the trance-logic hypothesis'. Hilgard had often demonstrated Orne's essential findings in front of his students, so he examined Johnson, Maher, and Barber's data with a magnifying glass to find out why they had obtained negative results.

What we really need to know, according to Hilgard, is the percentage of subjects who reported transparency and double hallucination, *from among those who met the stringent criterion of hallucination*. Subjects who did not meet the stringent criterion are irrelevant, because they were merely requested to *imagine* the assistant, and Orne's claims about trance logic do not apply to imaginings. But when Johnson and his colleagues reported data for subjects who met the stringent criterion, they did something very peculiar: they used as a base for their percentages of transparency and double hallucination *all* subjects, whether or not they experienced hallucinations. Remember what they said about those who did not hallucinate: they 'were scored as *not* exhibiting the transparent and double hallucinations no matter what their responses may have been'. Hilgard argued that this method of calculation was absurd. If all ten subjects in a group hallucinated, and one of these had a transparent hallucination, then 10 per cent would (correctly) be scored as transparent. But if only one subject in a group hallucinated, and she had a transparent hallucination, the answer would still be the same, that is, that 10 per cent had transparent hallucinations, because the other nine who did not hallucinate would be included in the calculation as not having transparent hallucinations no matter how they answered the questions.

In order to determine the percentage of subjects who said that they hallucinated and also reported transparency and double hallucinations, *relative to those who hallucinated*, we need to know how many subjects in each group met the stringent criterion of hallucination. These figures are missing from the paper, but Hilgard got hold of them by writing to the authors. It turned out that most of the simulators (nine out of ten in both high-suggestible and low-suggestible groups) met the stringent criterion as expected. In the hypnotic condition, six of the ten high-suggestible subjects and only two of the ten low-suggestible subjects met the stringent criterion. In the imagination condition only one single (high-suggestible) subject met the stringent criterion.

Hilgard re-computed the results using only these subjects – the ones who reported hallucinations. It turned out that in the hypnotic condition 50 per cent of hallucinations were transparent, and in the simulation condition 22 per cent were transparent. Since the imagination condition contained only one subject who reported a hallucination, Hilgard disqualified this as a legitimate control group, although in fact the 'hallucination' was transparent. Because of the very small numbers involved, the differences between the hypnotic and simulation conditions are not statistically significant. But the claim of Johnson and his colleagues that 'simulators reported the transparent hallucination as often as hypnotic [subjects]' is evidently refuted.

The double hallucination occurred in 40 per cent of hypnotic subjects who reported hallucinations and in 39 per cent of simulators who reported hallucinations.[69] Again, since the imagination condition contained only one subject Hilgard rejected it as a comparison group (although the subject did not in fact report a double hallucination). The differences are once again not statistically significant, but Johnson's and his colleagues' claim that simulators displayed double hallucinations *more* frequently than hypnotic subjects is certainly refuted.

Hilgard's re-computation of the results completely undermines the conclusions originally drawn from them. The re-computed results are all in the direction that Orne would predict. Hilgard commented: 'It is not difficult to mislead readers who are unfamiliar with the phenomena under investigation; had I not seen confirmation of the essential pehnomena reported by Orne in my own experience, I doubt that I would have been led to question the ... data analysis.'[70]

Hilgard made a number of other criticisms, of which the most telling are these. First, Orne's procedure calls for very highly susceptible subjects to be compared with very low-susceptible simulators, but Johnson and his colleagues included many subjects from the middle range of susceptibility in both groups. Second, the reason why no spontaneous transparency came to light, according to Hilgard, was probably that the subjects were merely asked to describe the hallucination. 'A far better procedure is to wait for the double hallucination and then to ask: "Can you tell which is really Joe?" Under that kind of questioning, it has been my experience that transparent hallucinations get reported spontaneously.' Third, the experimenters went on to ask the subjects, 'Do you, or do you not, see the back of the chair through Joe?' This has the disadvantage of giving non-hypnotized subjects a clue about how a hypnotic hallucination might look. Fourth, the data obtained under the 'liberal' criterion of hallucination, according to which subjects hallucinated if they merely *imagined* the assistant, are 'largely irrelevant to the issue at stake'.

Johnson[71] replied to Hilgard's critique as follows:

Hilgard's hypothesis is that when only those [subjects] are included in the analysis who met the stringent criterion for hallucination, real hypnotic [subjects] manifest trance logic somewhat more often than nonhypnotic [subjects]. This hypothesis differs in at least two ways from the one I considered. First, it considers for analysis only those [subjects] from each group who passed the stringent criterion for hallucination .... Second, it stresses that the relationship between trance logic and hypnosis is such that real hypnotic [subjects] simply exhibit trance logic somewhat more often than nonhypnotic [subjects]. Of course, Orne's original hypothesis was markedly different; Orne contended that *almost all* real hypnotic [subjects] and *very few* simulators show trance logic.

Hilgard had sought to show that the re-computed results were indeterminate because of small numbers 'but with trends all in favor of Orne's original findings'. Johnson called this conclusion misleading, because Hilgard's re-computation of the data 'does not consistently adhere to his own criterion for inclusion'; he did not include *all* subjects who met the stringent criterion for hallucination. To be specific, he ignored the imagination condition on the grounds that since only one subject met the stringent criterion it would not be used as a comparison. But since this one subject reported transparency, the proportion of transparent hallucinations in this condition, according to Hilgard's own method of computation, is one out of one (100 per cent), which is higher than the proportion in the hypnotic condition (50 per cent). This trend is not in favour of Orne's original finding but in the opposite direction, so it was wrong of Hilgard to say that the re-computed results were *all* in Orne's favour.

Johnson claimed that when the single subject who met the stringent criterion of hallucination in the imagination condition is included in the analysis, his original conclusion remains justified. In other words, trance logic occurs as often in non-hypnotic as in hypnotic subjects. This is so, according to Johnson, because when this subject is included, Hilgard's figures show some trends in Orne's favour, and some (actually just the one mentioned in the previous paragraph) in the opposite direction. With some results pointing one way and others pointing the opposite way, it is fair to conclude that, on the whole, hypnotic and non-hypnotic subjects display trance logic equally often.

Finally, Johnson attacked the special-state theory of hypnosis which, he thought, lay behind Hilgard's critique: 'Who is to be considered as a real hypnotic [subject]? ... Should we draw the line at the point at which a [subject] meets the stringent criterion for hallucination (as Hilgard does) or should we choose some other criterion?' A related problem, according to Johnson, arises from the implication of the special-state theory that there is a fundamental difference between the following three types of reports made by subjects: 'I see the person'; 'I see the person in my mind's eye'; and 'I vividly imagine the person'. In Johnson's opinion the difference is not really fundamental because there is no essential distinction between a hypnotic hallucination and an imagined image. Johnson concluded from this: 'Ambiguities concerning who is to be considered as a real hypnotic [subject] and who is to be considered as a hallucinator appear to be at the root of the disagreement between Hilgard and myself.' This last remark seems very much to the point, but nothing short of a negative hallucination is needed to ignore the distinctions that Johnson denies.

Later studies of trance logic[72] have not resolved the issues.

Differences of the kind that Orne identified between hypnotic subjects and simulators have often been reported, and when several different tests of trance logic have been used together the differences have been large and highly significant. In spite of this, hypnotic subjects do not all show trance logic, and highly susceptible subjects sometimes show it in non-hypnotic conditions. Trance logic does not seem to be the long-awaited touchstone of the hypnotic state, but it distinguishes between hypnotized and non-hypnotized subjects better than most other indices.

After two centuries of research, the quest for an objective index of the hypnotic trance state therefore remains only weakly fulfilled. This is a frustrating state of affairs, because hypnotized subjects generally report that their subjective experiences feel qualitatively different from the normal non-hypnotized state. However, a great deal has been learned about hypnosis since the Marquis de Puységur's accidental 'discovery' in 1784, and many superstitions about hypnosis have been laid to rest. With regard to some of the phenomena of hypnosis – hypnotic analgesia, in particular – I believe that accumulating evidence has made the extreme sceptical interpretation increasingly difficult to sustain. But different people will no doubt have different views about which side is winning the debate. I have tried to give both sides a fair hearing.

Notes

1 The best history of hypnosis is the book by Ellenberger (1970). My account is based mainly on this source, with additional material from Hull (1933), ch. 1; Boring (1957), ch. 7; Howells and Osborn (1984); and Edmonston (1986).
2 Boring (1957), p. 118.
3 A translation into English of one of the commission's reports is given in Shor and Orne (1965), pp. 3–7.
4 Boring (1957), p. 120.
5 ibid., p. 121.
6 Braid (1843), p. 13. Braid started with the word *neuro-hypnotism*, which he defined as 'nervous sleep', but suggested that the prefix 'neuro-' could be suppressed 'for the sake of brevity'.
7 Hull (1933). The quotation in the text is on p. ix.
8 Fellows (1985).
9 Sutcliffe (1960, 1961).
10 Eysenck (1957), p. 38.
11 Hilgard (1968), p. 126.
12 The evidence has been thoroughly reviewed by Hilgard and Hilgard (1983). For a brief account aimed at clinicians, see Ewin (1986).
13 The patient, Ainslie Meares, a prominent medical hypnotist and past president of the International Society for Clinical and Experimental Hypnosis, induced the anaesthesia himself through self-hypnosis. The case was first reported in the *Medical Journal of Australia* (McCay, 1963).

14 Knox, Morgan, and Hilgard (1974).
15 Sutcliffe (1961). See also Barber (1969), ch. 7, and Wagstaff (1987).
16 See Hilgard (1969), and Hilgard and Hilgard (1983) for thorough reviews of the literature.
17 Sutcliffe (1961).
18 Wagstaff (1981), p. 177. See also Wagstaff (1987).
19 Hilgard (1964), pp. 13–14, italics in original.
20 Knox, Morgan, and Hilgard (1974).
21 Bowers (1976), p. 24.
22 ibid., pp. 27–8.
23 Barber and Hahn, (1962).
24 Barber (1969), p. 133.
25 Hilgard (1964), pp. 14–16, italics in original.
26 Stern, Brown, Ulett, and Selten (1977).
27 Hilgard and LeBaron (1984).
28 The evidence is reviewed in Hilgard and Hilgard (1983).
29 Balthazard and Woody (1985).
30 Hilgard (1973). For a review of research into the hidden observer, see Hilgard (1979).
31 Sutcliffe (1961), p. 194, italics in original.
32 Hilgard (1973), italics in original.
33 See Hilgard (1979); Wagstaff (1981), pp. 179–85; Hilgard and Hilgard (1983), *passim*; and Kihlstrom (1985), pp. 400–1 for detailed reviews.
34 Wagstaff (1981), p. 181. See also Wagstaff (1987).
35 Knox, Morgan, and Hilgard (1974), p. 846.
36 Bowers (1976), p. 39. The quotations in the text above are from Knox, Morgan, and Hilgard (1974), pp. 845 and 846.
37 Kihlstrom (1985), p. 401.
38 Nogrady, McConkey, Laurence, and Perry (1983).
39 Hilgard, Hilgard, Macdonald, Morgan, and Johnson (1978).
40 Brief reviews of Barber's colossal output can be found in Barber (1969, 1972, 1979); Hilgard (1975); and Kihlstrom (1985).
41 In Britain, for example, Wagstaff (1981, 1987).
42 Meeker and Barber (1971). See also Barber (1986).
43 Barber (1972), p. 123.
44 Barber (1965a).
45 Underwood (1960).
46 Barber (1972), pp. 146–7.
47 Sarbin and Anderson (1963).
48 Barber (1969), pp. 173–4.
49 Barber (1969), pp. 175–7.
50 Barber (1969), p. 177.
51 These experiments are reviewed in Barber (1972), pp. 147–8.
52 Barber and Calverley (1964).
53 Gidro-Frank and Bowersbuch (1948).
54 Barber (1972), p. 144, italics in original.
55 True (1949). For a critique and reinterpretation of True's experiment, see Perry, Laurence, Nadon, and Labelle (1986).
56 Barber (1969), pp. 188–9.
57 Rochas (1911). A brief account of de Rochas's fantastic claims is given in Ellenberger (1970) p. 117. For a recent discussion of past lives regression, see Perry, Laurence, Nadon, and Labelle (1986).

58 Eysenck (1957), pp. 42–3.
59 This research is summarized in Barber (1969), pp. 204–5.
60 Fisher (1954).
61 Orne, Sheehan, and Evans (1968). The quotations in the text are from pp. 190 and 192.
62 See, for example, Hilgard (1964, 1965, 1975, 1979); Hilgard and Hilgard (1968); Bowers (1976); and Kihlstrom (1985).
63 Bowers (1967).
64 Spanos and Barber (1968).
65 Orne (1959). The quotations in the text are from pp. 295, 296, and 298.
66 Johnson, Maher, and Barber (1972). The first quotation in the text is from p. 214.
67 ibid., p. 219.
68 Hilgard (1972). The quotation in the text is from p. 221.
69 There is an arithmetic error in Hilgard's figures at this point. It is pointed out in a footnote by the journal editor. I have given the correct figures.
70 Hilgard (1972), p. 228. The following quotation in the text is from p. 229.
71 Johnson (1972). The long quotation is from p. 234, italics in original.
72 A brief review of these studies is given in Kihlstrom (1985), pp. 399–400. For a sceptical review of the same studies, see Wagstaff (1987).

6 Eating disorders: are anorexia nervosa and bulimia nervosa forms of depression?

The 'Case of Ellen West' is an uncommonly disturbing account of a disturbingly common mental disorder. Quotations from the patient's own diary and letters, in which she recorded her most intimate thoughts and feelings during her tragic psychological decline, give a three-dimensional quality to this classic case study, which was reported during the Second World War by the Swiss psychiatrist Ludwig Binswanger.[1]

Ellen West, the only child of middle-class Jewish parents, was an intelligent and ambitious schoolgirl, but by the time she was 17 her moods had begun to oscillate unpredictably between wretchedness and extreme elation. She gained weight during adolescence, her friends began to tease her about her plumpness, and something new and ominous entered her emotional life: a dread of becoming fat. She began dieting and going on strenuous hikes, and she developed a profound self-hatred. She wrote in a letter to a friend: 'Every day I get a little fatter, older, and uglier', and in her diary: 'I despise myself! ... But I am a human being with red blood and a woman with a trembling heart.' After an unhappy love affair with a student, leading to an engagement which her parents opposed, she began fasting and exercising with increased rigour, although her craving for food also intensified. She gradually became emaciated, but she felt increasingly convinced that starving herself was the key to her well-being. Eventually she grew weak, and her doctor prescribed rest in bed. Six weeks in bed caused her to gain weight, as a result of which she wept constantly. She hated her body so much that she often beat it with her fists.

She broke off her engagement, and three years later married a cousin. During her marriage she continued fasting and exercising in secret, and began taking laxative tablets in an effort to lose even more weight. She developed a conjuring trick of filling her plate at the dinner table and then surreptitiously emptying it into her handbag while no one was looking. She spent most of her free time copying out recipes of delectable puddings and desserts, and studying calorie charts. By this time her menstrual periods had ceased, and she had lost four and a half stones (29 kilograms) in weight; she was extremely emaciated and haggard looking.

Soon her weight had dropped to six and a half stones (41 kilograms) and she was swallowing sixty to seventy laxative tablets daily. Her diary during this period contains many psychologically significant comments. Notice, for example, that she did not consider her fear of becoming fat to be an obsession:

Fear of becoming fat acts as a brake .... The pleasure of eating is the real obsession .... It pursues me constantly and is driving me to despair .... In the end I usually dash out into the street. I run away from the bread in my larder .... One might say, 'Eat up the bread, then you will have peace.' But no; when I have eaten it I'm unhappier than ever .... I don't understand myself at all. It's terrible not to understand yourself. I confront myself as a strange person.

Her description of her emotional state at this time is poignant and chilling:

This is the horrible part of my life: it is filled with fear. Fear of eating, fear of hunger, fear of fear .... I can see nothing any more; everything is blurred; all the threads are tangled .... When I open my eyes in the morning, my great misery stands before me. Even before I am fully awake I think of – eating. Every meal is accompanied by anxiety and fear, and every hour between meals with the thought, 'When shall I get hungry again?'.

Even after starving herself down to skin and bone, Ellen West did not lose her craving for food:

I want to grow thinner and thinner, but I do not want to have to watch myself constantly, and I do not want to have to go without anything; it is this conflict between wanting to be thin and yet not wanting to miss any meals that is destroying me .... I am perishing in the struggle against nature. Fate wanted to have me fat and strong, but I want to be thin and delicate.

Ellen West was eventually admitted to hospital, where she spent ten weeks in the care of psychoanalysts and psychiatrists, including Eugen Bleuler who diagnosed schizophrenia (it was he who originally coined the term). During her stay in hospital she tried to make herself ill by standing naked on a windy balcony after a hot bath. Eventually, at her own request, she was discharged from hospital. On her third day at home she did something she had not done for many years: she ate a hearty lunch that satisfied her hunger and made her feel full, and during the afternoon she ate some chocolate creams and Easter eggs. Her husband thought she was truly happy, all the heaviness having lifted from her. But in the evening she swallowed a lethal dose of poison, and the following morning she was found dead. 'She looked as she had never looked in life – calm and happy and peaceful.'

Ellen West's symptoms are immediately recognizable today as those of anorexia nervosa, or what the popular press likes to call 'the slimmer's disease'. There is an interesting debate in the technical journals over the theory that anorexia nervosa, and a closely related eating disorder called bulimia nervosa, are forms of depression. Controversy has also centred on the claim that eating-disordered patients have disturbed body images, which might be the key to their problems. The arguments might seem rather abstract and scholastic out of the context of the eating disorders in question, so I must first discuss the necessary background information at some length.

Anorexia nervosa: 'the slimmer's disease'

Anorexia nervosa is classified by the World Health Organization as a mental disorder with the following symptoms:

The main features are persistent active refusal to eat and marked loss of weight. The level of activity and alertness is characteristically high in relation to the degree of emaciation. Typically the disorder begins in teenage girls but it may sometimes begin before puberty and rarely occurs in males. Amenorrhoea [absence of menstrual periods] is usual and there may be a variety of other physiological changes including slow pulse and respiration, low body temperature and dependent oedema [swollen ankles]. Unusual eating habits and attitudes toward food are typical and sometimes starvation follows or alternates with periods of overeating.[2]

Anorexia nervosa is not a new disorder or a new discovery. Written accounts can be traced back to a case study reported by the Persian physician Avicenna in the eleventh century.[3] In 1694 Richard Morton[4] suggested the name *phthisis nervosa* for a disorder that he had encountered in two of his patients. The symptoms were clearly those of anorexia nervosa: food avoidance, extreme emaciation, amenorrhoea, and overactivity. One of his patients, an 18-year-old English girl, died during a fainting fit, which 'preceded from Sadness and anxious Cares'.

The term 'anorexia nervosa' was introduced into the medical literature in 1874 by Sir William Gull of Guy's Hospital London, Physician Extraordinary to Queen Victoria and, curiously in view of his interest in problems of young women, a favourite suspect for the 'Jack the Ripper' murders of 1888.[5] Gull described a 'peculiar form of disease occurring mostly in young women, and characterized by extreme emaciation'. He illustrated the disorder with three strikingly similar case histories, the first of which related to a 17-year-old girl:

Her emaciation was very great. It was stated that she had lost 33 lbs. in weight. She was then 5 st. 12 lbs. Height 5ft. 5 in. Amenorrhoea for nearly a year .... Resp[iration], 12 [slow]; pulse, 56 [also slow]. No vomiting nor diarrhoea. Slight constipation. Complete anorexia for animal food and almost complete anorexia for everything else. Abdomen shrunk and flat, collapsed .... The condition was one of simple starvation. ... The patient complained of no pain, but was restless and active. This was in fact a striking expression of the nervous state, for it seemed hardly possible that a body so wasted could undergo the exercise which seemed agreeable.[6]

This patient eventually recovered, but Gull mentioned another who had died: 'Death apparently followed from starvation alone.'

Like Morton, Gull thought that the causes of anorexia nervosa were psychological rather than physical. In 1914, however, the German pathologist Morris Simmonds reported a case of emaciation and amenorrhoea in a girl whose pituitary gland was atrophied.[7] (The pituitary is an endocrine gland, that is, one that secretes hormones directly into the bloodstream. It functions as a link between the brain and the other endocrine glands, and in Simmonds' disease it ceases to function properly.) For the next twenty-five years most cases of anorexia nervosa were confused with Simmonds' disease and treated (unsuccessfully) with pituitary extracts. Eventually it became clear that Simmonds' disease produces rather different symptoms, such as lassitude and loss of pubic and axillary (underarm) hair, and that emaciation is unusual in Simmonds' disease except in terminal cases.[8] Since the early 1950s it had been generally accepted that anorexia nervosa does not have a purely physical cause, but that it stems from an interaction of psychological, social, and physical roots.

How is anorexia nervosa diagnosed?

There are no universally accepted diagnostic criteria for anorexia nervosa, although it is generally agreed that the main features of the disorder are an overwhelming desire to lose weight and various abnormal attitudes and activities that follow. Most doctors diagnose the disorder on the basis of intuitive impressions rather than by applying diagnostic criteria rigorously. Researchers, on the other hand, have to be rigorous so that others can replicate their investigations exactly. The diagnostic criteria suggested by Gerald Russell of the University of London Institute of Psychiatry are widely used by researchers; also very popular are those listed in the *Diagnostic and Statistical Manual of Mental Disorders* issued by the American Psychiatric Association. Russell's diagnostic criteria are as follows:

A   Behaviour leading to a marked loss of body weight, including the avoidance of fattening foods, and often (but not invariably) self-induced vomiting and/or laxative abuse and/or excessive exercise.
B   Endocrine disorder manifested by amenorrhoea in females and loss of sexual appetite in males.
C   Morbid fear of becoming fat.[9]

The diagnostic criteria listed in the most recent (third) edition of the *Diagnostic and Statistical Manual*, usually called DSM-III, are more specific:

A   Intense fear of becoming obese, which does not diminish as weight loss progresses.
B   Disturbance of body image, e.g., claiming to 'feel fat' even when emaciated.
C   Weight loss of at least 25% of original body weight or, if under 18 years of age, weight loss from original body weight plus projected weight gain expected from growth charts may be combined to make the 25%.
D   Refusal to maintain body weight over a minimal normal weight for age and height.
E   No known physical illness that would account for the weight loss.[10]

Criteria A and B in DSM-III, and Russell's criterion C, refer to psychological attitudes. A questionnaire, called the Eating Attitudes Test (EAT), is available for measuring abnormal eating attitudes and behaviour with some degree of objectivity.[11] The EAT comprises forty items; I have listed five of them below. People taking the test are asked to respond by answering *Always, Very Often, Often, Sometimes, Rarely,* or *Never* to each of them.

1   Am terrified about being overweight.
2   Find myself preoccupied with food.
3   Cut my food into small pieces.
4   Take longer than others to eat my meals.
5   Have the impulse to vomit after meals.

People who answer *Always, Very Often,* or *Often* to at least three out of four of the items in the complete EAT are almost certain to have abnormal eating attitudes and behaviour, and most of them are female.

In addition to abnormal eating attitudes and behaviour, there are various other signs of anorexia nervosa, many of them straightforward consequences of starvation, but not all patients display all the signs. Typically, the patient's skin is dry, dirty-looking, and rough like sandpaper, and her (rarely his) fingernails are brittle and cracked. Her menstrual periods may be very light or non-existent. Her cheeks, neck, forearms, and thighs are sometimes covered with a finy downy growth (lanugo hair). She may have lost some hair from her scalp, but her pubic hair is likely to be normal. Her breasts are probably normal in size, no matter how emaciated the rest of her body may be. She usually has a low basal temperature (hypothermia) and an abnormal intolerance of cold, and her fingers and toes may be cold and bluish in colour (cyanosis). The palms of her hands and soles of her feet, and the skin around the base of her nose, are often yellow-orange in colour. Her basal metabolic rate is generally about 30 per cent below normal, and her blood pressure, breathing, and heart rate correspondingly low. She usually sleeps less than most people and wakes early in the morning. Her sexual drive is reduced or non-existent. She is usually constipated, and she may have swollen ankles (peripheral oedema) if she is severely emaciated. If one of her methods of weight control is regular vomiting, then she probably has rotten teeth (dental caries), and she may also have chronic inflammation of the skin around her mouth (perioral dermatitis). She is likely to be a compulsive jogger or exerciser, or physically hyperactive in some other way. She probably loves cooking for others and is obsessed with cookery books, and she may be severely depressed. In spite of all this, she probably denies indignantly that there is anything the matter with her.

What is 'normal' body weight? A digression

Undoubtedly the most easily recognizable symptom of anorexia nervosa is the marked loss of body weight referred to in Russell's criterion A and in DSM-III's criteria C and D. Is it possible to define this symptom rigorously? DSM-III goes some way in this direction by specifying weight loss of at least 25 per cent of original body weight, and by referring to 'normal weight for age and height'. Loss of 25 per cent of original body weight does not seem to me to be a very helpful criterion. Leaving aside the quibble that every person's original body weight is that of a new-born baby or, better, the weight of a single fertilized cell at conception, what is meant by 'original body weight'? And surely a 25 per cent weight loss from a very fat body should not be accorded the same clinical significance as a similar percentage loss from an average or thin body? Should this be a universal criterion of anorexia nervosa? Surely not.

The phrase 'normal weight for age and height' is also less clear than it at first appears. For one thing, it should presumably read 'normal weight for age and height *and sex*' because, as everyone knows, men and women have quite different body builds and bone structures. Second, the word 'normal' probably means average, but it can also mean ideal, optimal, desirable, or healthy – that is, not pathological. Charts of 'ideal' weight for age, height, and sex used to be popular with doctors, but they are rapidly going out of fashion for two very good reasons. They are based on what are now known to be extremely unreliable data on life expectancies provided by life insurance companies;[12] and the concept of 'ideal' weight is now considered suspect by experts because different *set points* seem to be built into the self-regulating body metabolism of different people of the same age, height, and sex.

A simple formula, which does not rely on flawed survey data, for calculating 'ideal' weight according to height and sex, has been popularized in Germany recently by the women's magazine *Brigitte*. According to the formula, your ideal weight in kilograms is given by your height in centimetres, minus 100, minus 15 per cent (women) or 10 per cent (men). I have worked out an equivalent version in inches and pounds; your ideal weight in pounds is given by five times your height in inches, minus 180, minus 15 per cent (women) or 10 per cent (men). These formulae are less objectionable than the charts of ideal weights that are still routinely published in slimming magazines because they are not based on doubtful survey data. But they are quite arbitrary; they do not even take account of age, and they have no medical or scientific basis.

The concept of *average* weight for age, height, and sex, which is what DSM-III probably means by 'normal weight for age and height', is slightly (but only slightly) more useful. Reliable averages are notoriously difficult to determine: the first fully representative and properly controlled survey of the heights and weights of adults in Great Britain was published in 1984.[13] The average height of British men is 5 feet 8½ inches (173.9 centimetres) and their average weight is 11 stone 8 pounds (73.6 kilograms). The average height of

British women is 5 feet 3½ inches (160.9 centimetres) and their average weight is 9 stone 11 pounds (62.0 kilograms). White American men are, on average, just over half an inch (1.8 centimetres) taller, and 10 pounds (4.4 kilograms) heavier; white American women are just under half an inch (1.2 centimetres) taller, and 6 pounds (2.9 kilograms) heavier.[14] A portion of the data regarding average weight for age and height of British women is summarized below.[15]

Average (Unclothed) weights of British women

Height: ft & ins.	Age: years				
	16–19	20–29	30–39	40–49	50–64
5'0"–5'1"	8 st. 2 lb.	8 st. 8 lb.	8 st. 9 lb.	9 st. 5lb.	9 st. 8 lb.
5'1"–5'2"	8 st. 5 lb.	8 st. 13 lb.	9 st. 3 lb.	9 st. 7 lb.	9 st. 13 lb.
5'2"–5'3"	8 st. 12 lb.	9 st. 2 lb.	9 st. 6 lb.	9 st. 12 lb.	10 st. 5 lb.
5'3"–5'4"	8 st. 13 lb.	9 st. 5 lb.	9 st. 11 lb.	9 st. 13 lb.	10 st. 3 lb.
5'4"–5'5"	9 st. 6 lb.	9 st. 7 lb.	10 st. 1 lb.	10 st. 7 lb.	10 st. 8 lb.
5'5"–5'6"	9 st. 4 lb.	9 st. 12 lb.	10 st. 1 lb.	10 st. 11 lb.	10 st. 12 lb.
5'6"–5'7"	9 st. 11 lb.	9 st. 12 lb.	10 st. 2 lb.	10 st. 9 lb.	10 st. 4 lb.

The figures in the table are averages (means) based on huge representative samples. The average weight of 20- to 29-year-old women between 5 feet 1 inch and 5 feet 2 inches is 8 stone 13 pounds, for example. But there are more women in this group below the average than above it, and the same applies to all the averages in the table, because the weight distributions are positively skewed.[16] There are also anomalies in the table arising from the fact that just one or two extreme scores can drastically alter a mean, even in a very large sample.

A genuinely useful index of fatness, which correlates astonishingly closely with direct measures of body fat, is the Quetelet or Body Mass Index (BMI).[17] BMI is simply W/H^2, or weight in kilograms divided by the square of height in metres: divide your weight in kilograms by your height in metres, then divide the result by your height in metres again. If you prefer, use the following close approximation I have worked out for pounds and inches: BMI is approximately weight in pounds, multiplied by 700, divided by the square of height in inches. The average BMI of British women is 23.9, and the average for men is 24.3.[18] Although absolute thresholds are always arbitrary, it is generally agreed among biomedical researchers that anyone with a BMI less than 20 (14 per cent of women and 10 per cent of men) are underweight, those with BMI over 25 (32 per cent of women and 39 per cent of men) are overweight, and those with BMI over 30 (8.4 per cent of women and 6.1 per cent of men) are obese. Notice that according to these criteria more women than men are obese, and yet more women than men are underweight, which brings me back to my main theme, anorexia nervosa.

How common is anorexia nervosa?

The prevalence of a disorder in a specified population is the proportion of cases of the disorder in that population. Two factors make it difficult to establish reliable figures for the prevalence of anorexia nervosa. In the first place slimming diets are very popular nowadays: a recent survey of over 10,000 adults in Great Britain[19] revealed that 13 per cent of women and 5 per cent of men were currently on slimming diets, and 30 per cent of women and 10 per cent of men had dieted in the previous twelve months. Of course it is difficult to draw a sharp line between excessive dieting on the one hand and mild cases of anorexia nervosa on the other; the diagnostic criteria discussed earlier are helpful, but the distinctions they lead to are inevitably arbitrary. Second, most victims of anorexia nervosa tend to deny their symptoms and to maintain that there is nothing the matter with them – except that they are too fat! This creates further difficulties in recognizing mild cases. In spite of these problems, it is possible to say something about the prevalence of anorexia nervosa in various population groups.

Most strikingly, there is a huge sex difference. Numerous surveys have confirmed that 90 to 95 per cent of cases are female. This is especially puzzling when we recall that obesity – at the opposite end of the weight scale – is also much more common among women than among men: nearly 60 per cent of obese adults in Britain are female. There is also an age difference – the disorder is far more common among adolescents than among other age groups – and probably a class difference: about two-thirds of reported cases belong to the top two social classes (professional and managerial) although these classes make up less than one-fifth of the total population.[20]

In a detailed survey of schoolgirls between 16 and 18 years old in London, Crisp and his colleagues[21] found the overall prevalence of severe cases to be 1/250, or four per thousand. In independent schools the prevalence was more than twice as high – about one in every hundred schoolgirls. Among dancers and fashion models the prevalence is especially high. One Canadian study[22] found a prevalence of 1/15 or 6.7 per cent among female professional dance students, and 1/14 or 7.1 per cent among female fashion modelling students. It is probably not merely the extreme competitiveness of these professions or the performance anxiety associated with them that increases the risk, but the fact that they place a premium on slimness. The same study included a group of female music students at a highly competitive conservatory, and no cases of anorexia were found among them.

Most authorities believe that the prevalence of anorexia nervosa has increased in recent times and is still increasing, but the evidence for this is not very convincing. There is no doubt that more cases are being diagnosed, but this may merely reflect an increased awareness of the disorder among doctors, psychiatrists, clinical psychologists, and members of the general public. If anorexia nervosa is indeed on the increase, this may be connected with the fact that the female body shape that is generally considered desirable and is promoted in the mass media has been getting thinner and thinner in recent decades. Nowadays most people, especially women, want to be slim, and most men are attracted to slender women. Cyril Connolly's famous comment, 'Imprisoned in every fat man a thin one is wildly signalling to be let out', has been given a further twist by Katherine Whitehorn: 'And outside every thin girl a fat man is trying to get in.'

A group of Canadian researchers[23] examined the vital statistics of *Playboy* magazine centrefolds and Miss America Pageant contestants from 1959 to 1978. *Playboy* centrefolds in 1959 weighed 9 per cent less than the average for their age, height, and sex, and there was a gradual change over the next twenty years. By 1978 they weighed 17 per cent less than the average. During the same period centrefold bust measurements decreased from $36\frac{1}{2}$ inches to 35 inches, and hip measurements from 36 inches to $34\frac{1}{2}$ inches. Similar findings emerged from the study of Miss America Pageant contestants. During the 1970s, furthermore, the winners of this beauty competition weighed significantly less than the losing contestants. These findings should be seen in the light of the fact that during the 1960s and 1970s the average weight of ordinary women in the United States (and in the United Kingdom) rose significantly. The social pressures to become and stay slim must have increased as ordinary women drifted further and further away from the shrinking cultural ideal.

I suspect that the 1990s may see a change of fashion, with athletic female body shapes becoming more popular than the very slender cultural ideal of the 1960s and 1970s. This would be bad news for the hugely profitable slimming industry, but it might lead to a decrease in the prevalence of anorexia nervosa, or at least to a change in the way the disorder is manifested.

Body image disturbance

Anorexia nervosa patients often talk about their bodies in a way that is frankly astonishing to their friends and relatives. They tend to say that they look and feel fat even when they are so severely emaciated that they could pass as concentration camp inmates. The following remark, made by a woman who was five feet eight inches (173 centimetres) tall and weighed only five stone three pounds (33 kilograms) is typical: 'I look in a full-length mirror at least four or five times daily and I really cannot see myself as too thin .... Most of the time, odd as it may seem, I look in the mirror and believe that I am too fat.' Eventually this woman gave up weighing herself because the numbers never agreed with her body image. A different woman, who weighed 5 stones (32 kilograms), expressed disbelief when told that one of her fellow patients, whom she had described as 'very emaciated', was actually a stone and a half (9.5 kilograms) heavier than herself![24] Many patients apparently distrust both scales and mirrors, relying instead on arbitrary touchstones of their own. One of the commonest is the dreaded ruler test: Lie flat on your back and rest a ruler across your hips; if the ruler touches your belly you are too fat!

What does all this mean? Do anorexia nervosa patients have severely distorted body images? Many authorities think so. Hilde Bruch[25] has advanced an influential theory of anorexia nervosa in which body size misperception 'of delusional proportions' is fundamental, and she believes that correcting this misperception is 'a precondition for recovery'. According to Bruch, normal hunger awareness and body image awareness have to be learned through feedback from the social environment. Faulty hunger awareness and body image disturbance develop when an infant's signals regarding her internal states are ignored – when her mother fails to respond appropriately to her non-verbal signals and superimposes instead her own ideas about how the infant ought to be feeling. Inappropriate feedback of this kind, according to the theory, sows the seeds of three psychological abnormalities: disturbance of body image; inability to identify and respond appropriately to hunger and satiety; and an overwhelming sense of personal ineffectiveness. Bruch believes that children with these abnormalities are well on the way to developing anorexia nervosa in adolescence, though the theory seems powerless to explain why they are usually female.

Experimental studies of body size misperception have exploited three different techniques. The *moving-caliper* technique[26] is as follows. The subject stands facing a screen and is asked to imagine that the contours of her body are projected in silhouette on to the screen. She then adjusts a pair of sliding calipers or light beams to the width of the imagined silhouette in the regions of her face, shoulders, waist, and hips. Her estimates are then compared with her actual body measurements in the corresponding regions. A variation of this, the *image-marking* technique,[27] requires the subject to stand with a pencil in each hand facing a large sheet of paper, and to imagine that the paper is a mirror; she then uses the pencils to mark the width of the imagined mirror image at specified points. The *distorting-image* technique[28] is the most elaborate, but also the most realistic and reliable. A life-sized photograph or video image of the subject is projected on to a screen through an adjustable lens which allows the image to be distorted along the horizontal (thin–fat) dimension; the subject then adjusts the image of herself until it is as close to reality as possible.

The first controlled investigation of body size misperception in anorexia nervosa, using the moving-caliper technique, was reported by Slade and Russell of the University of London in 1973.[29] Their fourteen hospitalized patients overestimated their body widths by amounts varying from 25 to 55 per cent, although they estimated the widths of other objects, and their own heights, accurately. In sharp contrast, a control group of normal subjects made roughly accurate estimates of their body widths. Slade and Russell's paper excited a great deal of interest in psychological and psychiatric circles, because it seemed to show that body image disturbance lies at the heart of anorexia nervosa, and to provide an objective method of measuring it.

It would be pleasant to report that the psychological key to the mystery of anorexia nervosa had finally been found. But Slade and Russell's findings were swiftly challenged by other researchers. Crisp and Kalucy of St George's Hospital Medical School reported the results of their own investigation in 1974.[30] Using the moving-caliper technique, these researchers confirmed that their small group of anorexia nervosa patients tended to overestimate their body sizes, especially after eating a fattening meal, but their control group of normal subjects overestimated to a similar degree.

How can the discrepancy between these two investigations be explained? No one knows for sure; but one possible explanation centres on age differences in body perception. Shortly after the investigations were published it was discovered[31] that ordinary people tend to estimate their body sizes increasingly accurately as they grow older. In particular, older adolescent girls overestimate less than younger ones. This finding fits in nicely with Bruch's assumption, discussed earlier, that normal body image awareness develops with experience. Unfortunately, the subjects in Slade and Russell's normal control group were significantly older than their anorexia nervosa patients, and this age difference may possibly explain why the patient group overestimated their body sizes more than the control group of younger women.

Later investigations of body size misperception[32] have regrettably produced inconsistent results. Undaunted by Crisp and Kalucy's paper, Russell and his colleagues repeated their original conclusions in 1975,[33] but most researchers have found body size overestimation in various non-anorexic control groups as well as among anorexia nervosa patients. When age differences in body perception were discovered, Slade and two of his colleagues[34] replicated Slade and Russell's original investigation using a small group of patients with anorexia nervosa and a control group of similar age and found no differences between the two groups. The first investigation of body size misperception using large groups was reported in 1979.[35] Both the seventy-nine anorexia nervosa patients and the age-matched control subjects in this investigation tended to overestimate their body sizes, although overestimation was significantly greater, on average, in the patient group. The authors concluded that 'overestimation cannot be considered unique to anorexia nervosa'.

Results of investigations using the more realistic and reliable distorting-image technique[36] have not finally settled the argument about body size misperception, but they suggest the following tentative conclusions. A large proportion of patients with anorexia nervosa, but by no means all, overestimate their body sizes markedly, although most of them estimate the sizes of other people's bodies and non-human objects reasonably accurately. About one in three overestimate their body sizes by 10 per cent or more. But gross overestimation is by no means unknown among women without eating disorders, and may be quite common among obese and pregnant women. There is some evidence to suggest that anorexia nervosa patients who grossly overestimate their body sizes may be more severely disordered, and that their eating disorder may be less likely to improve, than those who do not.

Bulimia nervosa

During the late 1970s and early 1980s reports began to appear of an eating disorder related to anorexia nervosa which had not previously been described. It has been named *bulimia nervosa* in Britain[37] and *bulimia* in the United States.[38] I prefer the British term, because the word *bulimia* on its own means morbid hunger: it comes from the Greek words *bous* (ox) and *limos* (hunger). 'Bovine hunger' sounds more like a symptom than a disorder, and in any event it is not a necessary symptom of the disorder in question.

The cardinal symptom of bulimia nervosa is binge eating, usually followed by vomiting. This symptom is also found in about 50 per cent of anorexia nervosa patients, and in a small percentage of people suffering from obesity, although it may surprise you to learn that most obese people eat no more, and often less, than those of average weight.[39] In bulimia nervosa it occurs in an extreme form, among women whose body weights generally fluctuate within the 'normal' range for their age, height, and sex.

What is binge eating? Here is a brief description by a student undergoing treatment for bulimia nervosa:

I eat and eat, usually very fast, and without enjoyment, apart from the initial taste-pleasure, which anyway is tempered with guilt. Usually furtively and in one place – at home, the kitchen; at Oxford, my room. I eat until I physically cannot eat any more .... Immediately afterwards I am so physically bloated that emotions are dulled, but later I feel terrible.[40]

There is a fairly stereotyped pattern recognizable in most reports of eating binges. A binge usually follows a period of dieting, and almost invariably takes place in secret. It is often precipitated by stress, loneliness, or boredom, and it is sometimes planned in advance. A huge quantity of food, experienced at the time as grossly excessive, and usually consisting of fattening foods that are avoided at other times, is gobbled down rapidly with little or no chewing. The amount of food consumed during a binge varies, but 10,000 calories is quite common. This is equivalent to four large (500-gram) tins of baked beans, plus two dozen raw or boiled eggs, plus six large (100-gram) slabs of milk chocolate, plus fifteen slices of cream gateau, plus twenty half-pint cans of Coca Cola. (Bulimia nervosa can be an expensive disorder; it is hardly surprising that many sufferers are shoplifters.) There may be some enjoyment at first, but as more and more food is swallowed an unpleasant feeling of complete loss of control develops. The binge may be brought to an end by exhaustion of food supplies, abdominal pain, or interruption; the usual final act is self-induced vomiting, usually triggered by poking a finger or a toothbrush down the throat, although some women develop the ability to vomit without mechanical aids. If vomiting is planned, large quantities of liquid are usually consumed with the food. Sometimes the binge begins with a coloured 'marker' food, and after the binge vomiting is repeated until the marker re-emerges. The usual vomitorium is the lavatory; the cistern is flushed and taps are run to drown the sound of retching. Feelings of depression, guilt, and self-disgust invariably follow binge eating.

Russell, who coined the term 'bulimia nervosa', suggested the following diagnostic criteria:

A   A powerful and intractable urge to overeat.
B   Attempts to avoid the fattening effects of food through self-induced vomiting, laxative abuse, or both.
C   Morbid fear of becoming fat.[41]

The diagnostic criteria for 'bulimia' listed in the American Psychiatric Association's DSM-III are, once again, more specific:

A   Recurrent episodes of binge eating (rapid consumption of a large amount of food in a discrete period of time, usually less than two hours).
B   At least three of the following:
    (1)   consumption of high-calorie, easily ingested food during a binge
    (2)   inconspicuous eating during a binge
    (3)   termination of such eating episodes by abdominal pain, sleep, or self-induced vomiting
    (4)   repeated attempts to lose weight by severely restrictive diets, self-induced vomiting, or use of cathartics or diuretics
    (5)   frequent weight fluctuations greater than ten pounds due to alternating binges and fasts.
C   Awareness that the eating pattern is abnormal and fear of not being able to stop eating voluntarily.
D   Depressed mood and self-deprecating thoughts following eating binges.
E   The bulimic episodes are not due to Anorexia Nervosa or any known physical disorder.[42]

The clinical features of bulimia nervosa[43] resemble those of anorexia nervosa, but there are several important differences. Virtually all reported cases (about 99 per cent) are female, and most apparently belong to social classes I and II (professional and managerial). They score extremely highly on the Eating Attitudes Test (EAT) discussed earlier, and they are often profoundly disgusted by their own bodies. There are cases in the literature of women who undress only in complete darkness to avoid seeing their bodies, and of others who even keep some clothes on when taking a bath or a shower. Whereas anorexia nervosa patients are constantly fearful of losing control of their eating, those suffering from bulimia nervosa have chaotic eating habits and generally feel that they have already lost control. Many have a past history of anorexia nervosa, and most diet or fast between binges. They seldom minimize their symptoms in the manner characteristic of anorexia nervosa. The frequencies of binge eating and vomiting vary; in most cases episodes occur at least daily, and in some they occur several times a day. One of Russell's patients had callouses on the back of her hand caused by repeated friction against her front teeth when poking her finger down her gullet.[44] Because their weight tends to fluctuate wildly, some patients weigh themselves many times a day, especially before and after vomiting; Fairburn[45] described a patient who carried her bathroom scales in her rucksack on a hitch-hiking holiday round Europe. Others actively avoid weighing themselves but remain acutely anxious about their shape. A minority engage in unprepossessing eating habits such as habitual rumination: after a binge, food is repeatedly regurgitated, re-chewed, and re-swallowed.

Frequent vomiting or laxative abuse often leads to medical complications, including loss of potassium leading to cardiac problems or even epileptic seizures, dehydration, kidney damage, chronic hoarseness, and dental erosion caused by powerful digestive juices (especially hydrochloric acid) from the stomach. The medical complications of binge eating include acute dilation or rupture of the stomach. Binge eating and vomiting are not only dangerous; there is evidence to show that they are also habit-forming. This is presumably because they are mutually reinforcing: a full stomach make vomiting easier, and an empty stomach encourages binge eating.

The difficulty of estimating the prevalence of anorexia nervosa has already been discussed. Bulimia nervosa presents even more of a challenge to epidemiologists. Cases are more likely to go undetected because their body shape and weight are unremarkable and they are generally secretive about their bizarre eating habits, which they themselves consider thoroughly disgusting. But, in spite of the problems, researchers have managed to establish that it is a common disorder.

In 1980 a small advertisement appeared in the British edition of the popular women's magazine *Cosmopolitan* inviting letters from people who were using self-induced vomiting as a method of weight control.[46] So large was the response that the researchers who inserted the advertisement decided to follow up only the first 800 replies. A questionnaire was sent to these women, and their responses suggested that no fewer than 83 per cent of them fulfilled Russell's diagnostic criteria of bulimia nervosa, although less than 3 per cent were receiving treatment. In an attempt to estimate the prevalence of the disorder in the community, Cooper and Fairburn[47] persuaded 369 consecutive visitors to a family planning clinic in southern England to fill in a detailed questionnaire concerned with eating attitudes and habits. Women were classified as probable bulimia nervosa cases if they answered *Yes* to the questions 'In the past two months have you experienced an episode of uncontrollable and excessive eating?' and 'In the past two months have you used self-induced vomiting as a means of controlling your weight?', and *Always, Very Often,* or *Often* to the EAT item 'Am terrified about being overweight'. Seven women fulfilled these stringent criteria, which suggests a prevalence in the community of 1.9 per cent. A survey of American college students[48] has independently arrived at a similar estimate of the prevalence of the disorder. This evidence suggests that bulimia nervosa is even more common than anorexia nervosa.

Eating disorders and depression

In recent years, researchers have provided an enormous amount of descriptive information about anorexia nervosa and bulimia nervosa, but unfortunately very little about their underlying nature and causes. It has been suggested from time to time that eating disorders are merely disguised forms of other more familiar mental or physical disorders. I mentioned earlier that Ellen West was diagnosed by an eminent psychiatrist as suffering from schizophrenia. No reputable authority believes any longer that anorexia nervosa is related to schizophrenia. More recently, speculations have been offered that anorexia nervosa and bulimia nervosa are special kinds of phobias or obsessive-compulsive neuroses. Neither of these theories seems to harmonize with clinical experience and accumulating research evidence, and neither has won widespread acceptance among contemporary authorities. There is only one suggestion of this type that merits serious consideration: the theory that the eating disorders are essentially forms of depression. This theory has been accepted by many American authorities, and it has led to an interesting debate in the pages of the technical journals.

Several writers drew attention during the 1970s to aspects of the eating disorders that are suggestive of depression; but it was not until 1983 that a paper in the *British Journal of Psychiatry* by James

Hudson of the Harvard Medical School and three of his colleagues presented a detailed argument in favour of the depression theory of eating disorders.[49] On the first page of this paper, which is deceptively entitled 'Family History Study of Anorexia Nervosa and Bulimia', Hudson and his colleagues stated their intention of putting forward 'several lines of evidence' to show that the eating disorders 'may be related' to depression. Their summary presented the theory in a slightly stronger form, claiming that the evidence points to the disorders being 'closely related' to depression; and the final sentence of their paper asserted, more strongly still, that the eating disorders may be 'forms of' depression.

Hudson and his colleagues put forward, in fact, five lines of evidence in favour of the depression theory:

First, depressive symptoms are commonly described in patients with anorexia nervosa [and] depression is also frequently noted in patients with bulimia .... Second, outcome studies have found that patients with anorexia nervosa exhibit depressive symptoms at follow-up [although] comparable studies on the course of bulimia have not yet appeared. Third, biological tests have suggested a link between the eating disorders and affective [depressive] disorder .... Fourth, there are uncontrolled reports that anorexia nervosa may respond to amitriptyline [an antidepressant drug] .... With regard to bulimia, we have reported ... that six of eight patients responded to tricyclic antidepressants ... and that five of six patients responded to MAO inhibitors [another group of antidepressant drugs] .... Fifth, three family studies have found a higher than expected prevalence of affective disorder in the relatives of patients with anorexia nervosa .... In the case of bulimia, Pyle *et al.* (1981) found that 16 of 33 non-adopted bulimics reported depression in at least one first-degree relative [and we have found] that six of ten bulimics had at least one first-degree relative with DSM-III major affective disorder.[50]

The paper by Hudson and his colleagues went on to report further evidence that depression tends to run in the families of patients with anorexia nervosa or bulimia nervosa.

The depression theory of eating disorders was swiftly and comprehensively challenged by two British researchers, Peter Cooper and Christopher Fairburn, in a letter in a later issue of the same journal.[51] Cooper and Fairburn tackled each of Hudson's lines of evidence in turn. First, they acknowledged that depressive symptoms are indeed common in the eating disorders; but they drew attention to something that Hudson had failed to mention: 'In anorexia nervosa it is well recognised that restoration of body weight is associated with a decrease in depressive symptoms.' This suggests that depression is a by-product of malnutrition rather than a primary symptom of anorexia nervosa. In the case of bulimia nervosa, 'since the depression lifts in response to measures which enhance control over eating, the mood disturbance is likely to be a secondary phenomenon'. These comments put Hudson's first argument in proper perspective, but they certainly do not refute it. Even if – or perhaps especially if – the eating disorders are forms of depression, the depressive symptoms ought to disappear when they are successfully treated. The fact that depressive symptoms tend to decrease when anorexia nervosa patients regain weight, and when bulimia nervosa patients regain control over eating, does not prove that depression is a secondary by-product of the disorders. After all, depressive symptoms tend to decrease when patients with ordinary depressive disorders recover, and in those cases the depression is certainly a primary symptom. As we shall see, stronger arguments against Hudson's first line of evidence emerged later in the debate.

Hudson's second line of evidence was based on outcome studies, which show that many anorexia nervosa patients display depressive symptoms at follow-up. At face value, this is not a second line of evidence at all, but merely a consequence of the first. Since depressive symptoms are common in anorexia nervosa, many patients who have not fully recovered are likely to continue to display these symptoms at follow-up. And if, as Cooper and Fairburn suggested, the depressive symptoms are merely by-products of malnutrition, then it is hardly surprising that many patients continue to display them at follow-up because many still suffer from the effects of malnutrition, and those whose body weight has returned to normal are not usually depressed. But Hudson may have meant to imply that depressive symptoms tend over time to *replace* the psychological symptoms characteristic of anorexia nervosa – the pursuit of thinness and the morbid fear of fatness – which would suggest that anorexia nervosa tends to *develop into* the more familiar depressive disorder. It is this second interpretation, which would certainly constitute a powerful new line of evidence, that Cooper and Fairburn challenged. Outcome studies, they argued, 'have failed to support the contention that the condition is a form of depressive disorder .... With one exception, the outcome studies have found that the eating disorder does not evolve into an affective disorder [but that] the illness "breeds true" '.

The most important biological test that Hudson referred to in his third line of evidence is the *dexamethasone suppression test* (DST). This is a rather technical issue, and some background information is needed.

I referred earlier to the small pea-shaped gland in the centre of everyone's skull called the *pituitary*, which secretes a number of hormones into the bloodstream. Hormone levels are controlled by feedback mechanisms, triggered by receptors in the brain which are sensitive to the various hormones circulating in the blood. When the level of any pituitary hormone rises above a certain threshold, secretion of this hormone is switched off by the feedback mechanism, and when it falls below the threshold, secretion is switched back on, rather like a central heating thermostat. One of the hormones secreted by the pituitary is *adrenocorticotrophic hormone* – to avoid tongue-twisting it is nearly always called simply ACTH. Among its many functions, ACTH stimulates the adrenal glands, which are situated on top of the kidneys, to secrete *cortisol* into the bloodstream. When a person is stressed or injured, the level of ACTH – and consequently also the level of cortisol – in the bloodstream increases; this helps to prevent collapse from shock. Overactivity of the adrenal gland, often caused by a tumour, can lead to the disease called *Cushing's syndrome* with its familiar 'moon-face' clinical picture.

It was discovered in the early 1960s that many patients with severe depression have abnormally high levels of circulating cortisol, and that the levels usually return to normal on recovery.[52] More recently, the dexamethasone suppression test (DST) became widely used as crude index of abnormal cortisol secretion. Dexamethasone is a potent synthetic hormone (a steroid) which inhibits secretion of ACTH by the pituitary, and consequently also secretion of cortisol by the adrenals, by triggering the cortisol feedback mechanism in the brain. Normal people injected with dexamethasone suppress cortisol secretion for up to twenty-four hours, but patients with Cushing's syndrome do not; the DST is therefore routinely used in the diagnosis of Cushing's syndrome. The evidence[53] shows that *some* patients with *some* types of depressive disorder also fail to suppress cortisol secretion after being injected with dexamethasone, and it has been suggested that the DST may provide 'a specific laboratory test for the diagnosis of melancholia [a type of depression]'.[54] Finally, it was discovered in the early 1980s that some patients with anorexia nervosa respond to the DST in a similar way to depressives,[55] and so do some patients with bulimia nervosa.[56] These are the findings that Hudson put forward as the third line of evidence linking eating disorders to depression.

Cooper and Fairburn's reply was that the abnormal response of patients with anorexia nervosa and bulimia nervosa to the DST may be 'a secondary physiological response to these patients' abnormal eating habits or their low body weight'. In fact, Hudson and his colleagues had conceded in an earlier publication that 'subjects more than 20% below ideal body weight may show false positive DSTs'; but they claimed that bulimia nervosa patients with normal body weights also tend to respond abnormally to the DST: 'The most parsimonious explanation for these findings would appear to be that bulimia is closely related to affective disorder.'[57] Cooper and Fairburn offered another explanation, which is not obviously less parsimonious: the abnormal eating habits of patients with bulimia nervosa may cause sufficient stress to interfere with normal cortisol levels in the bloodstream. As we shall see, other authorities also consider this to be a more cogent explanation for the DST findings.

Cooper and Fairburn then turned to Hudson's fourth line of evidence – the claim that patients with eating disorders benefit from antidepressant medication. They pointed out that, in the case of anorexia nervosa, 'no study had even met the minimal requirements of proper evaluation', and that, as far as bulimia nervosa is concerned, 'the only controlled outcome study found that adequate dosage of [an antidepressant drug] had no specific effect on eating habits and attitudes, or indeed on mental state'. Cooper and Fairburn's rebuttal seems unanswerable. None of the drug studies with anorexia nervosa patients was *double-blind* – the patients and the experimenters both being ignorant as to which were receiving the drug and which were receiving placebos (pills containing inactive substances) – to rule out the biasing effects of prior expectations. And the only double-blind study with bulimia nervosa patients, which Hudson did not refer to, led its authors to the following conclusion: 'These data suggest that bulimia is not a manifestation of an underlying affective disorder as such but that mood changes are more likely to be a secondary part of the syndrome.'[58]

Cooper and Fairburn also argued that 'it is questionable whether response to antidepressant medication is a legitimate basis for assigning patients to a particular diagnostic category'. To see this point clearly, consider the fact that the symptoms of rheumatism and the common cold are both relieved by aspirin. But no one would claim this as evidence that these two illnesses are related, or that one is a form of the other.

Finally, Cooper and Fairburn commented briefly on Hudson's fifth line of evidence – the allegedly high prevalence of depressive disorder among close relatives of people with eating disorders. Without challenging the validity of this finding, they questioned its value as evidence: 'The only conclusion that can be drawn from this observation is that a family history of affective disorder predisposes individuals to develop an eating disorder.'

If there is a link between eating disorders and depression, then of course we should expect eating-disordered patients to show depressive symptoms. As we have seen, Hudson's first, and perhaps most crucial, line of evidence for the depression theory rested on the fact that depressive symptoms are 'commonly described' or 'frequently noted' in clinical reports and case studies of eating-disordered patients. Cooper and Fairburn suggested, on the basis of rather debatable evidence, that the depressive symptoms of these patients are secondary by-products rather than primary symptoms of the eating disorders. A few years later they strengthened their case by carrying out the first systematic comparison of the frequency, nature, and severity of depressive symptoms among patients with bulimia nervosa on the one hand and major depressive disorder on the other.[59] The results showed that there were important differences between the two groups as to the *pattern* of depressive symptoms. In particular, the depressive symptoms of the eating disordered patients tended more often to be associated with anxiety, and in three-quarters of cases this anxiety focused on eating in the presence of other people or being seen in public when 'feeling fat'. Although the eating disordered patients were indeed depressed, their depression was closely linked to their eating problems. These findings were interpreted as further evidence that the depressive symptoms of eating-disordered patients 'are likely to be secondary to the eating disorder itself, rather than of primary significance.'

Some of Hudson's lines of evidence have been attacked by other writers too. Jane Wolf,[60] for example, questioned Hudson's interpretation of the evidence from the dexamethasone suppression test. Recall that Hudson had rested his third line of evidence chiefly on the abnormal responses to the DST of patients with bulimia nervosa, because the equally abnormal responses of patients with anorexia nervosa can be explained by their low body weights. Wolf reminded her readers that ACTH and cortisol secretion tend to increase in response to stress or injury, and then commented: 'It would be reasonable to wonder whether the physiological stresses of vomiting several times a day (as these patients often do) would not also influence the [pituitary functioning].' Hudson and his colleagues replied as follows: 'Unfortunately, we do not have precise data on the frequency of binging and vomiting for the patients reported in the study .... We have subsequently studied the

DST in an additional 35 patients for whom we knew the frequency of binging.... We found no correlation between frequency of binging (1–35 times a week) and post-DST plasma cortisol level.'[61] One has to be alert to notice that Hudson and his colleagues have not, in fact, responded to Wolf's criticism. They began by referring to the 'frequency of binging and vomiting', and then they went on to deny that 'frequency of binging' is related to abnormal DST response. Wolf's question, however, was whether frequency of *vomiting* might be related to abnormal DST response.

Finally, Stephen Stern and several colleagues[62] reported the results of a carefully controlled investigation into the prevalence of depressive disorders among the families of a group of twenty-seven women with bulimia nervosa and a control group of normal women. The results showed that 9 per cent of the patients' relatives, and 10 per cent of the normal group's relatives, had suffered from depressive disorders at some time in their lives. The difference was not statistically significant, and in any event was in the opposite direction to expectation based on the depression theory of eating disorders. There are numerous studies showing that the prevalence of depressive disorders among relatives of patients with anorexia nervosa is higher than expected, and a family history of depression is recognized as a probable risk factor in anorexia nervosa. But Stern's data suggest that the same may not be true of bulimia nervosa. Stern and his colleagues interpreted their findings like this: 'Our findings do suggest that eating disorders may be quite heterogeneous and that individuals with normal weight bulimia may differ genetically from patients with anorexia nervosa.'[63]

What conclusions can be drawn from the debate over the depression theory of eating disorders? None of Hudson's lines of evidence has been decisively confirmed or refuted, and the opinions of experts remain divided. The balance of evidence and argument seems tilted against the depression theory; I do not feel persuaded that anorexia nervosa or bulimia nervosa are forms of depression, or even that they are closely related to depression, although it seems clear that eating disordered patients are often depressed. Above all, the depression theory cannot explain the huge sex difference: depression is rather more common among women than men, but this cannot account for the vast preponderance of women among eating-disordered groups – the largest sex difference I know of in the whole of psychology. But the question remains open. A deeper understanding of eating disorders may one day lead to better methods of prevention and treatment. It is even conceivable that our understanding of depression could be deepened through research into eating disorders.

Notes

1 Binswanger (1944-5). A translation can be found in May, Angel, and Ellenberger (1958), pp. 237–364. I used both sources, and corrected and improved the translation of some of the passages quoted below.

2 World Health Organization (1978), p. 46. The definitions in brackets were added by me. The best popular account of anorexia nervosa is the book by Palmer (1980).

3 Sours (1980), p. 205. See Stone (1973) for a detailed account of anorexia nervosa in the medieval period.

4 Morton (1694).

5 Rumbelow (1975), pp. 150–4; Knight (1976).

6 Gull (1874). The comments in square brackets are mine.

7 Simmonds (1914).

8 Sheehan and Summers (1949). The distinction between Simmonds' disease and anorexia nervosa began to emerge in the late 1930s; see Sours (1980), pp. 209–10, and Garfinkel and Garner (1982), pp. 60–1.

9 Summarized from Russell (1970).

10 American Psychiatric Association (1980), p. 69.

11 Garner and Garfinkel (1979). See also Garfinkel and Garner (1982), pp. 29–30 and 37–9.

12 The life insurance survey data are thoroughly demolished in *Spiegel* (1985); see especially pp. 37, 50. Some people in the samples were weighed with their clothes on and others naked; some were measured in their shoes and others barefoot; many people entered the statistics twice; and so on. Also, of course, members of some social classes and ethnic groups were hardly represented in the samples because they do not usually take out life assurance of sufficient value to require medical examinations; but Knight (1984, pp. 7, 8, 21) has shown that these factors are strongly associated with height and weight.

13 Knight (1984).

14 Abraham (1979).

15 Knight (1984), pp. 26–9. I have converted centimetres to feet and inches (to convert back to centimetres, multiply inches by 2.54) and kilograms to stones and pounds (to convert back to kilograms, multiply pounds by 0.45359). The first and last weights in the column labelled '16–19' were estimated from the regression equation given in Knight (1984), p. 31. The height range of the table given here covers 84 per cent of British women.

16 Consider a group of ten people weighing 7, 8, 8, 9, 9, 9, 10, 11, 12, and 13 stones respectively. This distribution is also positively skewed. The mean (average) weight is somewhere between 9 and 10 stones; but six of the ten weigh less than this, as you can see.

17 Garrow (1979); Garrow (1983); Goldbourt and Medalie (1974); Knight (1984).

18 Knight (1984), p. 33. The figures given below are also from this source.

19 Knight (1984), p. 37.

20 Garfinkel and Garner (1982), p. 167.

21 Crisp, Palmer, and Kalucy (1976).

22 Garfinkel and Garner (1982), pp. 112–17.

23 Garner, Garfinkel, Schwartz, and Thompson (1980).

24 Both examples are taken from Garfinkel and Garner (1982), pp. 125–6.

25 Bruch (1962). See also Bruch (1973).

26 This technique was originally introduced by Reitman and Cleveland (1964).

27 This technique was introduced by Askevold (1975).
28 Glucksman and Hirsch (1969).
29 Slade and Russell (1973).
30 Crisp and Kalucy (1974).
31 Halmi, Goldberg, and Cunningham (1977).
32 Details are given in Garfinkel and Garner (1982), pp. 127–43.
33 Russell, Campbell, and Slade (1975).
34 Button, Fransella, and Slade (1977).
35 Casper, Halmi, Goldberg, Eckert, and Davis (1979).
36 Garner, Garfinkel, Stancer, and Modlofsky (1976); Garfinkel, Modlofsky, Garner, Stancer, and Coscina (1978); Garfinkel and Garner (1982), pp. 133–9.
37 Russell (1979).
38 American Psychiatric Association (1980), pp. 69–71.
39 Fairburn (1983); Spiegel (1985).
40 Fairburn (1982), p. 3.
41 Summarized from Russell (1979).
42 American Psychiatric Association (1980), pp. 70–1.
43 See Russell (1979); Pyle, Mitchell, and Eckert (1981); Fairburn (1982); Fairburn (1983).
44 Russell (1979).
45 Fairburn (1982), p. 8.
46 Fairburn and Cooper (1982).
47 Cooper and Fairburn (1983b).
48 Pyle, Mitchell, Eckert, Halvorson, Neuman, and Goff (1983).
49 Hudson, Pope, Jonas, and Yurgelun-Todd (1983).
50 ibid., pp. 133–4 (material in brackets added by me).
51 Cooper and Fairburn (1983a). All quotations in the text are from p. 35.
52 The evidence is discussed by Kendell (1983), pp. 306–7.
53 A summary and critique is given in ibid., p. 306.
54 Carroll, Feinberg, Greden, *et al.* (1981). The quotation is from the title of the paper.
55 Gerner and Gwirtsman (1981).
56 Hudson, Laffer, and Pope (1982a).
57 ibid., p. 686.
58 Sabine, Yonace, Farrington, Barratt, and Wakeling (1983), p. 200S.
59 Cooper and Fairburn (1986). The quotation at the end of the paragraph is from p. 268.
60 Wolf (1982). The quotation below is from p. 1524; the phrase in square brackets is mine.
61 Hudson, Laffer, and Pope (1982b), p. 1524.
62 Stern, Dixon, Nemzer, *et al.* (1984). The quotation is from p. 1227.
63 Further drug trials are discussed by Fairburn (1985), who concludes that 'the evidence that antidepressants are an effective treatment for bulimia nervosa is both insubstantial and inconclusive' (p. 470). The whole debate has been reviewed by Swift, Andrews, and Barklage (1986), who concluded that eating disorders and depression are related, but that 'the nature of the relationship is unclear and open to dispute' (p. 297).

7 Extra-sensory perception: is there any solid evidence?

On 7 December 1918 Lieutenant David McConnel, an 18-year-old officer in the Royal Air Force, died in an air crash in the north of England. The testimony of his roommate and fellow officer Lieutenant J. J. Larkin, backed up by signed statements from other witnesses, provides one of the most impressive cases of a spontaneous paranormal phenomenon on record.[1] The facts of the McConnel case, according to the written testimony, are briefly as follows.

McConnel told Larkin that he had been ordered to fly a military aircraft from Scampton, near Lincoln, where they were both stationed, to Tadcaster, half-way between Leeds and York, and that he expected to be back in time for tea. He left Scampton airfield at about 11.30 a.m. After lunch, Larkin sat in front of a fire writing letters and reading. This is his account of what happened:

I heard someone walking up the passage; the door opened with the usual noise and clatter which David [McConnel] always made; I heard his 'Hello boy!' and I turned half round in my chair and saw him standing in the doorway, half in and half out of the room, holding the door knob in his hand .... I remarked, 'Hello! Back already?' He replied, 'Yes. Got there all right, had a good trip.' ... I did not have a watch, so could not be sure of the time, but was certain it was between a quarter and a half-past three, because shortly afterwards Lieut. Garner-Smith came into the room and it was a quarter to four. He said, 'I hope Mac (David) gets back early, we are going to Lincoln this evening.' I replied, 'He *is* back, he was in the room a few minutes ago!'

That night Larkin learned that McConnel had died at 3.25 p.m. – at almost the exact moment that the apparition had appeared in Larkin's room. The weather was fair when McConnel left Scampton, but he ran into dense fog between Doncaster and Tadcaster, and crashed near Tadcaster airfield. The first on the scene was a young woman who saw the aircraft going into a nose dive. She ran to the spot where it crashed and 'found the officer dead'. His watch, which had apparently been stopped by the impact, registered 3.25. Larkin could not at first believe that his roommate had been killed. When it became clear that the story was true, he was at a loss to explain his experience: 'I am of such a sceptical nature regarding things of this kind that even now I wish to think otherwise, that I did not see him, but I am unable to do so.' His account of events was corroborated in written statements by Lieutenant Garner-Smith and others.

If this story is true, and there is no reason to doubt that Larkin himself believed it, then it is obvious that something interesting happened on that foggy afternoon in 1918. Parapsychology is a branch of psychology devoted to examining and seeking to explain such apparently supernatural or paranormal (beside or beyond the normal) phenomena. There is an abundance of written evidence of spontaneous paranormal phenomena, or psi phenomena as they are often called (from the Greek letter psi, which stands for *psyche*, 'soul', and hence 'psychical'). And, of course, there are many more putative cases of spontaneous psi that have never been recorded in writing; most of us have heard accounts of psi experiences from relatives, friends, and acquaintances. The early history of parapsychology was devoted mainly to collecting and examining reports of alleged spontaneous psi. But, impressive though some of these cases are, they are not nowadays regarded as scientific evidence for psi. There are three reasons for this.

First, spontaneous phenomena are, by their very nature, unrepeatable, and this makes it difficult for independent researchers to check them. There are perfectly respectable sciences devoted to the study of inherently unrepeatable phenomena – seismology (the study of earthquakes) is one obvious example – but most sciences, and most branches of psychology, rely heavily on replications. If a psychologist working on hypnosis, for example, discovers an experimental procedure that produces analgesia in certain subjects, then independent researchers can replicate the experiment, and then vary the original procedure systematically in order to throw more light on the phenomenon. This is, in fact, how research into hypnotic analgesia has proceeded (see Chapter 5) and it is the usual procedure in psychology and also in experimental parapsychology. But no one can replicate the circumstances that led to the spontaneous apparition of Lieutenant McConnel. The inherent unrepeatability of spontaneous psi, coupled with a lack of theory as to when and where it should occur, excludes it from proper scientific investigation. Seismologists, in contrast, have a rather deep understanding of the nature and causes of earthquakes.

Second, it is generally difficult or impossible to determine the likelihood that some perfectly normal process could explain an ostensible case of spontaneous psi. In the McConnel case, for example, Lieutenant Larkin apparently saw an apparition of his friend at the moment of his death. But there is no way of gauging the likelihood that the apparition was the product of some perfectly normal psychological process – perhaps Larkin dozed off in front of the fire and dreamt that McConnel came into the room, for example – and that the coincidence of McConnel's death was due to chance. Larkin may have had a natural foreboding of his friend's death: he knew that McConnel was flying a 'notoriously dangerous aircraft',[2] and he probably knew that the weather was very bad. It is simply impossible to exclude a normal explanation in this instance, and the same problem arises in interpreting other reports of spontaneous psi. And, of course, the accumulation of similar examples does not necessarily strengthen the case for psi, because there may be even more instances of apparitions that went unreported because they did *not* coincide with anything interesting. It is instructive in this connection to note that Sigmund Freud never encountered a paranormal dream in twenty-seven years of psychoanalytic work with patients, many of whom were firm believers in the paranormal. Freud commented: 'Events such as accidents or illnesses of near relatives, in particular the death of one of the parents, have often enough happened during treatment and interrupted it; but not on one single occasion did these occurrences, eminently suitable as they were, afford me the opportunity of registering a single telepathic dream.'[3]

Third and most important, cases of spontaneous psi inevitably rest on the testimony of those who report them. More than two centuries ago the Scottish philosopher David Hume put forward an argument for rejecting all testimony of supernatural or paranormal events.[4] 'I flatter myself', he wrote, 'that I have discovered an argument ... which, if just, will, with the wise and learned, be an everlasting check to all kinds of superstitious delusion, and consequently, will be useful as long as the world endures.' It is worth examining Hume's argument carefully, because contemporary philosophers consider it to be substantially correct.[5]

Hume pointed out that when we are confronted with testimony of a paranormal phenomenon, or of anything else, for that matter, there are three possibilities to be considered. Either the report is true, or it is false because the informant is mistaken, or it is false because the informant is dishonest. One of these explanations must be correct, but how should we decide between them? According to Hume, we ought to weigh the likelihood of the informant's being deceived or a deceiver against the intrinsic likelihood of whatever the informant reports. If the informant reports something intrisincally unlikely, then the crucial question is whether it is more or less unlikely than that the informant is mistaken or dishonest. Now for the nub of the argument: if the informant reports a supernatural or paranormal event, it must be literally contrary to the laws of nature, which implies that it is as unlikely as anything could be. (If it is not contrary to the laws of nature, then the claim that it is supernatural or paranormal collapses.) It must therefore be more likely that the informant is mistaken or dishonest, because that would not be contrary to any law of nature. Consequently, there are never good grounds for believing the testimony. Perhaps surprisingly, Hume's arguments also applies to someone who experiences a paranormal event at first hand, because even the testimony of one's own senses can be mistaken without violating any law of nature.

It is important to understand that Hume did not seek to prove that supernatural or paranormal events never occur, or that they never could occur. What he argued was simply that we never have good reasons for believing testimony of their occurrence. Many commentators have misunderstood this point. John Beloff of the University of Edinburgh, a prominent parapsychologist, has tried to show that Hume's argument is 'fallacious' and 'obvious nonsense' because 'it presupposes, in fact, that every proposition has, if we could ascertain it, a certain definite probability of being true', whereas, in reality, 'the *most* we can ever hope to do is to give an honest opinion as to which of two alternatives we deem the more likely. But this is an act of personal judgment, not a statement of objective probabilities'.[6] But Hume's conclusion was precisely that we never have good reasons for believing, 'as an act of personal judgment', testimony of a supernatural event. When we are forced by his argument to conclude that such an event is intrinsically more unlikely than the alternative – that the informant is mistaken or dishonest – this conclusion is admittedly relative to a body of background information. New information might persuade us that the reported event was not, after all, contrary to the laws of nature, and was not therefore maximally unlikely. We might then believe that what was reported indeed happened, but we would no longer have good grounds for believing that it was paranormal.

I hope I have said enough to convince you that there are several good reasons why reports of spontaneous psi are insufficient to establish the reality of the paranormal. Evidence for the paranormal, if it is to escape the full force of Hume's argument, must be based on experiments, carefully designed to control for the operation of normal (non-psi) processes, which can be scrutinized for errors and repeated by independent investigators. Extraordinary claims require extraordinary standards of evidence. Before discussing the experimental evidence and some of the controversies that it has generated, it will be useful to say a few words about the classification of psi phenomena and the historical background of parapsychological research.

Classification and historical background

The paranormal or psi phenomena that are the subject matter of experimental parapsychology fall into two classes: extra-sensory perception (ESP) and psychokinesis (PK). Extra-sensory perception is defined by the *Journal of Parapsychology* as 'experience of, or response to, a target object, state, event, or influence without sensory contact'. In other words, ESP is perception without the use of sense organs. It can be subdivided as follows. Extra-sensory perception of other people's mental processes is called telepathy; extra-sensory perception of physical objects or events is called clairvoyance; and extra-sensory perception of mental processes, objects, or events in the future is called precognitive telepathy or precognitive clairvoyance, or simply precognition when the distinction is unimportant. The terms retrocognitive (referring to the past) and contemporaneous (referring to the present) telepathy and clairvoyance are also occasionally used.

Psychokinesis (from the Greek *psyche*, mind; *kinesis*, movement) is the movement or change of physical objects by purely mental processes, without the application of physical force. Distinctions are occasionally drawn according to the nature of the target object – whether it is animate or inanimate and whether it is microscopic or macroscopic. Mental influence on the growth of plants, for example, is PK involving animate macroscopic targets, and mental influence on the emission of electrons from radioactive materials is PK with inanimate microscopic targets, and so on.

There are two comments worth making about the classification and definitions of psi phenomena. First, the classification is to some degree arbitrary, and some parapsychologists nowadays prefer general terms such as ESP or psi to more specific terms such as telepathy or clairvoyance. The reason for this, to take a simple example, is that no demonstration of telepathy could be shown to exclude the possibility of clairvoyance, because it would always be possible that the subject used clairvoyance to observe the picture, playing card, or other target that the agent tried to transmit telepathically. Even if the target existed only in the agent's imagination, the subject might have used clairvoyance to observe the agent's physical brain processes. Analogously, if a subject were to predict the outcome of some random process, such as the spin of a roulette wheel, it would be impossible to know whether pre-cognition or psychokinesis had been demonstrated. Most contemporary parapsychologists consider these distinctions to be somewhat scholastic; what is crucial is whether *any* paranormal interaction between a subject and the environment can be demonstrated.

Second, there is an insidious tendency among some writers to weaken the definitions of psi phenomena in a way that removes the 'para' from 'paranormal'. In a recent popular book, for example, ESP is (re)defined as 'the reported ability to gain information about people, events or objects at some distant place and/or time by means as yet unknown to science'.[7] This is a debilitating definition because it encompasses types of perception that are not necessarily extra-sensory or paranormal, but merely 'as yet unknown to science'. If it were generally accepted as the definition of ESP, everyone would have to concede immediately, *without even considering the evidence of parapsychological research*, that ESP is an established fact, and that it is quite common in the animal kingdom. The ability of bats to gain information about obstacles in their flight paths is based on echo location, but this was 'unknown to science' before 1941.[8] The ability of nocturnally migrant birds such as European warblers to maintain their orientation depends on the use of the stars as a compass, but this means of bird navigation was 'unknown to science' before the mid 1950s.[9] Until quite recently, therefore, echo location by bats and star navigation by European warblers were genuine and uncontroversial examples of ESP according to the weak definition, although we now know that they involve nothing paranormal. Coming right up to the present, the ability of tadpoles to recognize siblings when they meet them for the first time involves 'means as yet unknown to science',[10] but researchers who have examined this phenomenon do not attribute it to ESP because, although it is very mysterious, there is no reason to believe that it is paranormal. In the decades ahead, science will explain many things that are currently unexplained, and will also uncover many new mysteries in search of explanations, irrespective of parapsychology. Parapsychology is devoted to ostensibly paranormal phenomena, not merely to phenomena that are as yet unexplained. Beloff himself has argued that *no* normal physical explanation could *ever* be given for a genuine psi phenomenon.[11]

The earliest record of an experiment in parapsychology is to be found in *The Histories* of Herodotus, the world's first history book.[12] The experiment was conducted by the rich king Croesus of Lydia in the middle of the sixth century BC. In order to test the powers of the most famous oracles, Croesus sent messengers with instructions to ask each oracle on a prearranged day, 'what Croesus, son of Alyattes and king of Lydia, was doing at that moment'. The answers were written down and brought back to him. According to Herodotus, 'Croesus had thought of something which no one would be likely to guess, and with his own hands, keeping carefully to the prearranged date, he cut up a tortoise and a lamb and boiled them together in a bronze cauldron with a bronze lid.' When the messengers showed Croesus the answers they had recorded, 'none had the least effect on him except the one which contained the answer from Delphi'. The priestess of that most famous of all oracles had answered, almost before the question was posed:

The smell has come to my sense of a hard-skulled tortoise
Boiling and bubbling with lamb's flesh in a bronze pot:
The cauldron underneath is of bronze, and of bronze the lid.

Encouraged by the outcome of this experiment, Croesus sent further messengers to Delphi to inquire of the oracle whether he should attack Persia. The answer was that if he attacked Persia he would destroy a mighty empire. This prophecy turned out to be correct, but not in the way that Croesus interpreted it. He attacked Persia, and the mighty empire that was destroyed was his own!

Systematic research into psi phenomena can be traced to the foundation of the Society for Psychical Research in Cambridge in 1882; the American Society for Psychical Research was founded in 1885. The early work of these societies was devoted to the investigation of spirit mediums, who claimed to receive messages from the dead, and to reports of spontaneous psi phenomena such as the McConnel case. Sophisticated experimental research, with careful control of normal, non-psi influences including chance, was begun by Joseph Banks Rhine at Duke University in the 1930s. The work of Rhine and his colleagues dominated parapsychology for several decades.

Most of Rhine's research was devoted to ESP, a term he coined in 1934.[13] In order to control for the effects of chance, he used a special deck of twenty-five cards devised by his colleague at Duke University, K. E. Zener. Each of the following five geometric symbols appears on the faces of five of the cards: circle, plus sign, square, star, and wavy lines. If the Zener cards, or ESP cards as they are now called, are thoroughly randomized by shuffling, then the probability of guessing a particular card by chance is one-fifth. Therefore, five target hits are expected by chance in twenty-five guesses. The significance of deviations above or below this chance expectation can be evaluated straightforwardly by simple statistics.

If an agent, or sender, usually in a distant room, looks at the ESP cards while the subject, or percipient, tries to call them, statistically significant results are generally regarded as evidence for telepathy, provided that other explanations are thought to have been ruled out by proper experimental controls. If no one looks at the cards while the subject calls them, significant results are generally attributed to clairvoyance. And if the cards are not shuffled until *after* the subject's calls have been recorded, significant results are usually interpreted as evidence for precognition.

Rhine published the results of his early experiments in 1934,[14] and some sixty critical papers were published in response. From 1934 to 1939 the Duke group published seventeen experiments specifically designed to meet the criticisms, and 88 per cent of these showed statistically significant evidence in favour of ESP. During this prewar period thirty-five experiments by researchers at other centres were published, and 61 per cent of these reported significant results. In spite of this, most psychologists remained unimpressed: funding for parapsychological research was not forthcoming, and publication in mainstream psychological journals was rare. The few researchers working in this area founded their own journals, starting with the *Journal of Parapsychology* in 1937, and continued to investigate psi phenomena on a relatively small scale.

After the mid 1960s parapsychology began to thrive, and by 1977 more than fifty journals specializing in the subject, and more than 150 parapsychological associations, had come into existence worldwide. In 1969, amid a welter of controversy, the American Association for the Advancement of Science (AAAS) decided to admit the Parapsychological Association of the United States as a member. By the mid 1980s several thousand experiments on telepathy, clairvoyance, precognition, and psychokinesis had appeared in print, and parapsychology was firmly established as a field of research.

Public opinion is generally quite favourably disposed towards the paranormal. A Gallup poll in the summer of 1984 showed that 59 per cent of teenagers in the United States believed in ESP. A survey of attitudes among the scientific elite in the United States, however, showed somewhat greater scepticism. Among council and section committee members of the American Association for the Advancement of Science, only 29 per cent believed in ESP: 4 per cent considered it an 'established fact' and a further 25 per cent 'a likely possibility'. The opinions of the remaining 71 per cent encompassed varying degrees of scepticism.[15] In sharp contrast to this, 88 per cent of members of the Parapsychological Association hold strong, positive beliefs about ESP.[16] On the other hand, several surveys have shown that psychologists who are not engaged in parapsychological research tend to hold more sceptical beliefs about ESP than virtually any other academic or professional group.[17]

What is the scientific basis for these beliefs? It is obviously impossible to discuss all of the experimental evidence for ESP, because there is simply too much of it. In fairness to parapsychology, however, any critical review should focus on the experiments that have been chosen by leading parapsychologists as persuasive evidence for ESP. One prominent parapsychologist has chastised critics who

confuse the thinking of the scientific community as a whole by a very simple procedure. Whenever questions come up as to what is wrong with the ESP experiments that have been performed, the tactic which has been followed – and I can only conclude it has been followed consciously – is to describe the weaknesses in those experiments which are not the best experiments ... and quietly to ignore the experiments which cannot be explained away.[18]

In a book co-authored by this exasperated parapsychologist in 1958[19] there is a chapter entitled 'Evidence that ESP Occurs' in which five experiments are cited. Among these are the Pearce–Pratt experiments from Rhine's laboratory at Duke University, and the Soal–Goldney experiments performed in London. These two were also among the four nominated by Rhine and Pratt in 1957[20] as providing 'conclusive evidence for ESP', and among the four described by Beloff in 1962[21] as the 'crème-de-la-crème of the experimental data'. The Pearce–Pratt and Soal–Goldney experiments are the only ones that were mentioned by all the distinguished parapsychologists in the books quoted, and I have therefore chosen them for critical examination.

More recently, a series of experiments on precognition in rodents enjoyed a brief spell in the parapsychological limelight. In 1974 Beloff[22] drew special attention to them in a chapter on 'the Current Status of Parapsychology', and John Randall,[23] another prominent British parapsychologist, commented on their 'remarkable degree of consistency which is unfortunately rare in parapsychological research'. In 1977 R. A. McConnell,[24] the scourge of the critics whose views I quoted in the previous paragraph, remarked that such near-perfect repeatability had never before occurred in para-psychology. I shall therefore discuss these experiments briefly.

In 1977 Scott Rogo[25] published 'The Case for Parapsychology' in which he recommended the psi Ganzfeld experiments as the most worthy representatives of the field. In 1982 Hans Eysenck and Carl Sargent[26] also singled out these experiments for special praise. I shall examine the debate over the psi Ganzfeld experiments in detail.

The fifth and last series of experiments to be discussed are the experiments on remote viewing published in 1974. I have decided to include these partly because they were published in *Nature*, arguably the world's most influential scientific journal, and partly because they received extensive coverage in the general news media.

The five series of experiments have all been certified at one time or another as *pièces de résistance* of parapsychology, and they have all been cited by parapsychologists as providing persuasive evidence for ESP. I believe that they provide a fair sample of the most influential parapsychological research of the last half-century. As we shall see, each series of experiments has been the subject of fierce controversy, and in some cases definite conclusions have emerged from the debates.

The Soal–Goldney experiments

Samuel G. Soal, a mathematician at the University of London, became interested in parapsychology after reading Rhine's first book, *Extrasensory Perception*, which appeared in 1934. He tried to replicate Rhine's experiments, introducing stricter controls, but although he tested 160 subjects, including a woman who had shown evidence of ESP in Rhine's laboratory, virtually all his results were negative. He wrote sceptically about ESP and became a harsh critic of Rhine's research. But in November 1939 someone suggested to him that he should re-examine his own data for possible cases of retrocognitive and precognitive ESP, that is, cases in which subjects' guesses corresponded to cards immediately preceding or following the target cards. A careful re-examination of his record sheets turned up two subjects whose scores were significant when these 'displacement effects' were taken into account. In collaboration with Mrs K. M. Goldney, a council member of the Society for Psychical Research, Soal began a fresh series of tests with one of these two, a professional photographer called Basil Shackleton. The results were first published by Soal and Goldney in the *Proceedings of the Society for Psychical Research* in 1943.[27]

Soal and Goldney went to greater lengths than any previous researchers to make their tests as rigorous as possible. The fact that their results were none the less highly significant created a worldwide sensation. A professor of philosophy at Cambridge University wrote that 'Soal's results are outstanding. The precautions taken to prevent deliberate fraud or the unwitting conveyance of information by normal means are described in great detail, and seem to be absolutely water-tight.'[28] A professor of biology at Yale University wrote that 'Soal's work was conducted with every precaution that it was possible to devise'.[29] Many people shared the view that Soal and Goldney had provided 'the most impressive data ever reported on the occurrence of extrasensory phenomena', as one psychologist put it.[30] Even Rhine himself, the doyen of parapsychology, described the Soal–Goldney experiments as 'one of the most outstanding researches yet made in the field .... Soal's work was a milestone in ESP research'.[31]

Here is a brief description of the Soal–Goldney experimental procedure. The subject, Shackleton, was tested with thirteen different agents, and throughout each testing session there were two experimenters present. Many of the sessions were also attended by eminent observers, including C. E. M. Joad (a well-known philosopher and Brain Trust member) and Sir Ernest Bennett (a member of parliament). Shackleton and the agent sat at tables in adjacent rooms, each accompanied by one of the experimenters. The connecting door was left ajar so that Shackleton could hear the experimenter who was sitting with the agent call out the trial numbers, indicating when he should record his responses, but Shackleton and the agent were positioned so that they could not have seen each other even if the door had been left wide open.

Five cards, each bearing a picture of a different animal – an elephant, a giraffe, a lion, a pelican, or a zebra – were arrayed in a box in front of the agent, shielded from everyone's view except the agent's. The cards were shuffled and placed face down in a row in the box before each batch of fifty trials. Opposite the agent, separated by a screen with a small hole in it, sat the experimenter (usually Mrs Goldney) who controlled the running of the experiment. At the beginning of each batch of fifty trials she consulted a list containing fifty digits (1s, 2s, 3s, 4s, and 5s) in random order – these lists were prepared in advance, usually by Soal, and concealed until the last moment. She looked at the first number on the list, held a card bearing this number up to the hole where the agent on the other side of the screen could see it, and called out, so Shackleton could hear, 'one' (the serial number of the trial). The agent turned over the corresponding picture card in his box – the second from the left if the experimenter had displayed a 2 at the hole in the screen, for example – looked at it, and replaced it face down in its original place. After a pause the whole procedure was repeated for the second trial, and so on for fifty trials. Whenever the serial number of a trial was called out, Shackleton wrote down E, G, L, P, or Z, according to whether he thought the agent was looking at the elephant, giraffe, lion, pelican, or zebra. The experimenter who was sitting with him checked that he wrote the letters on the correct lines of the record sheet. After each batch of fifty trials, the picture cards were turned over and their order was noted on the list of random digits, as a key to translate the digits into animals for scoring purposes. The cards were then shuffled and replaced face down for the next batch of trials, which used a new list of random digits. Eight batches of fifty trials were usually completed in a sitting.

The purpose of the complicated cipher system was to ensure that no one but the agent could know, except through ESP, which card was the target on each trial until the batch of trials was over. The experimenter who called out the trial numbers, in particular, could not know which cards the agent was looking at, and could not therefore give any deliberate or unintentional vocal cues that might help Shackleton to guess the target card.

The results were sensational. Shackleton obtained statistically significant scores with three of the thirteen agents with whom he was tested. His scores on the target cards were, on the whole, not significant, but with two of the agents his precognitive 'one-ahead' scores were significant, and with another both his precognitive and retrocognitive 'one-behind' scores were significant. The odds against chance were astronomical. With one of the agents, for example, Shackleton's score was 1101 precognitive hits out of 3879 trials. The number expected by chance, since on each trial one of five cards was the target, is obviously 3879/5, which is 776 hits. Simple statistical calculations confirm that the odds against getting a score as high as Shackleton's by chance alone are greater than 10^{35} to 1, that is, 100 million billion billion billion to one!

Critics of parapsychology often point out that if enough experimenters perform enough ESP experiments, the results are bound occasionally to be statistically significant purely by chance, because rare events *do* occur occasionally. Perhaps positive results reported by some investigators are counterbalanced by negative results obtained by others, but not reported because they are negative. But as Soal and Bateman commented with obvious pride some years later, if experiments like the Soal–Goldney series were repeated 'once every minute during the entire history of the earth ... it would still be fantastically improbable that results of the significance of those actually obtained could have been encountered by chance'.[32] Since Soal was a mathematician, we had better take his word for it.

In 1955 an extraordinary paper entitled 'Science and the Supernatural' by George Price, a medical researcher at the University of Minnesota, appeared in the influential American journal *Science*.[33] Price began by commenting that 'believers in psychic phenomena – such as telepathy, clairvoyance, precognition, and psychokinesis – appear to have won a decisive victory and virtually silenced the opposition'. The most impressive evidence, he said, was the Soal–Goldney series. 'I might select Rhine's work for discussion, but it apparently has not impressed critics nearly so much as Soal's.' He went on to describe the Soal–Goldney procedure in detail, and to argue that the results allow only two possible conclusions. The first – that Soal and Goldney had established the reality of ESP – he considered unlikely in the extreme. But the second – that they had been guilty of fraud, trickery, or deception – he admitted was unpleasant. He stopped short of an outright accusation of fraud: 'I am not stating here that Soal or any of his associates was guilty of deliberate fraud. All that I want to do is to show that fraud was easily possible.' Price described six possible methods of fraud that he himself might have used to duplicate the Soal–Goldney results. He concluded that the original Soal–Goldney experiments had *not* been conducted 'with every precaution that it was possible to devise', and he therefore remained sceptical about ESP. 'The only answer that will impress me is an adequate experiment. Not 100 experiments with 10 million trials and by 100 separate investigators giving total odds against chance of 10^{1000} to 1 – but just one good experiment.'

A later issue of the journal contained an outraged reply from Soal, together with comments from Rhine and others. Soal began his reply: 'I have read with some amazement the article "Science and the Supernatural" .... It is, I think, safe to say that no English scientific journal would have published such a diatribe of unsupported conjecture.'[34] He then went on to argue that none of Price's six methods of fraud could possibly explain his results. In a separate comment on Price's attack, Rhine suggested, with his tongue in his cheek, that 'Price deliberately undertook to sell parapsychology to American scientists by disguising a really informative article as a slanderous critique, with charges so utterly exaggerated that they would not be believed even by skeptics of ESP'.[35] Paul Meehl (a psychologist) and Michael Scriven (a philosopher of science) suggested that Price's 'allegations of fraud' were 'irresponsible because Price has not made any attempt to verify them'.[36] In the same issue of *Science*, Price replied to his critics: 'Rhine, Soal, and Meehl and Scriven all complain that it was improper of me to discuss the possibility of fraud. Naturally I did this with considerable reluctance, but it was absolutely essential that this question be treated frankly in order to settle things one way or the other.'[37]

It took twenty years to settle things one way or the other, and the process occurred in steps. First, Soal and Goldney revealed in 1960 that Gretl Albert, one of the three agents with whom Shackleton had scored above chance, had told Goldney at the time that she had seen Soal 'altering the figures' during one of the sessions.[38] This had not been mentioned in the original experimental report. In fact, Soal and Goldney's public revelation, nineteen years after the event, came only when a critic who had interviewed Gretl Albert threatened to publish an account of the matter himself.[39] Second, when Mark Hansel, a prominent British critic of ESP research, asked in 1956 to see the original score sheets of the experiments, on which chemical tests would, of course, reveal any tampering, Soal told him that they had been left on a train and lost in 1946.[40] But Soal and Bateman had declared in print in 1954 that the original records had been preserved and 'could be rechecked at any future time'.[41] By now the Soal–Goldney experiments were beginning to smell fishy. As one commentator pointed out, Soal was being harassed by two enemies, Hansel and Gretl.

The matter was finally resolved by the statistician Betty Markwick in 1978.[42] With the help of a computer, Markwick was able to show that several of the sequences of 'random' digits used in the Soal–Goldney experiments closely matched one another, apart from extra digits which seemed to be interpolated at regular intervals. She was then able to demonstrate that Soal manipulated his results by inserting extra 'dummy' digits into the random digit lists, later altering them to 4s or 5s, or leaving them as they were, depending on Shackleton's guesses, to secure target hits. Most of the phoney digits corresponded to target hits, and when these were taken out of the data, Shackleton's scoring fell to chance levels. Markwick's conclusion corresponds exactly to the recollections of the sharp-eyed Gretl Albert, who reported that she had seen Soal changing 1s to 4s and 5s in the random digit lists.

Nearly everyone now accepts that the Soal–Goldney experiments were fraudulent, though the actual method of fraud was different, and much more devious, than any of the six suggested by Price in 1955. At least one parapsychologist, however, was not convinced by Markwick's evidence that Soal cheated. According to Rhine's close associate Pratt, it is more likely that Soal 'used precognition when inserting digits in the columns of numbers he was copying down, unconsciously choosing numbers that would score hits on the calls the subject would later make'. You might think that Pratt's preposterous theory was intended as a joke; but it evidently was not, for he went on to say: 'For me, this "experimenter psi" explanation makes more sense, psychologically, than saying that Soal consciously falsified his own records.'[43]

The Pearce–Pratt experiments

Few experiments in parapsychology have received higher praise than Rhine's card-guessing experiments. His most respected series of experiments, which he quoted repeatedly in his later writings, was the Pearce–Pratt or 'campus distance' series conducted in 1933–4. Hubert Pearce, the star subject, was a theology student, and Joseph Gaither Pratt, the principal experimenter, was at the time Rhine's research assistant. The fullest account of the Pearce–Pratt series appeared in the *Journal of Parapsychology*.[44] Commenting on Rhine's work many years later, Hans Eysenck drew attention to 'a small number of cast-iron experiments which left no loopholes whatsoever. One of these highly impressive experiments was carried out on Hubert Pearce, one of Rhine's star subjects .... Dr Pratt ... carried out the experiment'.[45]

The procedure was straightforward. Before each session, Pearce and Pratt met in Pratt's office at Duke University, synchronized their watches, and agreed on a time to begin the experiment. Then Pearce left the office and walked across a quadrangle to the university library, about a hundred yards from Pratt's office, where he sat in a cubicle in the stacks. Pratt sat at his table with a pack of twenty-five ESP cards. After shuffling the cards, he placed each one face down in front of him for one full minute. After going through the whole pack, he paused for five minutes and then repeated the procedure with a second ESP pack. Meanwhile, in the cubicle in the library, Pearce recorded his (presumably clairvoyant) guesses as to the identity of the fifty cards. Up to that point, neither Pearce nor Pratt had seen the faces of the cards. At the end of the session, Pratt turned over both packs of cards and wrote down their order. He then made a duplicate of this record, which he sealed in an envelope and gave to Rhine. Pearce sealed a duplicate record of his guesses in another envelope which he also gave to Rhine. There were thirty-seven sessions in all, with very small variations in procedure.

Pearce's scores throughout were quite spectacular. Overall, he achieved 558 target hits, compared to a chance expectation of 370. The odds against achieving such a high score by chance alone can be shown by simple statistics to be greater than 10^{22} to 1, that is, 10,000 billion billion to one. A prudent punter would not be willing to bet that Pearce's results were a set of flukes.

In designing the experiment, Rhine introduced elaborate safeguards, which it would be tedious to list, to rule out the possibility of collusion between Pearce and Pratt. But there was one crucial control missing from the experiment: neither Rhine nor Pratt did anything to check that Pearce stayed in his cubicle during the experimental sessions. This glaring flaw formed the basis of a critique by the British psychologist Mark Hansel[46] who visited Duke University at Rhine's invitation in 1960.

Hansel pointed out that Pearce could have sneaked out of his cubicle at the end of each session, crossed the quadrangle, and hidden in a vacant room across the corridor from Pratt's office. There he could have stood on a chair and peeked through the fanlight at the top of the door, which would have given a clear view through a window connecting Pratt's office to the corridor, to get a glimpse of the cards while Pratt was making a record of their order. While Hansel was at Duke University he asked a researcher on Rhine's staff to run through a pack of ESP cards, following Pratt's procedure as closely as possible, while Hansel sat in an office down the corridor. Hansel reported: 'I slipped back ... and saw the cards by standing on a chair and looking through a crack at the top of the door. I had a clear view of them and obtained 22 hits in 25 attempts.'[47] The researcher had no idea how he had done it until Hansel told him. Hansel provided no material evidence to show that Pearce cheated in this way, but he claimed that the *possibility* of this and other forms of bias rendered the whole Pearce–Pratt series highly suspect:

One would expect that anyone in Pratt's position would have examined the room carefully and taken elaborate precautions to ensure that no one could see into it. At least he might have covered the windows leading to the corridor. Also, the cards should have been shuffled after they were recorded, and the door of the room might have been locked during and after the tests. These experiments were not a first-year exercise. They were intended to provide conclusive proof of ESP and to shake the very foundations of science. If Pratt had some misgivings, there is no evidence that he ever expressed them. He took no precautions to ensure that Pearce stayed in the library or to prevent the cards being visible to anyone looking into his room.[48]

Rhine and Pratt published a joint reply[49] to Hansel's critique when it first appeared. They commented on two important facts: first, that it was possible to see from Pratt's office window when Pearce entered and left the library; and second, that for some of the sessions Rhine himself was present as an observer in Pratt's office, 'for the purpose of scrutinizing the entire procedure from that point of vantage, to ensure that it was faithfully executed'. Hansel's reply to this was that 'what is important here is not whether Rhine could have seen Pearce leave the library if he had been watching for him, but whether he actually did see him leave at the termination of the experiment each day'. Hansel also pointed out that 'Rhine could not have been watching the window leading into the corridor to see that no one was looking in and at the same time have been looking through the window on the opposite wall to see Pearce leave the library.'[50]

In an essay review first published in the *New York Review of Books* in 1966, Martin Gardner told the following story:

The most sensational result ever obtained by Rhine occurred during the Depression when he kept offering Hubert Pearce, one of his star subjects, a hundred dollars for each top card he could call correctly in a pack of ESP cards. They halted the test by mutual consent after Pearce had correctly named twenty-five cards in a row .... (I once tried to get a few easily remembered details out of Pearce by correspondence – he is now a Methodist Minister in Arkansas – but he flatly refused to discuss the incident.) ... Rhine always cites this in his lectures as the most remarkable demonstration of clairvoyance he has ever witnessed, giving the odds of 298, 023, 223, 876, 953, 125 to 1 that it could have happened by chance.[51]

Gardner felt sorry for Pearce, because he was poor and needed the money, but when the test was over and he was owed $2500, Rhine said he had only been joking.

Pratt replied to Gardner's review by saying[52] that he had information that Pearce had received *two* letters from Gardner. Pearce had answered the first letter, explaining that he did not wish to write about his ESP work at Duke, and when Gardner's second letter arrived he simply did not reply. 'Under the circumstances', said Pratt, 'his failure to write again is hardly a flat refusal to discuss the matter. Yet in the review the omission is treated – could anyone fail to get the implication? – as a sign of a guilty conscience.' In response to this, Gardner[53] called attention to a cryptic passage in Rhine's book *New Frontiers of the Mind*, concerning a letter received by Pearce which so distressed him that he was never again able to demonstrate his ESP powers. 'A full report by the Reverend Hubert Pearce', commented Gardner, 'on his sensational, unrivaled ESP work when he was a student at Duke, would make a dramatic book. … Since scientific truth is also God's truth, it seems to me that such a report would serve both God and man. But my precognition tells me that Pearce will never write it.'

Pearce died in 1973, Pratt in 1979, and Rhine in 1980. We shall therefore never know many of the crucial details surrounding the now controversial Pearce–Pratt experiments. It is unlikely that anyone will prove conclusively that Pearce cheated. But since it is now clearly established that he *could* have cheated very easily, the Pearce–Pratt experiments cannot any longer be included among the 'cast-iron experiments which left no loophole whatsoever'.

Precognition in rodents

Rhine continued to publish research for several decades, but the results were never as spectacular as those of the Pearce–Pratt experiments. Over the years, Rhine introduced tighter and tighter controls in an effort to rule out fraud on the part of the subjects and also the experimenters. In 1974 he published a paper on 'Security Versus Deception in Parapsychology' in which he described twelve cases of fraud in his own laboratory 'to illustrate fairly typically the problem of experimenter unreliability prevalent in the 1940s and 1950s'.[54] Four of his experimenters were caught red-handed falsifying results, four tacitly admitted fraud when challenged, and in the remaining four cases 'the evidence was more circumstantial, but it seemed to our staff that they were in much the same doubtful category as the other eight'. Rhine described how this type of chicanery had been virtually eliminated since the 1960s by the implementation of rigorous security checks.

Among the most impressive results to emerge under these stringent controls were the findings of a series of nine experiments on precognition in rodents conducted by Walter Levy, the director on Rhine's laboratory. Commenting on Levy's experiments, the prominent British parapsychologist John Randall wrote in 1974: 'The fully automated experiments with mice and gerbils have been replicated sufficiently often and yielded such clearly significant results that we are now justified in claiming this phenomenon as one of the most firmly established in parapsychology.'[55] John Beloff gave special prominence to these experiments in his book *New Directions in Parapsychology* in 1974, commenting that 'in the light of … recent automated experiments using small mammals and other work of this kind, it looks as if we shall have to start thinking of psi as a universal property of animal life'.[56]

A few months after Rhine's paper on experimenter fraud appeared, the parapsychological world was rocked by a second paper by Rhine in the *Journal of Parapsychology*. 'When I wrote my paper on deception in the March issue of the *Journal*', Rhine said, 'I had not expected to come back to the subject again in publication. … Accordingly, I was shocked to discover, only a few months later, a clear example of this same problem, not only right here in the Institute for Parapsychology, but involving an able and respected colleague and trusted friend.'[57] The unnamed culprit was none other than Walter Levy. What had happened was as follows. A suspicious research assistant had hidden himself in the laboratory, and had spied on Levy tampering with the automated recording apparatus in one of his experiments on animal psi. After discussing with other members of the research team what he had seen, he secretly hooked up parallel recording apparatus, and this conclusively proved that Levy was manipulating the data to 'improve' the results. Without this 'improvement' the results were entirely nonsignificant. Rhine promptly fired Levy and warned parapsychologists that judgement should be suspended on all of Levy's published work. Unfortunately, Levy's work included most of the published experiments on precognition in rodents that yielded 'such clearly significant results' and were among 'the most firmly established in parapsychology'. The only other significant results in this area had been reported by two anonymous French researchers.

Psi Ganzfeld experiments

In the early 1970s several researchers began investigating the effects of sensory deprivation on ESP. The most promising technique was pioneered by Charles (Chuck) Honorton at the Dream Laboratory of the Maimonides Medical Center in New York.

Honorton's technique was based on a historical survey of reported psi experiences, including the ancient Indian *Yoga Sutras* of Patanjali, spontaneous psi reports collected by the British Society for Psychical Research in the nineteenth century, and memoirs of professional mediums and psychics. It appeared from these accounts that the optimal conditions for psi were those in which the subject was relaxed and attentive, but free of distractions from the external environment. In an effort to reproduce these conditions in the laboratory, Honorton borrowed the Ganzfeld (from the German *Ganz*, whole; *Feld*, field) technique of mild and relaxing sensory deprivation from research on visual perception. The subject lies on a mattress or a reclining chair with halved ping-pong balls covering both eyes, sealed around the edges with sticking plaster. A dim red light is directed on to the ping-pong balls, creating for the subject a uniform, featureless visual field. In ESP experiments the subject also wears headphones which emit continuous white noise – a random combination of sounds which resembles the hissing noise of a television receiver tuned off station.

In Honorton and Harper's original psi Ganzfeld experiment,[58] thirty volunteer subjects were used. Each subject was placed in the Ganzfeld while an agent in another room looked at a picture, trying to transmit its contents to the subject telepathically. The subjects gave running commentaries on their mental images, and these were tape-recorded and written down by an experimenter. The halved ping-pong balls and headphones were then removed, and each subject was presented with a set of four pictures, one of which was the target picture, and was asked to choose the one that most closely tallied with mental images experienced in the Ganzfeld. Obviously, since each subject had to choose one out of four pictures, 25 per cent of the choices were expected to be correct by chance. But Honorton and Harper's subjects made thirteen correct choices out of thirty, which is more than 43 per cent, or 18 per cent in excess of chance expectation. Statistical calculations show that the odds against getting so many hits by chance are about forty-five to one. (The odds are not 'around 60 to 1' as sometimes stated.)[59] The quality of the matches between the target pictures and the subjects' verbal commentaries in the Ganzfeld was in some cases quite phenomenal.

In an article entitled 'The Case for Parapsychology', Scott Rogo chose the Honorton–Harper psi Ganzfeld experiment as an example of parapsychology at its best,[60] and his opinion was shared by many other parapsychologists. By the beginning of 1982 this classic experiment had been replicated (with variations) more than forty times, and over half of these replications had reportedly generated statistically significant results. Chuck Honorton and Carl Sargent, Britain's leading psi Ganzfeld researcher, had carried out one-third of the experiments, but many other investigators had also reported significant results. Very few experiments had produced any evidence of 'psi missing' – scoring significantly *below* chance. Eysenck and Sargent concluded that 'this massive majority in favour of positive ESP effects suggests that we are dealing with a "lawful" phenomenon' and that, if sceptics are looking for a repeatable experiment, 'the nearest we get to this in parapsychology is probably the Ganzfeld/relaxation studies, where some 50–60 per cent of experiments do produce results well above chance'.[61]

In 1985 a critical review of the psi Ganzfeld experiments appeared in the *Journal of Parapsychology*.[62] The author was Ray Hyman, a psychologist at the University of Oregon. As a highly respected critic, he had been asked to review the whole field of parapsychology, but had decided instead to concentrate on a series of experiments that parapsychologists considered especially promising: 'I felt it would be fairer to try to assess the case for parapsychology at its best.'

Hyman first quesioned the way in which Honorton and other parapsychologists counted successful replications in order to arrive at the conclusion that more than half the replications were successful. One of the replications classified as successful, for example, involved two groups of subjects who each made six attempts to identify six different target pictures. Only one of the twelve sessions produced a statistically significant result. Instead of counting this as one successful and eleven unsuccessful replications, however, Honorton and others counted it as a single successful replication. On Hyman's re-count, the proportion of successful replications among the forty-two published reports dropped from 55 per cent to 30 per cent. Bearing in mind the fact that researchers tend to publish significant results but to discard nonsignificant results because they are less interesting, Hyman argued that the true percentage of successful replications was probably far below 30 per cent.

Hyman's second criticism was directed at the use of multiple criteria for scoring hits. In the first published replication of the Honorton–Harper experiment, for example, the subjects achieved only three direct hits out of ten. This was *not* statistically significant, yet parapsychologists invariably classify this as a successful replication. What is the explanation? The answer is that the investigators used *two* criteria for scoring hits. At the end of each session the subjects were presented with a set of six pictures, one of which was the target, and were asked to rank them from best to worst according to how well they matched their mental images during the Ganzfeld period. A direct hit was scored if the target was ranked top, but this only happened three times. A 'binary hit' (sometimes called a 'partial hit') was scored if the target was ranked in the top half, that is, if it was ranked first, second, or third by a subject. The chance expectation of a binary hit is, of course 50 per cent, but in this experiment all ten subjects scored binary hits, and this result (100 per cent) is statistically significant. Hyman found that more than half the replications used two or more criteria for scoring hits. The more criteria one uses, of course, the better one's chances of producing a 'significant' result. A result is conventionally considered to be statistically significant if the odds against chance are greater than nineteen to one. But Hyman estimated that, because of the use of multiple criteria for scoring hits, the psi Ganzfeld experiments were able to achieve apparent significance when the true odds against chance were only about three to one. In one 'successful' replication, Hyman estimated that the chances of coming up with at least one 'significant' result, given the multitude of indices that were used, were well over eight in ten. Putting all this together with his estimate that less than 30 per cent of the replications were even ostensibly successful, Hyman concluded this part of his critique: 'This rate of "successful" replication is probably very close to what should be expected by chance given the various options for multiple testing exhibited in this data base.'

Hyman also drew attention to a number of procedural flaws in the psi Ganzfeld experiments. Thirty-one of the forty-two experiments did not include proper randomization procedures for selecting target pictures and for arranging the sets of pictures given to the subjects for judging after the Ganzfeld sessions; in these experiments the subjects may have been able to guess which were the target pictures without ESP. In twenty-three experiments the original copy of the target picture, rather than a duplicate, was inserted into the set presented to the subjects. The agent may have handled it during the Ganzfeld session and intentionally or unintentionally marked it in some way, with a fingerprint or a smudge, for example. Such clues could, of course, have helped the subjects to guess which pictures were the targets. Twelve of the experiments contained errors in the statistical analysis of the results. Finally, several of the experimental reports omitted important details necessary for assessing the adequacy of the procedures used. Hyman commented as follows: 'The existence of so many elementary defects in this data base is both disturbing and surprising. Only two studies were entirely free of ... procedural flaws. And if we include multiple-testing errors, not a single study in this data base was flawless. It is important to realize that the defects being discussed are not obscure or subtle.'

Here is Hyman's final conclusion: 'The ganzfeld psi data base, despite initial impressions, is inadequate either to support the contention of a repeatable study or to demonstrate the reality of psi. ... Indeed, parapsychologists may be doing themselves and their cause a disservice by attempting to use these studies as examples of the current state of their field.'

Honorton wrote a detailed reply to Hyman's critical review.[63] He began by saying, 'I believe the existence of psi will remain in dispute until putative psi effects can be produced and studied with some specifiable degree of replicability. I am therefore primarily concerned with the extent to which the psi ganzfeld paradigm represents a step in that direction.'

The first problem that Honorton turned to was the use of multiple criteria for scoring hits. He acknowledged that 'a number of authors did use multiple tests or indices without applying suitable corrections', and he dealt with this criticism in two ways. First he re-analysed the data, applying a suitable statistical correction. If three separate criteria were used to count hits, for example, the results of the experiment were considered significant only if their probability of occurrence by chance was less than one in *sixty*, rather than the conventional one in twenty. With this type of correction, the proportion of statistically significant studies went down only slightly from twenty-three out of forty-two (55 per cent) to nineteen out of forty-two (45 per cent). Second, Honorton applied a uniform criterion of direct hits across all experiments in the data base for which this information was available. The twenty-eight experiments that provided data on direct hits were reported by investigators from ten different laboratories. Twelve of these experiments, or 43 per cent, were statistically significant, and their combined effect was far beyond chance expectation. Honorton commented: 'When a single test is used as a uniform index of success, the result indicates a strong and highly significant overall psi ganzfeld effect.'

Could these results be due to a selective bias on the part of researchers to report 'successful' replications and to discard 'unsuccessful' ones, as Hyman suggested? Honorton presented three arguments against this criticism. First, the Parapsychological Association Council is explicitly opposed to the selective reporting of positive results and, as a consequence, negative findings are routinely reported in parapsychological journals. In fact, many of the published psi Ganzfeld studies reported negative results. Second, Susan Blackmore had managed to locate nineteen *unpublished* psi Ganzfeld experiments and she had found that 'the bias introduced by selective reporting of ESP Ganzfeld studies is not a major contributor to the overall proportion of significant results'.[64]

Finally, Honorton calculated that 423 experiments with completely negative results would have to come to light to cancel out the overall statistical significance of the twenty-eight published experiments containing scores for direct hits. Assuming approximately one hour per trial, including instructions, judging, and so forth, he estimated that this would translate into one psi Ganzfeld session per hour for six years, working forty hours a week without vacations!

Turning to procedural flaws in the published experiments, Honorton was severely critical of Hyman's analysis. One experiment, for example, had been assigned four procedural flaws by Hyman. Honorton agreed with only one of these: the original copy of the target picture was included in the set given to the subject for judging after the Ganzfeld session. But Hyman also accused this experiment of improper randomization although, according to Honorton, 'ironically, it has one of the most complete descriptions of randomization using random number tables in the data base, one that is as complete as any that Hyman has acquitted of randomization flaws'. The other alleged procedural flaws were also highly debatable:

Whereas Hyman has charged this study with four procedural flaws, consistent application of his flaw criteria suggests that it should be charged with only one .... It is clear that Hyman's assignment of flaws is itself seriously flawed .... Hyman has been inconsistent in his assignment of flaws, with the effect of spuriously increasing the flaw count in some studies that appear to satisfy his stated criteria and decreasing the flaw count in other studies that fail his criteria.

Honorton concluded his reply by claiming that the existing evidence justified the conclusion that the psi Ganzfeld effect was established, and that the Ganzfeld technique was a positive step towards a repeatable ESP experiment.

In the light of the psi Ganzfeld debate, it seems to me that it would be premature to draw any firm conclusions about the phenomenon and its replicability. If these experiments do indeed constitute the strongest available evidence for ESP, as parapsychologists and others have claimed, then the reality of ESP is clearly highly debatable. One firm conclusion at least can be drawn: that the carelessness with which most of the experiments in this most vaunted area of psi research have been designed and executed is appalling, given that the results, if valid, would have the most stupendous significance for the whole structure of modern science.

Remote viewing experiments

In 1974 a paper entitled 'Information Transmission Under Conditions of Sensory Shielding' appeared in the influential scientific journal *Nature*.[65] It contained the first report by Russell Targ and Harold Puthoff, physicists at the Stanford Research Institute (now called SRI International) in California, of experiments on what they call remote viewing. They claimed to have ensured that 'all conventional paths of sensory input were blocked', and they 'took measures to prevent sensory leakage and to prevent deception, whether intentional or unintentional'. The results were hailed as a major breakthrough in psi research, not only by parapsychologists but also by news media on both sides of the Atlantic; Targ and Puthoff became international celebrities almost overnight.

The subject in the original remote viewing experiments was Pat Price, a former police commissioner. In each of the nine experiments, Price sat with an experimenter while two or more other experimenters visited a randomly chosen remote place within half an hour's drive of the laboratory. The target sites included a swimming pool, a nature reserve, a boat marina, a radio telescope, a church, and the Hoover tower. Price and the experimenter who stayed behind with him were not told which target site had been chosen. While the outside experimenters were at the target site, Price described his mental images into a tape recorder. The investigators used natural geographical targets rather than conventional ESP cards or other artificial objects on the assumption that large structures which had been in existence for a long time would be 'more potent targets for paranormal perception'.

Price showed an astonishing ability to describe buildings, roads, gardens, and other features of the target sites, sometimes in great detail, but his descriptions contained inaccuracies as well as correct statements. To obtain a numerical evaluation of accuracy, five judges who were otherwise unconnected with the experiments were asked to match the nine target sites, which they visited independently, with the nine typed transcripts of Price's narratives. The transcripts were unlabelled and presented in random order. Twenty-four of the forty-five matches made by the judges were correct; the most successful judge made seven correct matches out of nine. For six of the nine target sites, a majority of the judges – three or more – made the correct match. Targ and Puthoff calculated that the odds against chance were 2000 to 1.[66]

A critique of Targ and Puthoff's remote viewing experiments

appeared in *Nature* in 1978.[67] David Marks and Richard Kammann, psychologists at the University of Otago, New Zealand, based their criticisms on two important aspects of the experiments which were not mentioned in Targ and Puthoff's report. First, the judges were given a list of the target sites in the serial order in which they had been used in the remote viewing sessions. Second, the transcripts of Price's narratives, which Marks and Kammann managed to borrow from one of the judges, contained a large number of clues as to the serial order of the narratives. In one narrative, for example, Price expressed apprehension about his ability to do this kind of experiment; this provides a clue that the narrative belongs with the first target site. In a second narrative, reference is made to the fact that this is the 'second place of the day'; this means that it does not belong with the first target site, and together with clues in different narratives, it rules out certain other matchings. In a third narrative, mention is made of 'yesterday's two targets'; this provides further useful information to the judges. In a fourth, Price refers to the marina, which had been one of the target sites on the previous day; this tells the judges at least that the marina does not belong with the current narrative. In a fifth, the comment 'nothing like having three successes behind you' occurs; who could miss the implication that this is fourth in the series?

Using these and other clues in the narratives, together with a knowledge of the serial order of the target sites – information that was available to the judges in Targ and Puthoff's experiments – Marks found it as easy as psi to match five of the transcripts to the five corresponding target sites without error. (The remaining four transcripts and target sites were excluded from this exercise because they had already been published, and Marks might have known the correct pairings in advance.) He calls this process of matching by common sense and deductive logic 'remote judging'. It is worth noting that Marks never visited any of the target sites. He performed his feat 12,000 kilometres from the target sites, purely by intelligent reading of the available clues.

Marks and Kammann repeated the Targ–Puthoff experiments, taking care to remove all clues from the transcripts and to conceal the serial order of the target sites and transcripts from the judges. Under these conditions the results were entirely negative – the judges were unable to match the narratives to the target sites better than chance. Marks and Kammann concluded: 'Our investigation of the ... remote viewing experiments forces the conclusion that the successful identification of target sites by judges is impossible unless multiple extraneous cues which were available in the original unedited transcripts are used.'

In 1980 *Nature* published a rejoinder to Marks and Kammann's critique by Charles Tart, Harold Puthoff, and Russell Targ.[68] Tart, a highly regarded parapsychologist at the University of California, Davis, had agreed to re-analyse the original transcripts of Price's narratives 'to test the validity of the Marks–Kammann hypothesis' that the judges' correct matches could be explained by clues in the narratives. Tart 'edited the transcripts carefully, removing all phrases suggested as potential cues by Marks and Kammann, and removing any additional phrases for which even the most remote *post hoc* cue argument could be made'. The laundered transcripts were then given, in random order, to a new independent judge who was unfamiliar with the original experiment. A list of the target sites, in a different random order, was also given to the new judge, who visited the target sites and then tried to match them to the transcripts. 'The results of the blind matching of transcripts to target sites ... was that seven of the nine were again correctly matched.' The odds against such accurate matching by chance were calculated to be more than 10,000 to 1.

Tart and company also commented that the Marks–Kammann critique had not addressed the quality of Price's descriptions of the target sites. When the target site was a boat marina, Price's narrative began: 'What I'm looking at is a little boat jetty or a boat dock along the bay.' When the target site was the Hoover tower, Price said: 'The area – I have a place – seems like it would be the Hoover Tower.' Whatever the shortcomings of the judging procedure, the transcripts themselves seem to contain remarkable evidence of ESP. Tart and company conclude that 'the data continue to confirm the original conclusion that remote viewing is a viable human perceptual capability'.

Marks replied to these comments in 1981.[69] According to Marks, Tart's rejudging exercise was open to criticism on two grounds. First, since Tart was himself aware of the correct target–transcript pairings, his procedure was vulnerable to bias. Second, it was not permissible to include previously published material in the rejudging process as Tart had done, because the judge might have had access to the published information as to the correct matches. A more serious problem, on which Marks did not comment, is the impossibility of verifying that Tart succeeded in removing all clues from the transcripts, because the expurgated versions were not published. Marks's final comments were these: 'The Targ–Puthoff researches conform to a long history in parapsychology of methodological flaws and mistaken conclusions. Unless proper controls and methods are used by impartial observers, the search for scientific proof of paranormal and spiritual beliefs remains a futile enterprise.' The edited and unedited transcripts were finally released by Puthoff in 1986. When Marks examined them,[70] he found that 'Tart failed to remove a number of potentially useful cues', including (for example) Price's apprehension about not being able to do this kind of experiment, which he voiced at the beginning of the very first session. Marks commented that 'Tart's failure to perform this basic task seems beyond comprehension'.

Puthoff and Targ's last contribution to the debate in *Nature* appeared in 1981.[71] 'In order to give the Marks' [*sic*] hypothesis its best chance' Puthoff and Targ performed an analysis in which they assumed that all of the clues available in the original experiment had been used by the judges to maximum advantage. Their analysis suggested that for one of the targets the chance probability of a correct target–transcript match was increased from one-ninth to one-third; for a second target it was increased from one-ninth to one-seventh; and for two other targets it was increased from one-ninth to one-eighth. In the remaining five cases there were no clues that gave any direct advantage to the judges in matching targets and transcripts. Puthoff and Targ calculated that the odds against chance in the judges' original matchings, assuming that they had used all available clues to maximum advantage, were still greater than 2500 to 1. 'Thus the Marks hypothesis that the presence of extraneous cues accounts for the significance of the Price series results receives no support.'

Unfortunately, there is no way of checking Puthoff and Targ's analysis, because they did not specify how they calculated the advantage to a judge of each of the available clues. In fact, their conclusion is difficult to reconcile with the fact that Marks was able to match five of the transcripts to their correct targets by using these clues, which Puthoff and Targ said were of relatively little help to the original judges. And subsequent evidence published by Marks in 1986 (which I mentioned earlier) suggests that Puthoff and Targ ignored many of the clues that were present in the transcripts, in spite of their protestations to the contrary.

Several remote viewing experiments have been reported since the original Targ–Puthoff experiment.[72] Some of these replications were well designed and free of the obvious methodological flaws that Marks and Kammann found in the original series, but none of these experiments produced significant results. In the absence of clues that enable the judges to match the transcripts to the target sites by common sense and logic, the remote viewing effect simply disappears and the results fall to chance levels. Other replications have reported significant results, but all of these experiments, many of which were conducted by Targ and Puthoff or by their close associates, were vitiated by serious methodological flaws which reduce their evidential value. The only reasonable conclusion seems to be that experiments on remote viewing have not provided any persuasive evidence for ESP.

ESP: errors surely present?

In 1957 Hans Eysenck wrote:

Unless there is a gigantic conspiracy involving some thirty University departments all over the world, and several hundred highly respected scientists in various fields, most of them originally sceptical to the claims of the psychical researchers, the only conclusion that the unbiased observer can come to must be that there does exist a small number of people who obtain knowledge existing in other people's minds, or in the outer world, by means as yet unknown to science.[73]

In 1982 Eysenck and Sargent repeated these remarks and added: 'The only revision necessary now would be that the number of people involved is larger than it was then!'[74]

Readers should by now be able to spot at least three inaccuracies in Eysenck's remarks, and I shall also point out a fourth. First, no one disputes that *all* people (and some other animals too) obtain knowledge by means as yet unknown to science – the means by which children acquire knowledge of language, for example, are certainly not adequately explained. What is in dispute is the claim that people can *perceive* objects or events *without sensory contact*; 'extra-sensory perception' means literally perception without sensation, and that is how it is defined by the *Journal of Parapsychology*. Second, the history of parapsychology is disfigured by numerous cases of fraud involving some of the most 'highly respected scientists', their research associates, and their subjects. The following remark by Eysenck and Sargent is disingenuous: 'Sceptics point with glee to the one established case of fraud by a *researcher* in parapsychology (in 1974: he worked on psi in animals).'[75] Eysenck and Sargent are evidently alluding coyly to the Levy affair; but what about Soal? And what about the twelve cases of fraud by researchers that Rhine uncovered in his own laboratory? In fact fraud has been a recurrent leitmotiv of parapsychology, but this does not force us to postulate a 'gigantic conspiracy' theory any more than the history of murder forces us to believe in a gigantic conspiracy among the world's killers. Third, misleading conclusions can arise from errors committed in good faith without any intention to deceive. Some of the most highly regarded experiments in parapsychology have turned out, on closer inspection, to contain serious methodological flaws which destroy their evidential value. Fourth, the claim that 'most' parapsychologists were 'originally sceptical' is highly debatable. My own impression is that sceptics seldom get involved in parapsychology, and surveys have confirmed that very few parapsychologists are sceptical. On the contrary, true believers often develop doubts after becoming involved in parapsychological research – Susan Blackmore, Antony Flew, Chris Scott, and John Taylor spring to mind. The sad fact is that after a century of parapsychological research no one has produced a single piece of evidence that impresses the sceptics, still less an experiment that reliably yields positive results when it is repeated by independent researchers.

In 1980 James Randi, a professional magician and Fellow of the Committee for the Scientific Investigation of Claims of the Paranormal (CSICOP, pronounced sigh-cop), launched an audacious research project to test the quality of parapsychological research in the United States.[76] Project Alpha, as it was called, focused chiefly on the newly established McDonnell Laboratory for Psychical Research at Washington University, which was funded by a grant from the chairman of the McDonnell-Douglas Aircraft Company. Randi recruited two young amateur conjurers, Steve Shaw and Michael Edwards, and encouraged them to present themselves to the McDonnell researchers as psychics capable of psychokinetic metal bending (PKMB) and other paranormal feats. They agreed that if they were ever asked directly by an experimenter how they performed their exploits, they would immediately admit that they used conjuring tricks.

For more than two years Shaw and Edwards demonstrated spoon-bending, telepathy, and a host of other seemingly paranormal phenomena to the apparent satisfaction of the McDonnell researchers, who described them as 'gifted psychic subjects'. Simple tricks, performed under conditions involving scandalously inadequate controls, were written up as successful experiments. In one ESP experiment, for example, Edwards was left alone with a 'sealed' envelope containing the target picture. The envelope's seal turned out to be a few staples, which Edwards was able to remove and replace (after peeking at the target picture, of course) without leaving any visible traces of tampering. A problem arose when he lost one of the staples, but he was able to improvise by offering to open the envelope himself – which the experimenter naively allowed him to do! On another occasion the 'gifted psychics' complained of 'bad vibes' from the electronic equipment in the laboratory, whereupon the experimenters obligingly reduced the video surveillance and correspondingly increased the scope for 'paranormal' happenings.

Before Shaw and Edwards presented themselves at the McDonnell laboratory, Randi wrote to its director listing eleven security controls designed to minimize trickery in parapsychological experiments, and he even offered to attend the testing sessions as a consultant at his own expense, but all his warnings were ignored and he was never invited.

Shaw and Edwards were also examined by researchers unconnected with the McDonnell laboratory. One of these independent researchers, a psychiatrist with a long-standing interest in parapsychology, found an unexplained 'swirl' on an eight-millimetre film which Shaw had shot. In it he discovered moving faces, a portrait of Jesus, a UFO, a woman's torso, a nipple, a breast, a thigh, and a baby being born. In fact, Shaw had produced these photographic miracles simply by spitting on the camera lens. When Project Alpha was abandoned in 1983 and the true story was revealed, another independent researcher who had tested Shaw and Edwards could not bring himself to believe that he had been duped. He asked a reporter, 'How do these kids *know* they're fakes?'

The moral of Project Alpha is clear. The phenomena studied by parapsychologists are, by definition, so extraordinary that extraordinarily strong evidence is required to establish their existence. Competent researchers therefore have a responsibility to ensure that their subjects do not cheat. If the necessary controls are neglected, then their experiments are worthless. There are signs that Project Alpha galvanized some researchers into improving their security controls, and the McDonnell laboratory was closed soon after the findings were revealed.

The scientific evidence for psi is much weaker than most people realize. Why do so many people none the less believe in ESP? Grossly misleading popular books, articles, and television programmes are no doubt partly to blame. A related reason is that many people apparently *want* to believe in ESP, partly because they think that 'normal' science is boring and unmysterious. (Readers of this book will know that I do not find 'normal' psychology boring or unmysterious.) In 1985 Susan Blackmore and Tom Troscianko of the University of Bristol suggested a third, less obvious, reason for people's belief in psi.[77] A random postal survey revealed that most believers were convinced that they had actually experienced paranormal phenomena at first hand. What convinced them that they had experienced these things? There are two possibilities: either they had indeed experienced paranormal phenomena, or they had interpreted normal events as paranormal. Blackmore and Troscianko investigated the second possibility in three experiments. Their results showed that believers (sheep) made more errors than disbelievers (goats) in tasks involving judgements of probability. One of the questions was this: 'How many people would you need to have at a party to have a 50:50 chance that two of them would have the same birthday (not counting year)?' Subjects had to choose one of the following possible answers: 22, 43, 98. The correct answer[78] is 22. Blackmore and Troscianko found that sheep gave significantly fewer correct answers than goats to questions like this which depend on judgements of probability; this suggests that belief in psi may arise from misjudgements of probability. They also found that sheep were more likely than goats to believe that they had exercised control over a computer simulation of coin-tossing, even when the computer had in fact operated perfectly randomly. This seemed to be due to the fact that sheep greatly underestimated the number of hits expected by chance: they believed that they had influenced the computer because they thought (wrongly) that it had exceeded the chance baseline. A person who consistently underestimates the effects of chance is likely to seek additional – perhaps paranormal – explanations for events such as coincidences that are in fact purely random. According to Blackmore and Troscianko, 'in this way errors in judgements of probability might underlie both the illusion of control and belief in psi'.

The possibility remains that some people believe in paranormal phenomena because they have experienced such things at first hand. Although there appears to be no persuasive scientific evidence for telepathy, clairvoyance, precognition, psychokinesis, or any other parapsychological phenomenon, it is only fair to point out that none of these things has been conclusively disproved either. The history of science is peppered with examples of important facts that were initially rejected or even considered impossible. Galileo, one of the greatest scientific thinkers of the seventeenth century, was scornful of Kepler's belief in astrology – the supposed influence of the stars and planets on human lives – but his scepticism extended to Kepler's belief in the influence of the moon on ocean tides, which Galileo regarded as similar moonshine. Around the turn of the century the American scientist Simon Newcomb stated flatly that a heavier-than-air flying machine was a physical impossibility. And in 1933 Ernest Rutherford, the pioneer of nuclear physics, laughed to scorn the suggestion that people might some day be able to make practical use of nuclear energy. The dogmatic asseverations of Galileo, Newcomb, and Rutherford were all overturned by science.

The belief of many contemporary psychologists that ESP is impossible may also be overturned one day. The nineteenth-century French philosopher Auguste Comte, arguing that there are facts that must forever remain beyond the reach of science, cited as a prime example the 'obvious impossibility' of ever determining the chemical composition of the stars. Within a few years astronomers had developed a method (stellar spectroscopy) of doing precisely what Comte had declared impossible. Parapsychologists may one day also confound their critics by producing persuasive evidence for ESP. Nothing is impossible; even the efficacy of taghairm – a method of divination defined by *Chambers Twentieth Century Dictionary* as 'inspiration sought by lying in a bullock's hide behind a waterfall' – may one day be established by science. But I, for one, will not put money on it.

Notes

1 The McConnel case was first reported in the *Journal of the Society for Psychical Research*, July 1919 (Vol. 19, No. 357, pp. 76–83). A full account appeared in Sidgwick (1922), pp. 152–60. The case was thoroughly re-examined by McCreery (1967), pp. 17–27.

2 McCreery (1967), p. 18 fn.

3 Freud (1922), p. 410.

4 Hume (1948/1902), Section 10, 'Of Miracles'. The quotation in the text is from paragraph 86.

5 Mackie (1982), ch. 1, contains the most detailed recent commentary on Hume's argument.

6 Beloff (1962), p. 217, italics in original.

7 Eysenck and Sargent (1982), p. 10. Eysenck is described on the jacket of this book as 'Britain's leading social scientist', and Sargent as 'a member of the Parapsychological Association ... widely regarded as an authority on the paranormal'.

8 Brown (1975), pp. 547–56.

9 ibid. pp. 572–5. Rhine (1951) considered such forms of animal behaviour to be probably paranormal.

10 Blaustein and O'Hara (1986).

11 Beloff (1980).

12 Herodotus (*c.* 429 BC/1972), pp. 58–60. The quotations in the text are from p. 58 of the 1972 edition.

13 Rhine (1934). A book by Pagentescher entitled *Aussersinnlicher Wahrnemung*, which means 'extra-sensory perception' in German, was published in 1924, so Rhine's coinage was not really novel.

14 ibid.
15 Frazier (1983).
16 Frazier (1981).
17 These surveys are reviewed in Alcock (1981), pp. 24–37.
18 These remarks were made by R. A. McConnell in a symposium on ESP. They were quoted in Wolstenholme and Millar (1956), p. 51.
19 Schmeidler and McConnell (1958).
20 Rhine and Pratt (1957).
21 Beloff (1962), p. 251. Beloff calls the Soal–Goldney experiments 'the Shackleton–Soal series'.
22 Beloff (1974), p. 8.
23 Randall (1974), p. 85.
24 Quoted in Alcock (1981), p. 139.
25 Rogo (1977).
26 Eysenck and Sargent (1982), pp. 81 and 182–3.
27 Soal and Goldney (1943).
28 Broad (1944), p. 261.
29 Hutchinson (1948), p. 291.
30 Lyons (1965), p. 205.
31 Rhine (1947), p. 168.
32 Soal and Bateman (1954), p. 311.
33 Price (1955).
34 Soal (1956), p. 9.
35 Rhine (1956), p. 11.
36 Meehl and Scriven (1956), p. 15.
37 Price (1956), p. 18.
38 Soal and Goldney (1960).
39 Scott and Haskell (1973). The critic who interviewed Gretl Albert was Christopher Scott.
40 Hansel (1980), p. 155.
41 Soal and Bateman (1954), pp. 346–7.
42 Markwick (1978).
43 Pratt's comment can be found in the *Proceeding of the Society for Psychical Research* immediately after Markwick's paper. It is quoted in Gardner (1981), p. 231.
44 Rhine and Pratt (1954).
45 Eysenck (1957), pp. 130–1.
46 Hansel (1961). See also Hansel (1980), ch. 10.
47 Hansel (1980), p. 116.
48 Hansel (1980), p. 117.
49 Rhine and Pratt (1961).
50 Hansel (1980), p. 118.
51 The article was first published in 1966. It is reprinted in Gardner (1981), pp. 217–22. The quotation in the text is from p. 218 of the 1981 reprint.
52 Pratt's reply is reprinted in Gardner (1981), p. 223.
53 Gardner (1981), p. 228.
54 Rhine (1974a), p. 104.
55 Randall (1974), p. 92.
56 Beloff (1974), p. 6.
57 Rhine (1974b), p. 215.
58 Honorton and Harper (1974).
59 Eysenck and Sargent (1982), p. 80.

60 Rogo (1977).
61 Eysenck and Sargent (1982), pp. 81, 182.
62 Hyman (1985). The quotations in the text are, in order, from pp. 2, 25, 29, and 38.
63 Honorton (1985). The quotations in the text, apart from the quotation from Blackmore which is separately noted, are, in order, from pp. 52, 56, 59, 79, and 80.
64 Blackmore (1980), pp. 217–18.
65 Targ and Puthoff (1974). The quotations in the text are from pp. 602 and 605.
66 There is a distinct tinge of the supernatural about some of their other statistics; see Hansel (1980), p. 292, where an elementary error is pointed out.
67 Marks and Kammann (1978). The quotation in the text is from p. 681.
68 Tart, Puthoff, and Targ (1980).
69 Marks (1981).
70 Marks and Scott (1986).
71 Puthoff and Targ (1981).
72 Critical reviews of these experiments have been given by Marks (1982) and Hyman (1984/85).
73 Eysenck (1957), p. 131.
74 Eysenck and Sargent (1982), p. 182.
75 ibid.
76 Randi (1983a, 1983b). My account is based mainly on these two papers.
77 Blackmore and Troscianko (1985). Quotations in the text are from pp. 468 and 466.
78 The probability that 22 people chosen at random have 22 *different* birthdays is (365/365) (364/365) ... (344/365) = $\frac{1}{2}$ approximately. For an explanation of the logic behind this, see Colman (1988), ch. 5.

References

Abraham, S. (1979). *Weight and Height of Adults 18–74 Years of Age, 1971–74*. Hyattsville, MD: US Department of Health, Education and Welfare.

Alcock, J. E. (1981). *Parapsychology: Science or Magic? A Psychological Perspective*. Oxford: Pergamon.

American Psychiatric Association. (1980). *Diagnostic and Statistical Manual of Mental Disorders* (3rd ed.). Washington, DC: Author.

Arendt, H. (1963). *Eichmann in Jerusalem: A Report on the Banality of Evil*. New York: Viking Press.

Aronson, E. (1980). *The Social Animal* (3rd ed.). San Francisco: W. H. Freeman.

Ashby, B., Morrison, A., & Butcher, H. J. (1970). The abilities and attainment of immigrant children. *Research in Education*, **4**, 73–80.

Askevold, F. (1975). Measuring body image: Preliminary report on a new method. *Psychotherapy and Psychosomatics*, **26**, 71–77.

Balthazard, C. G. & Woody, E. Z. (1985). The 'stuff' of hypnotic performance: A review of psychometric approaches. *Psychological Bulletin*, **98**, 283–296.

Barber, T. X. (1965a). Measuring 'hypnotic-like' susceptibility with and without 'hypnotic induction': Psychometric properties, norms, and variables influencing response to the Barber Suggestibility Scale (BSS). *Psychological Reports*, **16**, 809–844.

Barber, T. X. (1965b). Physiological effects of 'hypnotic' suggestions: A critical review of recent research (1960–64). *Psychological Bulletin*, **63**, 201–222.

Barber, T. X. (1969). *Hypnosis: A Scientific Approach*. New York: Van Nostrand Reinhold.

Barber, T. X. (1972). Suggested ('hypnotic') behavior: The trance paradigm versus an alternative paradigm. In E. Fromm & R. E. Shor (Eds), *Hypnosis: Research Developments and Perspectives* (pp. 115–182). Chicago: Aldine.

Barber, T. X. (1979). Suggested ('hypnotic') behavior: The trance paradigm versus an alternative paradigm. In E. Fromm & R. E. Shor (Eds), *Hypnosis: Developments in Research and New Perspectives* (pp. 217–271). Chicago: Aldine.

Barber, T. X. (1986). Realities of stage hypnosis. In B. Zilbergeld, M. G. Edelstien, & D. L. Araoz (Eds), *Hypnosis: Questions and Answers* (pp. 22–30). New York: W. W. Norton.

Barber, T. X. & Calverley, D. S. (1964). Experimental studies in 'hypnotic' behavior: Suggested deafness evaluated by delayed auditory feedback. *British Journal of Psychology*, **55**, 439–466.

Barber, T. X. & Hahn, K. W. Jr. (1962). Physiological and subjective responses to pain producing stimulation under hypnotically-suggested and waking-imagined 'analgesia'. *Journal of Abnormal and Social Psychology*, **65**, 411–418.

Baumrind, D. (1964). Some thoughts on ethics of research: After reading Milgram's 'Behavioral Study of Obedience'. *American Psychologist*, **19**, 421–423.

Baumrind, D. (1965). *Further Thoughts on Ethics After Reading Milgram's 'A Reply to Baumrind'*. Unpublished manuscript, University of California, Berkeley. [Summarized in A. G. Miller (Ed.), *The Social Psychology of Psychological Research* (p. 80). New York: Free Press, 1972.]

Baumrind, D. (1971). Principles of ethical conduct in the treatment of subjects. *American Psychologist*, **26**, 887–890.

Beloff, J. (1962). *The Existence of Mind*. London: MacGibbon & Kee.

Beloff, J. (Ed.). (1974). *New Directions in Parapsychology*. London: Elk Science.

Beloff, J. (1980). Could there be a physical explanation for psi? *Journal of the Society for Psychical Research*, **50**, 263–272.

Binet, A. (1909). *Les Idées modernes sur les Enfants*. Paris: Flammarion.

Binswanger, L. (1944–5). Der Fall Ellen West. *Schweizer Archiv für Neurologie und Psychiatrie*, **53**, 255–277; **54**, 69–117; **55**, 16–40.

Blackmore, S. (1980). The extent of selective reporting of ESP Ganzfeld studies. *European Journal of Parapsychology*, **3**, 213–219.

Blackmore, S. & Troscianko, T. (1985). Belief in the paranormal: Probability judgements, illusory control, and the 'chance baseline shift'. *British Journal of Psychology*, **76**, 459–468.

Blau, Z. S. (1981). *Black Children/White Children: Competence, Socialization, and Social Structure*. New York: Free Press.

Blaustein, A. R. & O'Hara, R. K. (1986). Kin recognition in tadpoles. *Scientific American*, January, **254**(1), 90–96.

Bodmer, W. F. (1972). Race and IQ: The genetic background. In K. Richardson & D. Spears (Eds), *Race, Culture and Intelligence* (pp. 83–113). Harmondsworth: Penguin.

Bodmer, W. F. & Cavalli-Sforza, L. L. (1970). Intelligence and race. *Scientific American*, October, **223**(10), 19–29.

Boring, E. G. (1957). *A History of Experimental Psychology* (2nd ed.). New York: Appleton-Century-Crofts.

Bowers, K. S. (1967). The effects of demands for honesty on reports of visual and auditory hallucinations. *International Journal of Clinical and Experimental Hypnosis*, **15**, 31–36.

Bowers, K. S. (1976). *Hypnosis for the Seriously Curious*. Monterey, CA: Brooks/Cole.

Bowers, K. S. & Meulen, S. van der. (1972). *A Comparison of Psychological and Chemical Techniques in the Control of Dental Pain*. Paper delivered at the Society for Clinical and Experimental Hypnosis Convention, Boston. [Summarized in Bowers (1976), pp. 27–28.]

Braid, J. (1843). *Neurypnology; or The Rationale of Nervous Sleep considered in relation with Animal Magnetism*. London: John Churchill.

Broad, C. D. (1944). Discussion: The experimental establishment of telepathic precognition. *Philosophy*, **19**, 261–275.

Brown, J. L. (1975). *The Evolution of Behavior*. New York: W. W. Norton.

Brown, R. (1965). *Social Psychology*. New York: Free Press.

Bruch, H. (1962). Perceptual and conceptual disturbances in anorexia nervosa. *Psychological Medicine*, **24**, 187–194.

Bruch, H. (1973). *Eating Disorders: Obesity, Anorexia Nervosa, and the Person Within*. New York: Basic Books.

Burks, B. S. (1928). The relative influence of nature and nurture upon mental development: A comparative study of foster parent–foster child resemblance and true parent–true child resemblance. *Yearbook of the National Society for the Study of Education* (Part 1), **27**, 219–316.

Buros, O. K. (Ed.). (1953). *The Fourth Mental Measurements Yearbook*. Highland Park, NJ: Gryphon Press.

Buros, O. K. (Ed.). (1959). *The Fifth Mental Measurements Yearbook*. Highland Park, NJ: Gryphon Press.

Buros, O. K. (Ed.). (1974). *Tests in Print* (Vol. 2). Highland Park, NJ: Gryphon Press.

Burt, C. (1955). The evidence for the concept of intelligence. *British Journal of Educational Psychology*, **25**, 158–177.

Burt, C. (1958). The inheritance of mental ability. *American Psychologist*, **13**, 1–15.

Burt, C. (1966). The genetic determination of differences in intelligence: A study of monozygotic twins reared together and apart. *British Journal of Psychology*, **57**, 137–153.

Button, E. J., Fransella, F., & Slade, P. D. (1977). A reappraisal of body perception disturbance in anorexia nervosa. *Psychological Medicine*, **7**, 235–243.

Carroll, B. J., Feinberg, M., Greden, J. F., Tarika, J., Albaia, A. A., Haskett, R. F., James, N. M., Kronfol, Z., Lohr, N., Steiner, M.,

De Vigne, J. P., & Young, E. (1981). A specific laboratory test for the diagnosis of melancholia: Standardization, validation, and clinical utility. *Archives of General Psychiatry*, **38**, 15–22.

Casper, R. C., Halmi, K. A., Goldberg, S. C., Eckert, E. D., & Davis, J. M. (1979). Disturbances in body image estimation as related to other characteristics and outcome in anorexia nervosa. *British Journal of Psychiatry*, **134**, 60–66.

Centerwall, B. S. (1978). Comment: The use of racial admixture as evidence in intelligence research: A critique. *Human Genetics*, **45**, 237–238.

Colman, A. M. (1972). 'Scientific' racism and the evidence on race and intelligence. *Race*, **14**, 137–153.

Colman, A. M. (1981). *What is Psychology?* London: Unwin Hyman.

Colman, A. M. (1983). Attitudes of British police officers: A rejoinder. *Sociology*, **17**, 388–391.

Colman, A. M. & Gorman, L. P. (1982). Conservatism, dogmatism, and authoritarianism in British police officers. *Sociology*, **16**, 1–11.

Cooper, P. J. & Fairburn, C. G. (1983a). Are eating disorders forms of affective disorder [Letter to the editor]? *British Journal of Psychiatry*, **143**, 96–97.

Cooper, P. J. & Fairburn, C. G. (1983b). Binge-eating and self-induced vomiting in the community: A preliminary study. *British Journal of Psychiatry*, **142**, 139–144.

Cooper, P. J. & Fairburn, C. G. (1986). The depressive symptoms of bulimia nervosa. *British Journal of Psychiatry*, **148**, 268–274.

Crawford, T. J. (1972). In defense of obedience research: An extension of the Kelman ethic. In A. G. Miller (Ed.), *The Social Psychology of Psychological Research* (pp. 179–186). New York: Free Press.

Crisp, A. H. & Kalucy, R. S. (1974). Aspects of perceptual disorder in anorexia nervosa. *British Journal of Medical Psychology*, **47**, 349–361.

Crisp, A. H., Palmer, R. L., & Kalucy, R. S. (1976). How common is anorexia nervosa? A prevalence study. *British Journal of Psychiatry*, **128**, 549–554.

Dewdney, A. K. (1986). Computer recreations: How a pair of dull-witted programs can look like geniuses on I.Q. tests. *Scientific American*, March, **254**(3), 10–13.

Dicks, H. V. (1972). *Licensed Mass Murder: A Socio-Psychological Study of Some S.S. Killers*. New York: Basic Books.

Edmonston, W. E. Jr. (1986). *The Induction of Hypnosis*. New York: Wiley.

Ellenberger, H. F. (1970). *The Discovery of the Unconscious: The*

History and Evolution of Dynamic Psychiatry. New York: Basic Books.

Elms, A. (1972). *Social Psychology and Social Relevance.* Boston: Little Brown.

Elms, A. & Milgram, S. (1966). Personality characteristics associated with obedience and defiance toward authoritative command. *Journal of Experimental Research in Personality,* **2**, 282–289.

Embree, E. R. (1931). *Brown America: The Story of a New Race.* New York: Viking.

Erickson, M. (1968). The inhumanity of ordinary people. *International Journal of Psychiatry,* **6**, 277–279.

Erlenmeyer-Kimling, L. & Jarvik, L. F. (1963). Genetics and intelligence: A review. *Science,* **142**, 1477–1479.

Etzioni, A. (1968). A model of scientific research. *International Journal of Psychiatry,* **6**, 279–280.

Ewin, D. M. (1986). Hypnosis and pain management. In B. Zilbergeld, M. G. Edelstien, & D. L. Araoz (Eds), *Hypnosis: Questions and Answers* (pp. 282–288). New York: W. W. Norton.

Eyferth, K. (1961). Leistungen verschiedener Gruppen von Besatzungskindern in Hamburg: Wechsler Intelligenztest für Kinder (HAWIK). *Archiv für die gesamte Psychologie,* **113**, 223–241.

Eysenck, H. J. (1957). *Sense and Nonsense in Psychology.* Harmondsworth: Penguin.

Eysenck, H. J. (1966). *Check Your Own I.Q.* Harmondsworth: Penguin.

Eysenck, H. J. (1971). *Race, Intelligence and Education.* London: Temple Smith.

Eysenck, H. J. (1973). *The Inequality of Man.* London: Temple Smith.

Eysenck, H. J. & Kamin, L. J. (1981). *Intelligence: The Battle for the Mind.* London: Macmillan.

Eysenck, H. J. & Sargent, C. (1982). *Explaining the Unexplained: Mysteries of the Paranormal.* London: Weidenfeld & Nicolson.

Fairburn, C. G. (1982). *Binge-eating and Bulimia Nervosa.* Welwyn Garden City: Smith Kline & French Publications. Vol. 1 No. 4.

Fairburn, C. G. (1983). Eating disorders. In R. E. Kendall & A. K. Zealley (Eds), *Companion to Psychiatric Studies* (3rd ed., pp. 535–547). Edinburgh: Churchill Livingstone.

Fairburn, C. G. (1985). The management of bulimia nervosa. *Journal of Psychiatric Research,* **19**, 465–472.

Fairburn, C. G. & Cooper, P. J. (1982). Self-induced vomiting and bulimia nervosa: An undetected problem. *British Medical Journal,* **284**, 1153–1155.

Fancher, R. E. (1985). *The Intelligence Men: Makers of the IQ*

Controversy. New York: W. W. Norton.

Farber, S. (1980). *Identical Twins Reared Apart: A Reanalysis*. New York: Basic Books.

Farina, A., Holland, C. H., & Ring, K. (1966). Role of stigma and set in interpersonal interaction. *Journal of Abnormal and Social Psychology*, **71**, 421–428.

Feldman, M. W. & Lewontin, R. C. (1975). The heritability hangup. *Science*, **190**, 1163–1168.

Fellows, B. J. (1985). Hypnosis teaching and research in British psychology departments: Current practice, attitudes and concerns. *British Journal of Experimental and Clinical Hypnosis*, **2**, 151–155.

Fisher, S. (1954). The role of expectancy in the performance of posthypnotic behavior. *Journal of Abnormal and Social Psychology*, **49**, 503–507.

Flynn, J. R. (1980). *Race, IQ and Jensen*. London: Routledge & Kegan Paul.

Frazier, K. (1981). Profiles of parapsychologists: Their beliefs and concerns. *Skeptical Inquirer*, **5**(4), 2–6.

Frazier, K. (1983). Survey of AAAS scientific 'elite': High skepticism toward ESP. *Skeptical Inquirer*, **7**(4), 2–4.

Freud, S. (1922). Dreams and telepathy. In S. Freud, *Collected Papers* (Vol. 4, pp. 408–435, C. J. M. Hubback, Trans.). London: Hogarth.

Friedrichs, R. W. (1973). The impact of social factors upon scientific judgment: 'The 'Jensen thesis' as appraised by members of the American Psychological Association. *Journal of Negro Education*, **42**, 182–186.

Fries, H. (1977). Studies on secondary amenorrhea, anorectic behavior and body image perception: Importance for the early recognition of anorexia nervosa. In R. A. Vigersky (Ed.), *Anorexia Nervosa* (pp. 163–176). New York: Raven Press.

Fromm, E. (1974). *The Anatomy of Human Destructiveness*. London: Jonathan Cape.

Fulker, D. W. (1975). Review of *The Science and Politics of I.Q.* by L. J. Kamin. *American Journal of Psychology*, **88**, 505–519.

Galton, F. (1869). *Hereditary Genius: An Inquiry Into its Laws and Consequences* (2nd ed., 1892, reprinted 1978). London: Julian Friedmann.

Gardner, M. (1981). *Science: Good, Bad and Bogus*. Buffalo, NY: Prometheus.

Garfinkel, P. E. & Garner, D. M. (1982). *Anorexia Nervosa: A Multidimensional Approach*. New York: Basic Books.

Garfinkel, P. E., Moldofsky, H., Garner, D. M., Stancer, H. C., &

Coscina, D.V. (1978). Body awareness in anorexia nervosa: Disturbances in body image and satiety. *Psychosomatic Medicine*, **40**, 487–498.

Garner, D. M. & Garfinkel, P. E. (1979). The Eating Attitudes Test: An index of the symptoms of anorexia nervosa. *Psychological Medicine*, **9**, 273–279.

Garner, D. M., Garfinkel, P. E., Schwartz, D., & Thompson, M.(1980). Cultural expectation of thinness in women. *Psychological Reports*, **47**, 483–491.

Garner, D. M., Garfinkel, P. E., Stancer, H. C., & Moldofsky, H. (1976). Body image disturbances in anorexia nervosa and obesity. *Psychosomatic Medicine*, **38**, 227–336.

Garrow, J. S. (1979). Weight penalties. *British Medical Journal*, **2**, 1171–1172.

Garrow, J. S. (1983). Indices of adiposity. *Nutrition Abstracts & Reviews of Clinical Nutrition* (Series A), **53**, 697–708.

Gerner, R. H. & Gwirtsman, H. E. (1981). Abnormalities of dexamethasone suppression test and urinary MPHG in anorexia nervosa. *American Journal of Psychiatry*, **138**, 650–653.

Gidro-Frank, L. & Bowersbuch, M. K. (1948). A study of the plantar response in hypnotic age regression. *Journal of Nervous and Mental Disease*, **107**, 443–458.

Glucksman, M. L. & Hirsch, J. (1969). The response of obese patients to weight reduction, III: The perception of body size. *Psychosomatic Medicine*, **31**, 1–7.

Goddard, H. H. (1920). *Human Efficiency and Levels of Intelligence*. Princeton, NJ: Princeton University Press.

Goldberg, S. C., Halmi, K. A., Casper, R. C., Eckert, E. D., & Davis, J. M. (1977). Pretreatment predictors of weight change in anorexia nervosa. In R. A. Vigersky (Ed.), *Anorexia Nervosa* (pp. 31–42). New York: Raven Press.

Goldbourt, U. & Medalie, J. (1974). Weight height indices. *British Journal of Preventive and Social Medicine*, **28**, 116–126.

Gould, S. J. (1981). *The Mismeasure of Man*. New York: W. W. Norton.

Gull, W. W. (1874). Anorexia nervosa (apepsia hysterica, anorexia hysterica). *Transactions of the Clinical Society, London*, **7**, 22–28.

Halmi, K. A., Goldberg, S. C., & Cunningham, S. (1977). Perceptual distortion and body image in adolescent girls: Distortion of body image in adolescence. *Psychological Medicine*, **7**, 253–257.

Hansel, C. E. M. (1961). A critical analysis of the Pearce-Pratt experiment. *Journal of Parapsychology*, **25**, 87–91.

Hansel, C. E. M. (1980). *ESP and Parapsychology: A Critical*

Reevaluation. Buffalo, NY: Prometheus.

Hausner, G. (1967). *Justice in Jerusalem*. London: Nelson.

Hearnshaw, L. S. (1979). *Cyril Burt: Psychologist*. London: Hodder & Stoughton.

Henderson, N. (1982). Human behavior genetics. *Annual Review of Psychology*, **33**, 403–440.

Herodotus. (*c.* 429 B.C./1972). *The Histories* (Trans. A. De Sélincourt). Harmondsworth: Penguin.

Hilgard, E. R. (1964). The motivational relevance of hypnosis. *Nebraska Symposium on Motivation*, **12**, 1–46. Lincoln, NB: University of Nebraska Press.

Hilgard, E. R. (1965). Hypnosis. *Annual Review of Psychology*, **16**, 157–180.

Hilgard, E. R. (1968). *The Experience of Hypnosis*. New York: Harcourt, Brace & World.

Hilgard, E. R. (1969). Pain as a puzzle for psychology and physiology. *American Psychologist*, **24**, 103–113.

Hilgard, E. R. (1972). A critique of Johnson, Maher, and Barber's 'Artifact in the essence of hypnosis: An evaluation of trance logic,' with a recomputation of their findings. *Journal of Abnormal Psychology*, **79**, 221–233.

Hilgard, E. R. (1973). A neodissociation interpretation of pain reduction in hypnosis. *Psychological Review*, **80**, 396–411.

Hilgard, E. R. (1975). Hypnosis. *Annual Review of Psychology*, **26**, 19–44.

Hilgard, E. R. (1979). Divided consciousness in hypnosis: The implications of the hidden observer. In E. Fromm & R. E. Shor (Eds), *Hypnosis: Developments in Research and New Perspectives* (pp. 45–79). New York: Aldine.

Hilgard, E. R. & Hilgard, J. R. (1983). *Hypnosis and the Relief of Pain* (rev. ed.). Los Altos, CA: Kaufmann.

Hilgard, E. R., Hilgard, J. R., Macdonald, H., Morgan, A. H., & Johnson, L. S. (1978). Covert pain in hypnotic analgesia: Its reality as tested by the real-simulator design. *Journal of Abnormal Psychology*, **87**, 655–663.

Hilgard, J. R. & LeBaron, S. (1984). *Hypnosis in the Treatment of Pain and Anxiety in Children with Cancer: A Clinical and Quantitative Analysis*. Los Altos, CA: Kaufmann.

Hoffmann, B. (1962). *The Tyranny of Testing*. New York: Crowell-Collier.

Hofling, C. K., Brotzman, E., Dalrymple, S., Graves, N., & Pierce, C. M. (1966). An experimental study in nurse–physician relationships. *Journal of Nervous and Mental Disease*, **143**, 171–180.

Honorton, C. (1985). Meta-analysis of psi Ganzfeld research: A response to Hyman. *Journal of Parapsychology,* **49**, 51–91.

Honorton, C. & Harper, S. (1974). Psi-mediated imagery and ideation in an experimental procedure for regulating perceptual input. *Journal of the American Society for Psychical Research,* **68**, 156–168.

Horn, J. M., Loehlin, J. C., & Willerman, L. (1979). Intellectual resemblance among adoptive and biological relatives: The Texas Adoption Project. *Behavior Genetics,* **9**, 177–207.

Hovland, C. I. & Sears, R. R. (1940). Minor studies in aggression: VI. Correlations of lynchings with economic indices. *Journal of Psychology,* **9**, 301–310.

Howells, J. G. & Osborn, M. L. (1984). *A Reference Companion to the History of Abnormal Psychology.* Westport, CT: Greenwood Press.

Hudson, J. I., Laffer, P. S., & Pope, H. G. Jr. (1982a). Bulimia related to affective disorder by family history and response to the dexamethasone suppression test. *American Journal of Psychiatry,* **139**, 685–687.

Hudson, J. I., Laffer, P. S., & Pope, H. G. Jr. (1982b). Dr Hudson and associates reply [Letter to the editor]. *American Journal of Psychiatry,* **139**, 1524.

Hudson, J. I., Pope, H. G. Jr, Jonas, J. M., & Yurgelun-Todd, D. (1983). Family history study of anorexia nervosa and bulimia. *British Journal of Psychiatry,* **142**, 133–138.

Hull, C. L. (1933). *Hypnosis and Suggestibility: An Experimental Approach.* New York: Appleton-Century-Crofts.

Hume, D. (1748/1902). *Enquiry concerning Human Understanding* (L. A. Selby–Bigge, Ed.). Oxford: Oxford University Press.

Hutchinson, G. E. (1948). Marginalia. *American Scientist,* **26**, 291.

Hyman, R. (1984/85). Outracing the evidence: The muddled 'Mind Race'. *Skeptical Inquirer,* **9**, 125–145.

Hyman, R. (1985). The Ganzfeld psi experiments: A critical appraisal. *Journal of Parapsychology,* **49**, 3–49.

Jensen, A. R. (1969). How much can we boost IQ and scholastic achievement? *Harvard Educational Review,* **39**, 1–123.

Jensen, A. R. (1970). Race and the genetics of intelligence. *Bulletin of the Atomic Scientists.* Reprinted in N. Block & G. Dworkin (Eds), *The IQ Controversy* (pp. 93–106). London: Quartet, 1977.

Jensen, A. R. (1972). *Genetics and Education.* London: Methuen.

Jensen, A. R. (1973a). *Educability and Group Differences.* London: Methuen.

Jensen, A. R. (1973b). *Educational Differences.* London: Methuen.

Jensen, A. R. (1980). *Bias in Mental Testing.* London: Methuen.

Jensen, A. R. (1981). *Straight Talk About Mental Tests.* London:

Methuen.

Johnson, R. F. Q. (1972). Trance logic revisited: A reply to Hilgard's critique. *Journal of Abnormal Psychology*, **79**, 234–238.

Johnson, R. F. Q., Maher, B. A., & Barber, T. X. (1972). Artifact in the 'essence of hypnosis': An evaluation of trance logic. *Journal of Abnormal Psychology*, **79**, 212–220.

Juel-Nielsen, N. (1965). Individual and environment: A psychiatric–psychological investigation of monozygous twins reared apart. *Acta Psychiatrica et Neurologica Scandanavica*, Monograph Supplement 183.

Kamin, L. J. (1974). *The Science and Politics of I.Q.* Harmondsworth: Penguin.

Kamin, L. J. (1977a). Comment on Munsinger's adoption study. *Behavior Genetics*, **7**, 403–406.

Kamin, L. J. (1977b). A reply to Munsinger. *Behavior Genetics*, **7**, 411–412.

Kelman, H. C. (1967). Human use of human subjects: The problem of deception in social psychological experiments. *Psychological Bulletin*, **67**, 1–11.

Kendell, R. E. (1983). Affective psychoses. In R. E. Kendell & A. K. Zealley (Eds), *Companion to Psychiatric Studies* (3rd ed., pp. 297–318). Edinburgh: Churchill Livingstone.

Kihlstrom, J. F. (1985). Hypnosis. *Annual Review of Psychology*, **36**, 385–418.

Kilham, W. & Mann, L. (1974). Level of destructive obedience as a function of transmitter and executant roles in the Milgram obedience paradigm. *Journal of Personality and Social Psychology*, **29**, 696–702.

Knight, I. (1984). *The Heights and Weights of Adults in Great Britain*. London: Her Majesty's Stationery Office.

Knight, S. (1976). *Jack the Ripper: The Final Solution*. London: Harrap.

Knox, V. J., Morgan, A. H., & Hilgard, E. R. (1974). Pain and suffering in ischemia: The paradox of hypnotically suggested anesthesia as contradicted by reports from the 'hidden observer'. *Archives of General Psychiatry*, **30**, 840–847.

Kudirka, N. K. (1965). *Defiance of Authority Under Peer Influence*. Unpublished doctoral dissertation, Yale University.

Leahy, A. M. (1935). Nature–nurture and intelligence. *Genetic Psychology Monographs*, **17**, 235–308.

Lewontin, R. C. (1970a). Race and intelligence. *Bulletin of the Atomic Scientists*. [Reprinted in N. Block & G. Dworkin (Eds), *The IQ Controversy* (pp. 78–92). London: Quartet, 1977.]

Lewontin, R. C. (1970b). Further remarks on race and intelligence. *Bulletin of the Atomic Scientists.* [Reprinted in N. Block & G. Dworkin (Eds), *The IQ Controversy* (pp. 107–112). London: Quartet, 1977.]

Lewontin, R. C. (1975). Genetic aspects of intelligence. *Annual Review of Genetics,* **9**, 387–405.

Lindgren, H. C. & Harvey, J. H. (1981). *An Introduction to Social Psychology.* St Louis: Mosby.

Loehlin, J. C., Lindzey, G., & Spuhler, J. N. (1975). *Race Differences in Intelligence.* San Francisco: W. H. Freeman.

Lyons, J. (1965). *A Primer of Experimental Psychology.* New York: Harper & Row.

McCay, A. R. (1963). Dental extraction under self-hypnosis. *Medical Journal of Australia,* June 1, 820–822. [Quoted in Hilgard (1968), p. 127.]

McCreery, C. (1967). *Science, Philosophy and ESP.* London: Hamish Hamilton.

Mackenzie, B. (1984). Explaining race differences in IQ: The logic, the methodology, and the evidence. *American Psychologist,* **39**, 1214–1233.

Mackie, J. L. (1982). *The Miracle of Theism: Arguments For and Against the Existence of God.* Oxford: Clarendon.

Mackintosh, N. J. (1975). Critical notice: Kamin, L. J., *The Science and Politics of I.Q. Quarterly Journal of Experimental Psychology,* **27**, 672–686.

Mackintosh, N. J. (1980). Review of *Cyril Burt: Psychologist* by L. S. Hearnshaw. *British Journal of Psychology,* **71**, 174–175.

Mackintosh, N. J. (1986). The biology of intelligence? *British Journal of Psychology,* **77**, 1–18.

Mackintosh, N. J. & Mascie-Taylor, C. G. N. (1985). The IQ question. In *Report of Committee of Inquiry into the Education of Children from Ethnic Minority Groups* (pp. 126–163). London: Her Majesty's Stationery Office.

Mantell, D. M. (1971). The potential for violence in Germany. *Journal of Social Issues,* **27**, 101–112.

Marks, D. F. (1981). Sensory cues invalidate remote viewing experiments. *Nature,* **292**, 177.

Marks, D. F. (1982). Remote viewing revisited. *Skeptical Inquirer,* **6**(4), 18–29.

Marks, D. F. & Kammann, R. (1978). Information transmission in remote viewing experiments. *Nature,* **274**, 680–681.

Marks, D. F. & Scott, C. (1986). Remote viewing exposed. *Nature,* **319**, 444.

Markwick, B. (1978). The Soal–Goldney experiments with Basil Shackleton: New evidence of data manipulation. *Proceedings of the Society for Psychical Research*, **56**, 250–277.

Masserman, J. (1968). Debatable conclusions. *International Journal of Psychiatry*, **6**, 281–282.

May, R., Angel, E., & Ellenberger, H. F. (1958). *Existence: A New Dimension in Psychiatry and Psychology*. New York: Basic Books.

Mayr, E. (1968). Biological aspects of race in man: Discussion. In M. Mead, T. Dobzhansky, E. Tobach, & R. E. Light (Eds), *Science and the Concept of Race* (pp. 103–108). New York: Columbia University Press.

Meehl, P. E. & Scriven, M. (1956). Compatibility of science and ESP. *Science*, **123**, 14–15.

Meeker, W. B. & Barber, T. X. (1971). Toward an explanation of stage hypnosis. *Journal of Abnormal Psychology*, **77**, 61–70.

Mercer, J. R. & Brown, W. C. (1973). Race differences in IQ: Fact or artifact? In C. Senna (Ed.), *The Fallacy of IQ* (pp. 56–113). New York: The Third Press-Joseph Okpaku.

Milgram, S. (1963). Behavioral study of obedience. *Journal of Abnormal and Social Psychology*, **67**, 371–378.

Milgram, S. (1964). Issues in the study of obedience: A reply to Baumrind. *American Psychologist*, **19**, 848–852.

Milgram, S. (1965). Some conditions of obedience and disobedience to authority. *Human Relations*, **18**, 57–76.

Milgram, S. (1968). Reply to critics. *International Journal of Psychiatry*, **6**, 294–295.

Milgram, S. (1972). Interpreting obedience: Error and evidence. In A. G. Miller (Ed.), *The Social Psychology of Psychological Research* (pp. 138–154). New York: Free Press.

Milgram, S. (1974). *Obedience to Authority: An Experimental View*. New York: Harper & Row.

Minton, H. L. & Schneider, F. W. (1980). *Differential Psychology*. Monterey, CA: Brooks/Cole.

Morton, R. (1694). *Phthisiologia: Or a Treatise of Consumptions*. London: Sam. Smith and Benj. Walford.

Munsinger, H. (1975). Children's resemblance to their biological and adopting parents in two ethnic groups. *Behavior Genetics*, **5**, 239–254.

Munsinger, H. (1977a). A reply to Kamin. *Behavior Genetics*, **7**, 407–409.

Munsinger, H. (1977b). The identical-twin transfusion syndrome: A source of error in estimating IQ resemblance and heritability. *Annals of Human Genetics*, **40**, 307–321.

Newman, H. H., Freeman, F. N., & Holzinger, K. J. (1937). *Twins: A Study of Heredity and Environment.* Chicago: University of Chicago Press.

Nogrady, H., McConkey, K. M., Laurence, J.-R., & Perry, C. (1983). Dissociation, duality, and demand characteristics in hypnosis. *Journal of Abnormal Psychology,* **92,** 223–235.

Orne, M. T. (1959). The nature of hypnosis: Artifact and essence. *Journal of Abnormal and Social Psychology,* **58,** 277–299.

Orne, M. T. & Holland, C. C. (1968). On the ecological validity of laboratory deceptions. *International Journal of Psychiatry,* **6,** 282–293.

Orne, M. T., Sheehan, P. W., & Evans, F. J. (1968). Occurrence of posthypnotic behavior outside the experimental setting. *Journal of Personality and Social Psychology,* **9,** 189–196.

Palmer, F. H. & Anderson, L. W. (1979). Long-term gains from early intervention: Findings from longitudinal studies. In E. Zigler & J. Valentine (Eds), *Project Head Start: A Legacy of the War on Poverty.* New York: Free Press.

Palmer, R. L. (1980). *Anorexia Nervosa: A Guide for Sufferers and their Families.* Harmondsworth: Penguin.

Paul, D. B. (1985). Textbook treatments of the genetics of intelligence. *Quarterly Review of Biology,* **60,** 317–326.

Perry, C., Laurence, J.-R., Nadon, R., & Labelle, L. (1986). Past lives regression. In B. Zilbergeld, M. G. Edelstien, & D. L. Araoz (Eds), *Hypnosis: Questions and Answers* (pp. 50–61). New York: W. W. Norton.

Pettigrew, T. F. (1964). *A Profile of the Negro American.* Princeton, NJ: Van Nostrand.

Price, G. R. (1955). Science and the supernatural. *Science,* **122,** 359–367.

Price, G. R. (1956). Where is the definitive experiment? *Science,* **123,** 17–18.

Puthoff, H. E. & Targ, R. (1981). Rebuttal of criticisms of remote viewing experiments. *Nature,* **292,** 388.

Pyle, R. L., Mitchell, J. E., & Eckert, E. D. (1981). Bulimia: A report of 34 cases. *Journal of Clinical Psychiatry,* **42,** 60–64.

Pyle, R. L., Mitchell, J. E., Eckert, E. D., Halvorson, P. A., Neuman, P. A., & Goff, G. M. (1983). The incidence of bulimia in freshman college students. *International Journal of Eating Disorders,* **2,** 75–85.

Randall, J. (1974). Biological aspects of psi. In J. Beloff (Ed.), *New Directions in Parapsychology* (pp. 77–94). London: Elk Science.

Randi, J. (1983a). The Project Alpha experiment: Part 1. The first two years. *Skeptical Inquirer,* **7**(4), 24–33.

Randi, J. (1983b). The Project Alpha experiment: Beyond the

laboratory. *Skeptical Inquirer*, **8**(1), 36–45.

Rao, D. C., Morton, N. E., & Yee, S. (1976). Resolution of cultural and biological inheritance by path analysis. *American Journal of Human Genetics*, **28**, 228–242.

Record, R. G., McKeown, T., & Edwards, J. H. (1970). An investigation of the difference in measured intelligence between twins and single births. *Annals of Human Genetics*, **34**, 11–20.

Reed, T. E. (1969). Caucasian genes in American Negroes. *Science*, **165**, 762–768.

Reitman, E. E. & Cleveland, S. E. (1964). Changes in body image following sensory deprivation in schizophrenic and control groups. *Journal of Abnormal and Social Psychology*, **68**, 168–176.

Report of Consultative Committee on Secondary Education. (1938). London: His Majesty's Stationery Office.

Rhine, J. B. (1934). *Extrasensory Perception*. Boston, MA: Bruce Humphries.

Rhine, J. B. (1947). *The Reach of Mind*. New York: Sloane.

Rhine, J. B. (1951). The present outlook on the question of psi in animals. *Journal of Parapsychology*, **15**, 230–251.

Rhine, J. B. (1956). Comments on 'Science and the Supernatural'. *Science*, **123**, 11–14.

Rhine, J. B. (1974a). Security versus deception in parapsychology. *Journal of Parapsychology*, **38**, 99–121.

Rhine, J. B. (1974b). A new case of experimenter unreliability. *Journal of Parapsychology*, **38**, 215–225.

Rhine, J. B. & Pratt, J. G. (1954). A review of the Pearce–Pratt distance series of ESP tests. *Journal of Parapsychology*, **18**, 165–177.

Rhine, J. B. & Pratt, J. G. (1957). *Parapsychology: Frontier Science of the Mind*. Springfield, IL: Charles C. Thomas.

Rhine, J. B. & Pratt, J. G. (1961). A reply to Hansel's critique of the Pearce–Pratt series. *Journal of Parapsychology*, **25**, 93–94.

Ring, K., Wallston, K., & Corey, M. (1970). Mode of debriefing as a factor affecting subjective reaction to a Milgram-type obedience experiment: An ethical inquiry. *Representative Research in Social Psychology*, **1**, 67–88.

Robinson, J. (1965). *And the Crooked Shall Be Made Straight*. New York: Macmillan.

Rochas, A. de (1911). *Les Vies Successives: Documents pour l'Etude de cette Question*. Paris: Chacornac.

Rogo, D. S. (1977). The case for parapsychology. *The Humanist*, November/December, **37**, 40–44.

Rose, S., Kamin, L. J., & Lewontin, R. C. (1984). *Not In Our Genes: Biology, Ideology and Human Nature*. Harmondsworth: Penguin.

Rosenhan, D. L. (1969). Some origins of concern for others. In P. H. Mussen, J. Langer, & M. Covington (Eds.), *Trends and Issues in Developmental Psychology* (pp. 134–153). New York: Holt, Rinehart & Winston.

Rotton, J. & Kelly, I. W. (1985). Much ado about the full moon: A meta-analysis of lunar–lunacy research. *Psychological Bulletin*, **97**, 286–306.

Rumbelow, D. (1975). *The Complete Jack the Ripper*. London: W. H. Allen.

Russell, G. F. M. (1970). Anorexia nervosa: Its identity as an illness and its treatment. In J. H. Price (Ed.), *Modern Trends in Psychological Medicine, 2* (pp. 131–164). London: Butterworths.

Russell, G. F. M. (1979). Bulimia nervosa: An ominous variant of anorexia nervosa. *Psychological Medicine*, **9**, 429–448.

Russell, G. F. M., Campbell, P. G., & Slade, P. D. (1975). Experimental studies on the nature of the psychological disorder in anorexia nervosa. *Psychoneuroendocrinology*, **1**, 45–56.

Russell, Lord. (1962). *The Trial of Adolf Eichmann*. London: Heinemann.

Ryan, J. (1972). IQ: The illusion of objectivity. In K. Richardson & D. Spears (Eds), *Race, Culture and Intelligence* (pp. 36–55). Harmondsworth: Penguin.

Sabine, E. J., Yonace, A., Farrington, A. J., Barratt, K. H., & Wakeling, A. (1983). Bulimia nervosa: A placebo controlled double-blind therapeutic trial of mainserin. *British Journal of Clinical Pharmacology*, **15**, 195S–202S.

Samelson, F. (1977). World War I intelligence testing and the development of psychology, *Journal of the History of the Behavioral Sciences*, **13**, 274–282.

Samelson, F. (1979). Putting psychology on the map: Ideology and intelligence testing. In A. R. Buss (Ed.), *Psychology in Social Context* (pp. 103–141). New York: Irvington.

Sarbin, T. R. & Anderson, M. L. (1963). Base-rate expectancies and perceptual alterations in hypnosis. *British Journal of Social and Clinical Psychology*, **2**, 112–121.

Scarman, Lord. (1981). *The Brixton Disorders 10–12 April 1981*. London: Her Majesty's Stationery Office.

Scarr, S. (1981). *Race, Social Class, and Individual Differences in IQ*. Hillside, NJ: Lawrence Erlbaum.

Scarr, S., Pakstis, A. J., Katz, S. H., & Barker, W. B. (1977). Absence of a relationship between degree of white ancestry and intellectual skills within a black population. *Human Genetics*, **39**, 69–86.

Scarr, S., Pakstis, A. J., Katz, S. H., & Barker, W. B. (1979). Reply to

Centerwall. *Human Genetics*, **47**, 225–226.

Scarr, S. & Weinberg, R. A. (1976). IQ test performance of black children adopted by white families. *American Psychologist*, **31**, 726–739.

Scarr, S. & Weinberg, R. A. (1977). Intellectual similarities within families of both adopted and biological children. *Intelligence*, **1**, 170–191.

Schmeidler, G. R. & McConnell, R. A. (1958). *ESP and Personality Patterns*. Westport, CT: Greenwood Press.

Scott, C. & Haskell, P. (1973). 'Normal' explanation of the Soal–Goldney experiments in extra-sensory perception. *Nature*, **245**, 52–54.

Sharma, R. (1971). Unpublished PhD thesis. [Cited in Mackintosh & Mascie-Taylor (1985) and Mackintosh (1986).]

Sheehan, H. L. & Summers, V. K. (1949). Syndrome of hypopituitarism. *Quarterly Journal of Medicine*, **18**, 319–378.

Sheridan, C. L. & King, R. G. (1972). Obedience to authority with an authentic victim [Summary]. *Proceedings of the 80th Annual Convention of the American Psychological Association*, **7**, 165–166.

Shields, J. (1962). *Monozygotic Twins Brought Up Apart and Brought Up Together*. Oxford: Oxford University Press.

Shockley, W. (1972). The apple-of-God's-eye obsession. *Humanist*, **32**, 16–17. [Cited in Taylor (1980), p. 3.]

Shor, R. E. & Orne, M. T. (Eds.) (1965). *The Nature of Hypnosis: Selected Basic Readings*. New York: Holt, Rinehart & Winston.

Shuey, A. M. (1966). *The Testing of Negro Intelligence* (2nd ed.). New York: Social Sciences Press.

Sidgwick, H. (1922). An examination and analysis of cases of telepathy between living persons printed in the 'Journal' of the Society since the publication of the book 'Phantasms of the Living' by Gurney, Myers and Podmore, in 1886. *Proceedings of the Society for Psychical Research*, **33**, 152–160.

Simmonds, M. (1914). Über Hypophysisschwund mit todlichem Ausgang. *Deutsche Medizinische Wochenschrift*, **40**, 332–340.

Skodak, M. & Skeels, H. M. (1949). A final follow-up study of one hundred adopted children. *Journal of Genetic Psychology*, **75**, 85–125.

Slade, D. D. & Russell, G. F. M. (1973). Awareness of body dimensions in anorexia nervosa: Cross-sectional and longitudinal studies. *Psychological Medicine*, **3**, 188–199.

Snow, C. P. (1961). Either-or. *Progressive*, February, p. 24.

Snyderman, M. & Herrnstein, R. J. (1983). Intelligence tests and the Immigration Act of 1924. *American Psychologist*, **38**, 986–995.

Soal, S. G. (1956). On 'Science and the Supernatural'. *Science*, **123**,

9–11.

Soal, S. G. & Bateman, F. (1954). *Modern Experiments in Telepathy*. London: Faber.

Soal, S. G. & Goldney, K. M. (1943). Experiments in precognitive telepathy. *Proceedings of the Society for Psychical Research, 47*, 21–150.

Soal, S. G. & Goldney, K. M. (1960). The Shackleton report. *Journal of the Society for Psychical Research, 40*, 378.

Sours, J. A. (1980). *Starving to Death in a Sea of Objects: The Anorexia Nervosa Syndrome*. New York: A. Jason Aronson.

Spanos, N. P. & Barber, T. X. (1968). 'Hypnotic' experiences as inferred from subjective reports: Auditory and visual hallucinations. *Journal of Experimental Research in Personality, 3*, 136–150.

Spiegel, Der. (1985). Schrei aus dem Tiefe des Bauches. 8 April, No. 15, pp. 36–56.

Stern, J. A., Brown, M., Ulett, G. A., & Selten, I. (1977). A comparison of hypnosis, acupuncture, morphine, valium, aspirin, and placebo in the management of experimentally induced pain. *Annals of the New York Academy of Science, 296*(1), 175–193.

Stern, S. L. Dixon, K. N. Nemzer, E., Lake, M. D., Sansone, R. A., Smeltzer, D. J., Lantz, S., & Schrier, S. S. (1984). Affective disorder in the families of women with normal weight bulimia. *American Journal of Psychiatry, 141*, 1224–1227.

Stone, M. H. (1973). Child psychiatry before the twentieth century. *International Journal of Child Psychotherapy, 2*, 264–308.

Sutcliffe, J. P. (1960). 'Credulous' and 'sceptical' views of hypnotic phenomena: A review of certain evidence and methodology. *International Journal of Clinical and Experimental Hypnosis, 8*, 73–101.

Sutcliffe, J. P. (1961). 'Credulous' and 'sceptical' views of hypnotic phenomena: Experiments on esthesia, hallucination, and delusion. *Journal of Abnormal and Social Psychology, 62*, 189–200.

Swift, W. J., Andrews, D., & Barklage, N. E. (1986). The relationship between affective disorder and eating disorders: A review of the literature. *American Journal of Psychiatry, 143*, 290–299.

Szasz, T. (1970). *Ideology and Insanity: Essays on the Psychiatric Dehumanization of Man*. New York: Doubleday.

Targ, R. & Puthoff, H. E. (1974). Information transmission under conditions of sensory shielding. *Nature, 251*, 602–607.

Tart, C. T. (1983). Parapsychology. In R. Harré & R. Lamb (Eds), *The Encyclopedic Dictionary of Psychology* (pp. 444–445). Oxford: Blackwell.

Tart, C. T., Puthoff, H. E., & Targ, R. (1980). Information transmission in remote viewing experiments. *Nature, 284*, 191.

Taylor, H. F. (1980). *The IQ Game: A Methodological Inquiry into the Heredity-Environment Controversy*. Brighton: Harvester.

Terman, L. M. (1916). *The Measurement of Intelligence*. Boston, MA: Houghton Mifflin.

Tizard, B., Cooperman, O., Joseph, A., & Tizard, J. (1972). Environmental effects on language development: A study of young children in long-stay residential nurseries. *Child Development*, **43**, 337–358.

Tobias, P. V. (1970). Brain-size, grey matter and race: Fact or fiction? *American Journal of Physical Anthropology*, **34**, 3–25.

True, R. M. (1949). Experimental control in hypnotic age regression. *Science*, **145**, 1330–1331.

Underwood, H. W. (1960). The validity of hypnotically induced hallucinations. *Journal of Abnormal and Social Psychology*, **61**, 39–46.

Vernon, P. E. (1969). *Intelligence and Cultural Environment*. London: Methuen.

Vernon, P. E. (1970). Review of *Environment, Heredity, and Intelligence*, by A. R. Jensen et al. *Contemporary Psychology*, **15**, 161–163.

Waddington, P. A. J. (1982). 'Conservatism, Dogmatism, and Authoritarianism in British Police Officers': A comment. *Sociology*, **16**, 591–594.

Wagstaff, G. F. (1981). *Hypnosis, Compliance and Belief*. Brighton: Harvester.

Wagstaff, G. F. (1987). Hypnosis. In H. Beloff & A. M. Colman (Eds), *Psychology Survey 6*. Leicester: British Psychological Society.

Witty, P. A. & Jenkins, M. D. (1936). Intra-race testing of Negro intelligence. *Journal of Psychology*, **1**, 179–192.

Wolf, J. M. (1982). Bulimia and the dexamethasone suppression test [Letter to the editor]. *American Journal of Psychiatry*, **139**, 1523–1524.

Wolstenholme, G. E. W. & Millar, E. C. (Eds) (1956). *Extrasensory Perception: Ciba Foundation Symposium*. London: Churchill.

World Health Organization (1978). *Mental Disorders: Glossary and Guide to their Classification in Accordance with the Ninth Revision of the International Classification of Diseases*. Geneva: Author.

Index

ABO blood types 56-7
Abraham, S. 164n
ACTH *see* adrenocorticotrophic hormone
acupuncture 120
admixture, racial 58-63
adoption studies 17, 18, 24, 39-47, 48, 61-3
adrenal gland 160
adrenocorticotrophic hormone (ACTH) 160
age-regression, hypnotic 110-11, 113, 114-15, 122, 126-8
Albert, G. 179
Alcock, J. E. 199n
American Indians 69, 70-1
American Psychological Association 24, 55, 92, 95
American Society for Psychical Research 172
anaesthesia, hypnotic 111, 113, 114-22, 130; spontaneous 115-16
analgesia, hypnotic 111, 113, 114-22, 130, 138; spontaneous 115-16
Anderson, L. W. 79n
Anderson, M. L. 125, 139n
Andrews, D. 165n
Angel, E. 164n
animal magnetism 112, 113
anorexia nervosa 143-6, 149-53, 155, 156, 157-63; body image disturbance in 151-3; case study 141-3; class differences 149; clinical features 143-6; confused with Simmonds' disease; diagnostic criteria 144-6; history of 143-4; prevalence 149-51; related to depression 155, 157-63; sex differences 149
Arendt, H. 83, 84, 85, 90, 104, 107n
Aronson, E. 88, 108n
Ashby, B. 79n
Asians (British) 68, 69, 71-2
Askevold, F. 165n
aspirin 118, 120, 161
assortative mating 34-5, 38, 51n
astrology 197
automatic writing 121
Avicenna 143

Babinski reflex 126-7
Bailly, J. S. 112
Balthazard, C. G. 139n
baquet 112
Barber Suggestibility Scale 124
Barber, T. X. 118, 119, 120, 122, 123, 124, 125, 126, 127, 128, 130, 131, 132-4, 139n, 140n
Barker, W. B. 78n
Barklage, N. E. 165n
Barratt, K. H. 165n
Bateman, F. 177, 179, 199n
bats, echo location by 171
Baumrind, D. 91-2, 93, 95, 96, 99, 106, 108n
Beloff, J. 169, 171, 174, 183, 198n, 199n
Ben-Gurion, D. 81-2
Bennett, E. 176
Besatzungskinder 62
Binet, A. 18-19, 20, 22, 32, 50n, 68
binge eating 154-7, 163
Binswanger, L. 141-3, 164n
bird navigation 171
Blackmore, S. 188, 195, 196-7, 200n
Blau, Z. S. 79n
Blaustein, A. R. 198n
Bleuler, E. 142
blood types 56-7, 58, 59, 60
Bodmer, W. F. 64, 75, 79n
body image disturbance 151-3
Body Mass Index (BMI) 148-9
Boring, E. G 138n
Bowers, K. S. 118, 121-2, 130, 139n, 140n
Bowersbuch, M. K. 126-7, 139n
boxing, analogy from 41
Braid, J. 114, 138n
brain size 56-7
Brigitte magazine 147
Broad, C. D. 199n
Brotzman, E. 108n
Brown, J. L. 198n
Brown, M. 139n
Brown, R. 78n
Brown, W. C. 79n
Bruch, H. 151, 153, 164n
bulimia nervosa 153-63; clinical features 155-6; diagnostic criteria 155; prevalence 156-7; related to depression 157-63; sex differences 155
Burks, B. S. 40-2, 44, 51n
Buros, O. K. 107n
Burt, C. 22, 26-9, 32, 33, 35, 36, 37, 38, 43-4, 49, 50n, 74
Butcher, H. J. 79n
Button, E. J. 165n

Calverley, D. S. 126, 139n
Campbell, P. G. 165n
campus distance series 174, 180-3
Carroll, B. J. 165n
case studies 13
Casper, R. C. 165n
catelepsy, hypnotic 113
causal relationships 13-14
Cavalli-Sforza, L. L. 64, 79n
Centerwall, B. S. 60, 61, 78n

Index

Child Health and Education Study 67-8, 71-2, 73

clairvoyance 170, 173; *see also* extra-sensory perception

Cleveland, S. E. 164n

cold pressor pain 116, 119, 120, 121

Colman, A. M. 14n, 53, 78n, 80n, 108n, 200n

compensatory education 74-5

complementary-colour afterimages 125-6

Comte, A. 198

Connolly, C. 150

Conway, J. 28

Cooper, P. J. 157, 158-9, 160-2, 165n

Cooperman, O. 78n

Corey, M. 95-6, 105, 108n

corn, heritability in 64-5

correlation: explanation of 13-14; height-weight 13; intraclass 24, 50n; invariant, in Burt's data 27

cortisol 160, 162-3

Coscina, D. V. 165n

Cosmopolitan magazine 156

Crawford, T. J. 94, 108n

Crisp, A. H. 149, 152, 153, 164n, 165n

Croesus (King of Lydia) 172

crossing, racial 58-63

culture-fair tests 68-9

culture-free tests 68-9

culture-reduced tests 68-9

Cunningham, S. 165n

Cushing's syndrome 160

Dalrymple, S. 108n

Darwin, C. 17

Darwin, E. 17

Davis, J. M. 165n

deafness, hypnotic 122, 126

delayed auditory feedback (DAF) 126

Delphi, oracle of 172

dentistry, use of hypnosis in 116, 118

dependent variable, definition 11

depression 155, 157-63

Dewdney, A. K. 50n

dexamethasone suppression test (DST) 159-60, 161, 162-3

Dicks, H. V. 104, 108n

distorting-image technique 152

Dixon, K. N. 165n

dominance, genetic 38

Dutton, D. 106-7, 108n

Eating Attitudes Test (EAT) 145-6, 157

Eaves, L. J. 38

Ebers papyrus 111

echo location 171

Eckert, E. D. 165n

Edmonston, W. E. Jr 138n

Edwards, J. H. 79n

Edwards, M. 195-6

Ehrenstein illusion 124-5

Eichmann, A. 81-4, 90, 101, 104, 107, 107n; psychological normality of 83, 84

eleven-plus examination 22, 48-9

Ellen West, case of 141-3, 157

Ellenberger, H. F. 138, 139n, 164n

Elliotson, J. 113

Elms, A. 94-5, 105, 108n

Embree, E. R. 58, 78n

Erickson, M. 94, 108n

Erlenmeyer-Kimling, L. 35-7, 38, 51n

Esdaile, J. 113, 114

ESP *see* extra-sensory perception

Etzioni, A. 94, 108n

eugenics 17, 20

Evans, F. J. 140n

Ewin, D. M. 138n

experiments: controlled 11; quasi 11, 12

extra-sensory perception 166-200; classification 170-1; definitions 170, 194; history 171-3; opinions regarding 173-4; Pearce-Pratt experiments 74, 180-3; Project Alpha 195-6; psi Ganzfeld experiments 175, 184-9; remote viewing experiments 175, 190-4; rodent experiments 174, 183-4; Soal-Goldney experiments 174, 175-80; sources of belief 196-7; spontaneous cases 166-9

Eyferth, K. 62, 78n

Eysenck, H. J. 24-5, 26, 27, 28, 34, 35, 36, 38, 40, 47, 48, 49n, 50n, 51n, 52n, 54, 55, 56, 58, 59, 63, 64, 66, 69, 70, 71, 72, 74, 75, 76, 77, 78, 78n, 80n, 138n, 140n, 175, 180, 185, 194, 198n, 199n, 200n

Fairburn, C. G. 156, 157, 158-9, 160-2, 165n

Fancher, R. E. 50n

Farber, S. 33, 51n

Farina, A. 106, 108n

Farrington, A. J. 165n

Feinberg, M. 165n

Feldman, M. W. 79n

Fellows, B. J. 138n

Figgins, D. B. 21

Fisher, S. 128-9, 140n

Flew, A. 195

Flynn, J. R. 78n

four sports problem 15-16

France, A. 56

Franklin, B. 112

Fransella, F. 165n

Frazier, K. 199n

Freeman, F. N. 31-2, 33, 51n

Freud, S. 168, 198n

Friedrichs, R. W. 78n

Fromm, E. 104, 108n

Fulker, D. W. 38, 41-2, 48, 51n, 52n

Galileo 197, 198

Galton, F. 17-18, 22, 50n, 54, 78n
Gardner, M. 182, 183, 199n
Garfinkel, P. E. 164n, 165n
Garner, D. M. 164n, 165n
Garner-Smith, Lt 166, 167
Garrow, J. S. 164n
Gedankenexperiment 64-5
genealogy 59, 61
Germany 22, 62, 81-4, 90-1, 102-4, 105, 106
Gerner, R. H. 165n
Gidro-Frank, L. 126-7, 139n
Gillie, O. 28
Glucksman, M. L. 165n
Goddard, H. H. 20, 21, 22
Goff, G. M. 165n
Goldberg, S. C. 165n
Goldbourt, U. 164n
Goldney, K. M. 175, 176, 178, 179, 199n
Gorman, L. P. 53, 78n
Gould, S. C. 50n, 51n, 78n
Graves, N. 108n
Greden, J. F. 165n
Guillotin, Dr 112
Gull, W. 143-4, 164n
Gwirtsman, H. E. 165n

Hahn, K. W. Jr 119, 120, 139n
Haiti 57
hallucinations, hypnotic 113, 114-15, 122, 124-6, 132, 133, 134, 135, 136, 137; double 132, 133, 134, 135, 136; transparent 131-2, 133, 134, 135, 136
Halmi, K. A. 165n
Halvorson, P. A. 165n
hand lock test 109, 124
Hansel, C. E. M. 179, 181, 182, 199n, 200n
Harper, S. 185, 199n
Harvey, J. H. 108n
Haskell, P. 199n
Hausner, G. 84, 107n
Hearnshaw, L. S. 28, 51n
Henderson, N. 39, 51n
heritability: defined 23-4; IQ and 23-49, 63-6; misunderstood 25; race differences and 63-6; socio-political implications 63-6
Herodotus 172, 198n
Herrnstein, R. J. 50n
hidden observer 120-2
Hilgard, E. R. 117, 119, 120, 121, 134-6, 137, 138n, 139n, 140n
Hilgard, J. R. 138n, 139n, 140n
Hirsch, J. 165n
Hispanics, American 69-70, 72-3
Hoffmann, B. 15, 49n
Hofling, C. K. 101, 102, 108n
Holland, C. C. 96-9, 100, 101, 102, 108n
Holland, C. H. 106, 108n

Holocaust, Nazi 22, 82-4, 90-1, 102-4, 106
Holzinger, K. J. 31-2, 33, 51n
Honorton, C. 184, 185, 186, 188, 189, 199n, 200n
Horn, J. M. 46-7, 52n
Hovland, C. I. 14n
Howard, M. 28, 38
Howells, J. G. 138n
Hudson, J. I. 158, 159, 160, 161, 162, 163, 165n
Hull, C. L. 114, 138n
human plank demonstration 111, 123
Hume, D. 168-9, 198n
Hutchinson, G. E. 199n
Hyman, R. 186, 1987, 188, 189, 200n
hypnosis 109-38, 167; age regression in 110-11, 113, 114-15, 122, 126-8; anaesthesia and analgesia in 111, 113, 114-22, 130, 138, 167; deafness in 122, 126; dentistry use in 116, 118; hallucinations in 113, 114-15, 122, 124-6, 132, 133, 134, 135, 136, 137; hand lock test 109, 124; hidden observer in 120-2; history of 111-14; human plank demonstration 111, 123; induction procedures 109-10, 118-19, 122; obstetrics, use in 115-16, 117; post-hypnotic suggestion 124, 128-30; stage performance of 109-11, 123; state of, controversy over 122-31; surgery under 113-14, 116, 117, 118; trance logic in 131-8

identical twins 25-34
image-marking technique 152
immigration laws 21-2
independent variable, definition 11
informed consent, principle of 92, 93, 94
intelligence 15-80; adoption studies of 17, 18, 24, 39-47, 48; brain size and 56-7; definition of 16-17; environmental influences on 72-6; heritability of 23-49, 63-6; historical background of 17-22; IQ tests 15-22, 66-9; kinship correlations of 17, 24, 34-9, 40, 48; race and 53-78; twin studies of 17, 18, 24, 25-34, 38-9, 48
intelligence quotient *see* IQ
IQ: definition 19-20; highest recorded 60; *see also* intelligence
ischaemic pain 116, 117, 120
Israeli secret service (Mossad) 81

Jack the Ripper 144
James, W. 120
Jarvik, L. F. 35-7, 38, 51n
Jenkins, M. D. 59-60, 78n
Jensen, A. R. 24, 26, 27, 28, 34, 35, 36, 38-9, 48, 50n, 51n, 54, 55, 56, 58, 63, 64, 66, 67, 68, 69, 70, 72, 74, 76, 77, 78, 78n, 79n, 80n
Jinks, J. L. 38
Joad, C. E. M. 176
Johnson, L. S. 139n

Johnson, R. F. Q. 132-4, 135, 136-7, 140n
Jonas, J. M. 165n
Joseph, A. 78n
Juel-Nielsen, N. 32-3, 51n
Jurgelun-Todd, D. 165n
'just world' effect 106

Kalucy, R. S. 153, 164n, 165n
Kamin, L. J. 25, 27, 29, 30, 32, 36, 38, 39, 40-5, 46, 47, 48, 50n, 51n, 52n, 78n, 79n, 80n
Kammann, R. 191, 192, 193, 200n
Katz, S. H. 78n
Kelly, I. W. 14n
Kelman, H. C. 94, 96, 108n
Kendell, R. E. 165n
Kepler, J. 197
Kihlstrom, J. F. 122, 139n, 140n
Kilham, W. 105, 108n
kin recognition, in tadpoles 171
King, R. G. 105, 108n
kinship correlations 17, 24, 34-9, 40, 48
Klement, R. (Adolf Eichmann) 81
Knight, I. 14n, 164n
Knight, S. 164n
Knox, V. J. 121, 139n
Kudirka, N. 100-1, 108n

Labelle, L. 139n
Laffer, P. S. 165n
Larkin, J. J. 166, 167, 168
laughter, in hypnosis 110
Laurence, J.-R. 139n
Lavoisier, A. L. 112
Leahy, A. M. 40-2, 44, 51n
LeBaron, S. 139n
Levy, W. 183, 184, 194
Lewontin, R. C. 64-5, 66, 78n, 79n, 80n
Lindgren, H. C. 108n
Lindzey, G. 78n, 79n
lobotomy, frontal 118
Loehlin, J. C. 46-7, 52n, 78n, 79n
lynching 13
Lyons, J. 199n

McCay, A. R. 138n
McConkey, K. M. 139n
McConnel, D. 166, 167, 168, 172, 198n
McConnell, R. A. 174, 199n
McCreery, C. 198n
Macdonald, H. 139n
McDonnel Laboratory for Psychical Research 195, 196
Mackenzie, B. 61, 78n, 79n
McKeown, T. 79n
Mackie, J. L. 198n
Mackintosh, N. J. 28, 30, 31, 45, 50n, 51n, 52n, 63, 78n, 79n
Maher, B. A. 132-4, 140n

Mann, L. 105, 108n
Mantell, D. M. 105, 108n
Marks, D. F. 191, 192, 193, 200n
Markwick, B. 179, 180, 199n
Mascie-Taylor, C. G. N. 78n, 79n
Masserman, J. 108n
May, R. 164n
Mayr, E. 57, 79n
Meares, A. 138n
Medalie, J. 164n
Meehl, P. E. 179, 199n
Meeker, W. B. 139n
mental age, definition 19
Mercer, J. R. 79n
Mesmer, F. A. 111, 112
Milgram, S. 85, 86, 88, 89, 90, 91, 92, 93, 94, 95, 96, 97, 98, 99, 100, 101, 102, 103, 104, 105, 106, 107, 107n, 108n
Millar, E. C. 199n
Miller, A. G. 108n
Minnesota interracial adoption study 46-7, 62-3
Minton, H. L. 79n
miracles, Hume's argument on 168-9
miscegenation 57-63
Miss America Pageant 150
Mitchell, J. E. 165n
Moldofsky, H. 165n
monozygotic twins 25-34
moon madness 13
Morgan, A. H. 139n
morphine 118, 120
Morrison, A. 79n
Morton, N. E. 38, 51n
Morton, R. 143, 144, 164n
moving caliper technique 152
Munsinger, H. 42-4, 52n

Nadon, R. 139n
National Child Development Study 37, 71, 73
National Front 76
Nazi Germany 22, 81-4, 90-1, 102-4, 106
Nemzer, E. 165n
nepotism 18
Neuman, P. A. 165n
Newcomb, S. 197-8
Newman, H. H. 31-2, 33, 51n
Nogrady, H. 122, 139n
number-sequence problems 16, 49-50n
Nuremberg trials 83

obedience 83-4, 85-107; counterintuitive nature of 87-8, ethical justification of research into 91-6; Milgram's experiments on 85-90; national differences in 105; personality and 105-6; prods, use of in experiments 87; proximity of victim and 89; relevance to Nazi atrocities 83-4, 103-4; sex differences in 105; stress in

experiments on 88-9, 91, 92-3; surveillance and 89-90; validity of experiments on 96-104
obesity 149, 154
obstetrics, use of hypnosis in 115-16, 117
O'Hara, R. K. 198n
oracle of Delphi 172
Orientals (American) 69, 71
Orne, M. T. 96-9, 100, 101, 102, 108n, 129, 131-2, 136, 137, 138, 138n, 140n
Osborne, M. L. 138n

pain *see* analgesia; hypnotic; cold pressor pain; ischaemic pain
Pakstis, A. J. 78n
Palmer, F. H. 79n
Palmer, R. L. 164n
Parapsychological Association 174, 188
parapsychology 167; *see also* extra-sensory perception
passing (racial) 70-1
past lives regression 127-8
Paul, D. B. 36-7, 51n
Peabody Picture-Vocabulary Test 69-70
Pearce, H. 180, 181, 182, 183
Pearce-Pratt experiments 174, 180-3
Perry, C. 139n
Pettigrew, T. F. 55, 78n
phantom limb 118
phenylketonuria 48, 49
Pierce, C. M. 108n
pituitary gland 144, 160
Plato 17
Playboy magazine 150
police, attitudes of 53, 77
Pope, H. G. Jr 165n
post-hypnotic suggestion 124, 128-30
Pratt, J. G. 174, 181, 182, 183, 199n
precognition 170, 171, 173, 177, 180, 183-4; *see also* extra-sensory perception
prejudice, racial 52-3, 70-1, 77, 105-6
premonitions 166-7, 168
Price, G. R. 178, 179, 180, 199n
Price, P. 190, 191, 192, 193
prods, use of in obedience experiments 87
Project Alpha 195-6
psi Ganzfeld 175, 184-9
psychokinesis 170, 171, 173, 195
psychokinetic metal bending (PKMB) 195
psychology: academic research 11; applied 11; definition 10-11
Puthoff, H. E. 190, 191, 192, 193, 194, 200n
Puységur, A. M. Marquis de 113, 138
Pyle, R. L. 165n

quasi-experiments 11, 12

race: admixture 58-63; definition 56-8; intelligence and 53-80

Race, V. 113
Randall, J. 174, 183, 199n
Randi, J. 195-6, 200n
randomization, logic behind 11
Rao, D. C. 38, 51n
Raven's Progressive Matrices 69
Record, R. G. 79n
Reed, T. E. 78n
reincarnation 127
Reitman, E. E. 164n
remote judging 191
remote viewing 175, 190-4
Rhine, J. B. 172, 173, 174, 175, 176, 178, 179, 180, 181, 182, 183, 184, 194, 198n, 199n
Ring, K. 95-6, 105, 106, 108n
Rochas, A. de 127, 139n
Rogo, D. S. 175, 185, 199n, 200n
Rose, S. 78n, 79n, 80n
Rosenhan, D. L. 100, 102, 108n
Rotton, J. 14n
Rumbelow, D. 164n
rumination 156
Russell, G. F. M. 145, 146, 152, 153, 155, 156, 157, 165n
Russell, Lord 107n
Rutherford, E. 198
Ryan, J. 67, 79n

Sabine, E. J. 165n
Samelson, F. 50n
Sarbin, T. R. 125, 139n
Sargent, C. 175, 185, 194, 198n, 199n, 200n
Scarman, Lord 53, 78n
Scarman report 53
Scarr, S. 46-7, 52n, 60, 61, 62-3, 78n
Schmeidler, G. R. 199n
Schneider, F. W. 79n
Schwartz, D. 164n
Scott, C. 195, 199n, 200n
Scott, W. 96-7
Scriven, M. 179, 199n
Sears, R. R. 14n
Selten, I. 139n
sex differences: in eating disorders 149, 155; in obedience 105
Shackleton, B. 175, 176, 177, 179
Sharma, R. 79n
Shaw, S. 195-6
Sheehan, H. L. 164n
Sheehan, P. W. 129, 140n
Shelton, L. G. 106-7, 108n
Shields, J. 29-31, 33, 51n
Shirer, W. 107
Shockley, W. 77, 80n
Shor, R. E. 138n
Shuey, A. M. 78n
Sidgwick, H. 198n
Simmonds' disease 144, 164n

Simmonds, M.   164n
Simon, T.   19, 20
Skeels, H. M.   44-5, 52n
skin colour   59
Skodak, M.   44-5, 52n
Slade, D. D.   152, 153, 165n
slavery   58, 60-1, 95
sleep, compared to hypnosis   113, 131, 138n
Snow, C. P.   107, 108n
Snyderman, M.   50n
Soal, S. G.   175, 176, 177, 178, 179, 180, 194, 199n
Society for Psychical Research   172, 184
sociologist's fallacy   74
somnambulism, artificial   113
Sours, J. A.   164n
South Africa   58, 76, 88, 109
Spanos, N. P.   130, 140n
Spartacus   95
Spiegel magazine   164n, 165n
Spuhler, J. N.   78n, 79n
Stancer, H. C.   165n
standardization   19, 32, 66-7
stars, chemical composition of   198
statistical significance, definition   12
statistics: mathematical model   51n; purpose of   12
Statue of Liberty   14, 21
sterilization: statutory   20-1; voluntary   77
Stern, J. A.   139n
Stern, S. L.   163, 165n
Stern, W.   19, 20
Stone, M. H.   164n
stress, in obedience experiments   88-9, 91, 92-3
Suedfeld, P.   106-7, 108n
Summers, V. K.   164n
superior orders, defence in war crimes trials   82-3, 107n
surgery, use of hypnosis in   113-14, 116, 117, 118
survey methods   12-13
Sutcliffe, J. P.   115, 117, 118, 120, 138n, 139n
Swift, W. J.   165n
Szasz, T.   107n
Szondi, L.   84, 107n
Szondi Test   84, 107n

tadpoles   171
taghairm   198
Targ, R.   190, 191, 192, 193, 194, 200n
Tart, C. T.   192, 193, 200n
Taylor, H. F.   33-4, 37, 38, 39, 51n, 52n, 79n, 80n

Taylor, J.   195
telepathy   170, 173; *see also* extra-sensory perception
Terman, L. M.   20, 21, 22, 50n
test bias   66-9
Texas Adoption Project   46-7
Thompson, M.   164n
tides, effect of moon on   197
Tizard, B.   62, 78n
Tizard, J.   78n
Tobias, P. V.   56, 78n
trance logic   131-8
triplets   75
Troscianko,T.   196-7, 200n
True, R. M.   127, 139
twin studies   17, 18, 24, 25-34, 38-9, 48, 51n, 75

Ulett, G. A.   139n
Underwood, H. W.   124-5, 139n

validity, definition   96
Valium   120
variance, definition   23
Vernon, P. E.   79n, 80n
vomiting   154-7, 163

Waddington, P. A. J.   78n
Wagstaff, G. F.   117, 118, 121, 139n, 140n
Wakeling, A.   165n
Wallston, K.   95-6, 105, 108n
Ward, W. S.   113, 114
Wechsler, D.   32, 68
weight: average   147-8; 'ideal'   147, 150, 164n; normal   146-9, 154
Weinberg, R. A.   46-7, 52n, 62-3, 78n
West, E.   141-3
West Indians (British)   53, 55, 57, 58, 62, 67-9, 71-2, 73
Whitehorn, K.   150
Whitlow, J. E.   123
Wilde, O.   9
Willerman, L.   46-7, 52n
Witty, P. A.   59-60, 78n
Wolf, J. M.   162-3, 165n
Wolstenholme, G. E. W.   199n
Woody, E. Z.   139n
World Health Organization   143, 164n

Yee, S.   38, 51n
Yerkes, R.   20
Yonacae, A.   165n

Zener, K. E.   172